WEBSTER'S NEW WORLD™

PUNCTUATION

Simplified and Applied

Geraldine Woods

Wiley Publishing, Inc.

For Kyra, the first of the next generation.

Webster's New World® Punctuation: Simplified and Applied

Copyright © 2006 by Wiley, Hoboken, NJ

Published by Wiley, Hoboken, NJ
Published simultaneously in Canada

For general information on our other products and services or to obtain technical support, please contact our Customer Care Department within the U.S. at 800-762-2974, outside the U.S. at 317-572-3993, or fax 317-572-4002.

Wiley also publishes its books in a variety of electronic formats. Some content that appears in print may not be available in electronic books. For more information about Wiley products, please visit our web site at www.wiley.com.

Library of Congress Cataloging-in-Publication Data:

Woods, Geraldine.
  Webster's New World punctuation : simplified and applied / Geraldine Woods.
    p. cm.
  ISBN-13: 978-0-7645-9916-3 (isbn-13 : pbk.)
  ISBN-10: 0-7645-9916-X (isbn-10 : pbk.)
  1. English language—Punctuation—Handbooks, manuals, etc. I. Title.
  PE1450.W66 2006
  428.2—dc22

                                        2005023688

Manufactured in the United States of America
10 9 8 7 6 5 4 3 2 1

Contents

PART II: Punctuation in Common Writing Formats

Introduction

A popular French entertainer once explained that "a kiss can be a comma, a question mark, or an exclamation point." This sort of "punctuation" easily attracts interest, but until recently many grammarians and copy editors assumed that their passion for a properly placed semicolon was rare. Yet a substantial number of people do care about punctuation and would indeed like to know, for example, when a comma is called for. Moreover, everyone should care because punctuation is the roadmap that tells the reader how to arrive at the writer's meaning.

Imagine that a worried student goes to a fortuneteller for advice about an important exam and receives this note:

> The way you are studying you will take the test and pass not experiencing a miserable failure.

How is the student to react? Should the worrier open the book and study madly in an effort to avert disaster? Should the student, reassured by the prediction, take in a movie instead? The answer depends on the punctuation:

> The way you are studying, you will take the test and pass, not experiencing a miserable failure.

> The way you are studying, you will take the test and pass not, experiencing a miserable failure.

The preceding example illustrates what American writer Edgar Allan Poe meant when he said, "The writer who neglects punctuation, or mispunctuates, is liable to be misunderstood." The primary reason to place a punctuation mark in your text is to clarify the message, making sure that the reader grasps what you are trying to say.

Proper punctuation, like good grammar, has another purpose as well. The quality of your writing influences the impression you make on your boss, your teacher, or your personal correspondents. A job application letter or a note to a child's teacher that is marred by punctuation errors will, rightly or wrongly, make you less likely to be taken seriously. The reverse is also true: to attract and keep the reader's serious attention, you must write—and therefore punctuate—correctly.

Learning how to punctuate is relatively easy these days, but such was not always the case. The modern system of punctuation did not become standardized until the late 18th century. The preference of individual writers and printers determined the placement of punctuation, not the needs of the reader. In the works of Shakespeare, for example, periods, colons, and semicolons appear with seemingly little reason for one rather than the other. At various times polite but fierce battles broke out over the standards and practices of various punctuation marks. Thomas Jefferson, as he wrote the Declaration of Independence, joined a long-running dispute over apostrophes, placing an apostrophe in *it's* (the possessive pronoun) in that document. In Jefferson's draft, the new government was "organizing it's powers." The "non-apostrophists" eventually won their point, and Jefferson was obliged to omit the apostrophe from *its*.

Jefferson's struggle illustrates an important point about punctuation: Each little symbol gets its meaning from an agreement between readers and writers. Educated people today have decided that the possession shown by the word *its* may be turned into a contraction with the addition of an apostrophe (*it's*). Thus, *its* and *it's* have different meanings. Had the standard been decided otherwise, *it's* might have fulfilled both functions.

Although many punctuation rules clarify meaning, some exist for no reason at all apart from custom. With meaning not at stake, you may wonder why a writer should worry about where to place the period or whether a comma belongs inside or outside the quotation marks. The value of these punctuation customs is the sense of stability they provide. Seeing the period inside some quotation marks and outside others in the same piece of writing would be disconcerting. Proper punctuation works on an almost subconscious level. It guides the reader to the intended meaning without becoming too intrusive. Variations catch attention and distract the reader from the writer's message. So arbitrary or not, punctuation customs are worth learning.

Unfortunately, the rules for punctuation are still not completely uniform. They change over time and according to location. Years ago writers placed far more commas and semicolons in their work than modern writers do. Also, punctuation sometimes varies depending on country or context. British and American writers follow different rules—and even use different names—for some punctuation marks. Scientists' customs differ from historians', and business has its own traditions.

This book explains both the generally accepted rules as well as the major variations. The recommendations of the major style manuals, the texts that codify the preferences for each academic discipline, are included. If you are writing in a particular field, take note of the style manual that governs your work: *The Publication Manual of the American Psychological Association* (APA, science and social science), *The Modern Language Association Handbook* (MLA, the humanities), and *The Chicago Manual of Style* (CMS, general). This punctuation manual also highlights current business practices. In addition, the British and American language gap is addressed. Where British and American punctuation customs differ, the American style is explained first, followed by the British custom.

This book is divided into three parts, each giving you a different path to the information you seek. In Part I, every punctuation mark is treated separately. The rules are explained and illustrated, and common pitfalls are described. If you are puzzling over a colon, for instance, you can turn to the chapter on colons (Chapter 6) to find the rules governing this punctuation mark and examples of its most common usage. Part II provides samples of all sorts of writing. If you are writing a business letter or an absence note for school, you can look at a prototype to see how this sort of writing is punctuated and why. Parts I and II also highlight the most frequent errors. Part III features citations: how to identify sources (both print and electronic) and format entries in the major bibliographic styles. If you are writing a term paper, a dissertation, or a professional article, you will find the proper punctuation of footnotes, endnotes, and parenthetical notes in Part III.

One last point about punctuation: not everything about punctuation is written in stone. At times the insertion or deletion of a comma is a matter of preference, not correct usage. Plus, the best writers, the true geniuses, break the rules at some point. For those who understand what is expected and who can show that they know what is expected, the unexpected is a good option. To surprise and delight the reader with originality is a wonderful achievement!

For the ordinary, everyday writer, however, the rules are a safety device; obeying the rules ensures that you are within the accepted practice of educated people. American author Ernest Hemingway put it best:

> My attitude toward punctuation is that it ought to be as conventional as possible. The game of golf would lose a good deal if croquet mallets and billiard cues were allowed on the putting green. You ought to be able to show that you can do it a good deal better than anyone else with the regular tools before you have a license to bring in your own improvements.

Part I

THE PUNCTUATION MARKS

1

The Period

What Americans call a "period" is named "full point" or "full stop" in Britain. The second British term gives a good idea of the period's main function. Like the red sign at the end of a road, a period orders the reader not just to slow down briefly but to come to a true halt. Probably the only sign in a piece of writing that makes a sharper separation between one idea and another is the blankness at the end of a line preceding a new paragraph or the unfilled page at the end of a chapter.

The period's primary function is to signal the end of any sentence that makes a statement or gives a command. Periods also appear in most abbreviations. In recent years this punctuation mark has picked up a new and important function as part of Web addresses.

Though the rules governing the period are fairly straightforward, problems do arise when a period at the end of a sentence tangles with the period of an abbreviation or with quotation marks. This chapter addresses those intricacies and other special cases, including the use of a period in titles, lists, and slide presentations.

AS AN ENDMARK

A complete sentence that states an idea always ends with a period. A sentence that gives a command normally concludes with a period as well. To put this rule another way: Any sentence that does not ask a question, exclaim, or command with extra emphasis needs a period. Every sentence in this chapter

thus far, and nearly every sentence in this book, finishes up
with a period. Some examples follow:

> The toy duck is resting atop the child's dresser. (statement)
>
> Turn left at the corner. (command)
>
> Stop what you are doing and help me. (command)
>
> No house is truly a home until it is lived in. (statement)
>
> A penny saved is a penny earned. (statement)

The period's emotional tone is neutral. To see the contrast,
imagine the above sentences punctuated differently:

> The toy duck is resting atop the child's dresser?
>
> Turn left at the corner!
>
> Stop what you are doing and help me!
>
> No house is truly a home until it is lived in!
>
> A penny saved is a penny earned?

The first sentence leads one to think that the writer is
puzzled or perhaps even upset about the presence of the toy
duck on the dresser. Why is the duck there, you imagine the
writer pondering. The next two sentences are much more
urgent than the versions ending with a period. Perhaps the
writer is angry or intent on securing complete obedience. The
fourth sentence sounds like a protest. Any one of a number
of situations comes to mind: a new house, a family not yet
settled, a conversation about the meaning of "home." In the
last example, you may imagine a spendthrift child answering
a parent's scolding with a bit of sarcasm. Whatever scenario
you come up with for these sentences, the issue is the same.
The period has a more neutral effect on meaning than other
endmarks.

In placing a period at the end of a sentence, be sure that
you've actually written a complete sentence. A true "complete
sentence" in grammatical terms includes a subject and a verb

and expresses a coherent thought. The subject is the person or thing being talked about in the sentence and the verb is the action or state of being of the subject. A coherent thought means that the sentence may stand alone and make sense. The reader may not have every piece of information possible, but neither is the reader left hanging halfway through an idea. Below are some samples of complete and incomplete thoughts. Several of the examples include subjects and verbs, but only the complete thoughts are true sentences:

Complete: The stadium is filled to capacity. (subject = *stadium,* verb = *is filled*)

Incomplete: The fans are. (subject = *fans,* verb = *are*)

Why it is incomplete: The fans are what? The statement isn't finished.

Revised, complete: The fans are thrilled by the team's success.

Complete: Despite altering the dress three times, the tailor was still dissatisfied with the fit. (subject = *tailor,* verb = *was*)

Incomplete: Sewing for hours and hours to make ends meet. (no subject or proper verb)

Why it is incomplete: There is a verb form, *sewing,* but no subject. No one *is sewing.* If sewing is taken as a thing, a hobby, perhaps, it may be a subject. In that case the sentence still needs a verb.

Revised, complete: Sewing for hours and hours to make ends meet, Eloise dreamed of a better life.

IN PARENTHESES

A number of rules govern the interaction between periods and parentheses (what the British call "round brackets").

Entire Sentence Inside Parentheses

If an entire sentence making a statement or giving a command is in parentheses, place a period inside the closing mark:

> (The appendix contains more information on closing costs and mortgage rates.)

> (See page 12 for more information.)

Complete Sentence Inserted into Another Sentence

If the parenthetical statement appears inside another sentence, there is no period in the parentheses. The logic behind this rule is that there is only one sentence, of which the parenthetical information is a part, and thus only one endmark.

> This situation is not acceptable (I have told you so several times) and must be remedied immediately.

> When the cleaners have finished their work (they generally leave before midnight), only the security staff remain on campus.

Citations in Parentheses

Citations of source material are sometimes placed in parentheses at the end of the ideas or quotations being cited. The major style manuals allow this citation format and even at times recommend it over footnotes or endnotes. The general principle is simple: Parenthetical citations are part of the sentence but not part of the quotation, if there is one. Therefore the parentheses come before the endmark of the sentence (usually a period) but after any quotation marks. Note the punctuation in these examples:

> As Smith reached the Pole, he "staked the claim of a sovereign nation" (Smith 203).

> A sailor on the supply boat later said that Smith admitted his trek had not been a success because of the high fatality rate (Morganstern 44).

For more information on the punctuation of cited sources, see Part III.

IN QUOTATIONS

The rules governing where a period should be placed in quoted material have very little to do with meaning. The arbitrary nature of these rules is made clear by the fact that they are different on each side of the Atlantic Ocean. In fact, British and American period and quotation mark placement is exactly opposite. In most cases British and American quotation marks vary in another respect as well. In Britain single quotation marks generally enclose quoted material; double quotation marks are reserved for quotations within other quotations. In American usage the order is reversed, with double quotation marks enclosing the primary quotation and single marks surrounding an interior quotation.

Quotation at the End of a Sentence

When quoted material appears at the end of a sentence and a question mark or exclamation point is not called for, the period resides inside the closing quotation mark (American English) or outside the quotation mark (British English).

Some examples in American English follow:

> Laura replied, "I visited the museum yesterday and toured the Asian galleries."

> Olivia mentioned that Tang Dynasty art presents an "age of splendor."

> One piece of art was called "Autumn Moon."

Some examples in British style:

> 'Laura, as an art buff you are more likely to be in a museum than anywhere else'.

> Oliver commented that he plans to see the new Rubens exhibit this weekend 'or die trying'.

> I'm looking forward to the curator's essay for this exhibit, 'Rubens: A Reassessment'.

When the quotation ending the sentence is a question, a question mark appears inside the quotation marks, but no period ends the sentence. The logic here is that the sentence should not have two endmarks, so the question mark does double duty. Some examples follow:

> Arthur asked, "Are you feeling ill today?"
>
> Amy replied, "Why are you asking?"

In British style these sentences would employ single quotation marks (inverted commas), but otherwise appear the same:

> Arthur asked, 'Are you feeling ill today?'
>
> Amy replied, 'Why are you asking?'

The question mark, following both American and British usage, goes inside the closing quotation mark if the quoted material is a question and outside the closing quotation mark if the sentence, but not the quoted material, is a question. The period, on the other hand, always goes outside the quotation mark (British style) or inside (American style).

Quotation Within a Sentence

If a quoted statement normally calls for a period but the sentence continues on after the quotation, replace the period with a comma:

> "The tapestry is slightly frayed," observed the curator.

The tapestry is slightly frayed is a complete sentence. Because it is a statement, it would normally end with a period. Yet *observed the curator* is part of the same sentence. A period should follow *curator* to signal the end of the entire sentence. Had you placed a period after frayed, the sentence would have two endings, a clearly impossible situation:

> **Wrong:** "The tapestry is slightly frayed." observed the curator.

Here is another example:

> The ski instructor remarked that his class "must be willing to fall" in order to master the correct posture.

Here the quotation is not a complete sentence, but some writers may still be tempted to insert a period after the instructor's statement. Once again, the rule is that no sentence should have two endmarks. A period should not be inserted after *fall* because the sentence continues:

> **Wrong:** The ski instructor remarked that his class "must be willing to fall." in order to master the correct posture.

Quotation Within Another Quotation

If the sentence ends with a quotation within another quotation, place the period inside both the single and the double quotation marks (American usage). In British usage, the period normally goes outside both marks:

> **American usage:** Canwell explained, "My favorite saying is 'just do it.'"

> **British usage:** Canwell explained, 'My favorite saying is "just do it"'.

For more information on quotation marks, see Chapter 7.

IN ABBREVIATIONS

A period often takes the place of letters that have been omitted in an abbreviation. However, not all abbreviations include periods. If you are unsure about a particular abbreviation, the dictionary is a good guide. The major style manuals also include lists of abbreviations, showing which should include periods and which should not. If you are writing an academic paper, check the style manual if you are in doubt about the conventions of abbreviations in your field. This section explains only the most common forms.

Most Common Abbreviations

Two of the most common abbreviations are a.m. and p.m., indicating morning and afternoon times. These abbreviations are sometimes capitalized and written without periods: AM and PM. Both forms are correct and quite common, so you may choose either. Take care to be consistent in one piece of writing. Regardless of how they are written, these forms are always placed after the time, separated by a space.

Names and Titles

When a name or title is abbreviated, insert a period:

W. B. Yeats (William Butler Yeats)

F.D.R. (Franklin Delano Roosevelt)

John F. Kennedy (John Fitzgerald Kennedy)

Msgr. Robert Agnow (Monsignor Robert Agnow)

Sen. Henry Dosworth (Senator Henry Dosworth)

Some Common Abbreviations for Titles

The abbreviations in the following chart are generally written with periods:

Atty. Gen.	Attorney General
Dr.	Doctor
Esq.	Esquire
Gov.	Governor
Jr.	Junior
Pres.	President
Rep.	Representative

Note: Academia and the military now prefer to omit periods from abbreviated ranks or degrees (*LT* for "Lieutenant," *PhD* for "Doctor of Philosophy," and so forth). Many titles, such as "Medical Doctor" may be abbreviated with or without periods (*M.D.* or *MD*).

The most common titles—Mr., Mrs., and Ms.—have traditionally been followed by periods. However, this style is changing, perhaps in recognition of the fact that the words abbreviated are never spelled out and, in the case of the female titles, never even pronounced as a whole word. In Britain, the period is always omitted in these titles.

Latin Terms

Abbreviations derived from Latin words commonly include periods:

e.g. (for example)

i.e. (that is)

cf. (compare)

et al. (and others)

etc. (and so forth)

When any abbreviation ends a sentence, only one period is inserted. The period following the abbreviation (if there is one) does double duty, as in the following examples:

The best article was written by Peterson et al.

The temperamental artist was always complaining about the lack of time, space, energy, etc.

Sic Is Not an Abbreviation

A small word, *sic,* alerts the reader to an error in a quotation—a misspelled word, a faulty grammatical construction, and the like. *Sic* is not an abbreviation and thus is not followed by a period. *Sic* should be placed in brackets next to the error.

Original: She had gave it to me yesterday before I went to the movies.

Quoted: The witness reported that "she had gave it [sic] to me" but the jury did not believe him.

Lowercase Words

Most abbreviations that end with a lowercase letter include periods:

> fig. (figure)
>
> illus. (illustration)
>
> Sp. (Spanish)
>
> Inc. (Incorporated)
>
> Ltd. (Limited)
>
> irreg. (irregular)

When these abbreviations occur at the end of a sentence, only one period is inserted. The period at the end of the abbreviation also serves as an endmark, as in these examples:

> Helen invested in Burbank, Ltd.
>
> The towels on sale were marked "irreg."

Abbreviations Without Periods

As noted earlier in this chapter, the trend today is to stream-line writing by omitting the periods in many abbreviations, as in AM (morning) and PM (afternoon). The same trend applies to the abbreviation for the United States of America, which may be written with periods but which increasingly appears without punctuation (*USA*). Acronyms—"words" created from the first letters of each word of a name—don't include periods:

> NATO (North Atlantic Treaty Organization)
>
> OPEC (Organization of Petroleum Exporting Countries)

The United States Postal Service abbreviations for American states and territories should not include periods. A sampling:

> NY
>
> AK

AL

MS

You may see the older state abbreviations (*Ind.* for "Indiana," *Penn.* for "Pennsylvania," for example) from time to time. The two-letter abbreviations are preferred.

Note: Abbreviations and acronyms multiply almost as fast as a supercomputer. Because the placement or omission of a period is often governed by custom, not logic, you may want to check the standard usage in your company or school before writing a particular abbreviation. If you're unsure and the dictionary is no help, simply spell out the term you need. If more than one option is open to you, be sure to use the same abbreviated form throughout the document.

Abbreviations in a Sentence

When an abbreviation containing a period occurs within a sentence, the period remains. When the same abbreviation occurs at the end of the sentence, one period serves two purposes—to mark the abbreviation and to signal the end of the sentence. Some examples follow:

> I bought this stationery from Johnson's Inc. and compared it to a store brand. (abbreviation within the sentence)

> In my opinion the best quality stationery is from Johnson's Inc. (one period for the abbreviation and endmark)

If the abbreviation is tucked into the sentence at a spot where a comma or semicolon is called for, the period of the abbreviation is followed—never preceded—by those marks:

> I bought this stationery from Johnson's Inc., which is going out of business.

> I thought you invested wisely in Johnson's Inc.; I was wrong.

One Endmark Only

Never place two periods at the end of a sentence.

Wrong: Return unused merchandise to the Macalister Co..

Right: Return unused merchandise to the Macalister Co.

WITH AN ELLIPSIS

An *ellipsis* is a series of three dots, each separated from the next by a space, indicating that material has been left out of a quotation. An ellipsis may also signal a trailing thought. (For more information on ellipses, see Chapter 10.) When an ellipsis occurs at the end of a sentence expressing a statement or command, the three dots are joined by a fourth, which is the period, as in this example:

> The author goes on to say that we should "take advantage of each day. . . ."

In the above example the period is placed immediately after the concluding word, *day,* and the three dots for the ellipsis follow, each separated by one space.

If the quotation is cited parenthetically in the text, the period follows the parentheses. In the quotation below, the three dots after *anger* indicate missing words, and the period after the parentheses functions as an endmark.

> The author writes, "None of the rulers understood the nature of the peasants' anger . . ." (Sneeman 23).

IN LISTS AND SLIDE PRESENTATIONS

When items in a list on paper or in a slide presentation are complete sentences, each item ends with a period:

Follow these steps in assembling your new Robotype G-3:

(1) Unpack and count all pieces. You should have twelve.

(2) Assemble all side slats according to figure 1.

(3) Place the roof over slats 1–5.

(4) Connect the power supply cord to slat 3.

If the items are not complete sentences, no period is called for. Note the difference between this list and the preceding list:

Each camper should bring these supplies:

- sleeping bag

- canteen

- water purification tablets

- snacks

- sunscreen

Numbers, Letters, and Periods

If the items in a list are numbered or preceded by letters, the numbers and letters are usually followed by periods or enclosed in parentheses. The choice is a matter of style. Don't mix parentheses and periods in the same list, and don't place periods inside parentheses. Some examples follow:

Incorrect:

(1.)

(2.)

(3.)

Correct:

1.

2.

3.

Correct:

  A.

  B.

  C.

Correct:

  (1)

  (2)

  (3)

IN TITLES AND HEADINGS

If a title or subtitle is centered on a title page or in a heading, no periods are needed even if the title sounds like a complete sentence.

> **Wrong:** The Sun Also Rises. (centered title)
>
> **Right:** The Sun Also Rises (centered title)

IN MEMOS AND E-MAILS

In writing a memorandum or an e-mail, the text is punctuated normally. Periods signal the end of complete sentences in the usual way. The heading of the memo or e-mail contains no periods unless one is called for in an abbreviation or an e-mail address. The subject line contains no periods. Note these excerpts from a memo and an e-mail:

To:	Alexander McSorley
From:	Eileen Enders
Re:	The Company Picnic

Next month the company picnic will be held in McCarron Park. All departments are responsible for collecting fees from members.

To: absmith@havad.edu

Subject: Term Paper

Please submit the rough draft no later than February 27, 2006.

IN WEB ADDRESSES

Periods, more commonly called "dots" in this context, separate various parts of Web addresses or Internet addresses.
Because these addresses are sometimes extremely long, you
may need to divide one between two lines. Take care to separate the Web address at a natural break—after a slash or before
a period. If a Web address is mentioned in your text and ends
a sentence, place a period at the end of the sentence in the
normal way.

> **Wrong:** The data we need for next month's
> product launch can be found at www.hav
> ad.edu

> **Right:** The data we need for next month's
> product launch can be found at
> www.havad.edu.

IN NUMBERS

The period acts as a decimal point, as in these examples:

> 15.44 (15 and 44 hundredths)

> 2.033 (2 and 33 thousandths)

In Britain, the separation between hours and minutes is
also indicated by a period, or full stop. (In American usage, a
colon replaces the period for this function.) Examples in
British style:

> 5.15 (15 minutes past 5)

> 2.30 (half past 2)

The same times would be written differently in American style:

> 5:15 (15 minutes past 5)
>
> 2:30 (half past 2)

In drama, a period also separates the number of an act, scene, and line:

> 1.2.33–34 (Act 1, scene 2, lines 33–34)

When a Period Is Not Appropriate

Periods are not called for after centered titles, following dates and addresses, or in short captions that do not form complete sentences. A signature should not be followed by a period.

2

The Question Mark

During the Middle Ages, the question mark began to appear in the form of a shorthand version of the first and last letters of the Latin word for question, *quaestio,* written one on top of the other. Gertrude Stein, a famously eccentric American author, believed that question marks were fine as "a brand on cattle" or "in decoration" but were not needed in sentences because "the question is already there in the writing." Stein was a literary star and thus permitted to ignore normal punctuation rules. Ordinary people, however, must follow certain conventions in placing question marks. Fortunately this particular bit of punctuation poses few problems.

The function of a question mark is simple: It generally indicates a request or expresses doubt. Most question marks appear at the end of the sentence, but under specific circumstances—when a question is in parentheses or embedded in a statement, for example—a question mark may be placed within a sentence.

TO ASK A QUESTION

The question mark is one of three endmarks; the other two are the period and the exclamation point. Question marks take the place of the rising intonation of the voice when someone asks a question orally.

Normal Word Order

As Gertrude Stein observed, the order of words usually signals that a sentence is a question instead of a statement. Nevertheless, the question mark makes life easier for the reader when the question is written. Take a look at these examples:

> What time is the party?
>
> When will we learn that war is not the answer?
>
> Will you help me clean the gutters?

The word order of these examples makes it impossible for the sentences to be anything other than questions. Sentence one is a true request for information. Sentence two is not really a question at all but a disguised statement of the writer's beliefs about war and aggression. This sort of statement is called a rhetorical question and is a traditional tactic in persuasive speeches, essays, or letters. The reader or audience is not supposed to answer the question but rather to accept the writer's point of view. Sentence three is a request for assistance. Said by an authority figure, sentence three's answer is a foregone conclusion. Regardless of the amount of free will involved, however, sentence three is still technically a question.

Statements as Questions

Not every question has a word-order pattern that immediately signals its identity. In these sentences, the punctuation makes all the difference in meaning. Some examples:

> I'm next in line?
>
> You want me to clean my room?

These sentences represent a less common form of question. With a period, the first example would state a fact. The question mark allows you to imagine a bit of doubt. Perhaps the speaker is in a confusing situation, wondering where her place is. She may be tentatively asserting a possibility, hoping that someone will clarify that she is indeed next. Perhaps the "I" in the sentence is not ready and is really expressing surprise that she's come to the head of the line so quickly. Similarly, in the second example the question mark creates a vastly different emotional tone. Now you may picture a disbelieving teenager who can't accept that his private domain is subject to parental control. Alternatively, this sentence may come from someone with an urge to please, begging for a way to be useful. Whatever the context, the question mark creates a scenario that is not at all related to the tone signaled by a period.

Mixed Statements and Questions, Question Last

Sometimes a statement and a question are combined in the same sentence. In such sentences, conclude with a question mark if the question appears at the end of the sentence. Some examples:

> He mused, where do I fit it?

> The committee argued all morning on the question, how much money should be spent on advertising and how much on development?

> As you begin the college application process, take a moment to consider, How important is campus atmosphere to you?

> The deliberations of the other jurors receded into the background while Martha thought, Could the police officer have lied?

Notice that in each sentence a comma separates the statement from the question. The first word of the question may be capitalized for emphasis or left in lowercase, according to the writer's preferences.

Multiple Endmarks

Comedians and comic book artists like to string several endmarks together to indicate strong emotion or simply to achieve a humorous effect:

> Did you eat my sandwich!!?!?

> What????

These combinations are fine for a laugh, but not for standard, formal English. In formal writing, no sentence should conclude with two endmarks.

Mixed Statements and Questions, Question First

Endmarks, by definition, appear at the end of a sentence. However, a question may be embedded in a sentence that ends with a statement. Usually this sentence structure occurs when the question is quoted, but not always. (For more information on punctuating questions in quotations, see "In Quotations" later in this chapter.) Embedded questions may also appear in parentheses.

Embedded Questions, No Parentheses

If a question appears inside a sentence and is not set off from the rest of the sentence by parentheses, a question mark separates the question from the statement. The statement is followed by a period, as in these examples:

> Did the roses arrive? was the first thing he asked the florist.
>
> What role did his parents play in organizing the surprise party? he wondered.
>
> No matter how many schools she visited, How can I get into an Ivy League college? was her constant worry.

The logic here is simple. The entire sentence, taken overall, is a statement, so a period is appropriate after the final word. The embedded question is set apart from the rest of the sentence so that the reader is not confused. In the first two examples, the question mark signals the separation. In the last example, a comma marks the beginning of the question, and a question mark signals the end of the question.

In the third sentence, *How* is capitalized. The writer may capitalize or lowercase the question, according to personal preference. The capital letter makes the question more formal and emphatic.

You may also add a string of similar questions to one sentence if you are sure that the reader will understand your meaning:

What time did he send the message? from where? to whom?

In the preceding example, the reader understands that the last two questions mean:

From where did he send the message?

To whom did he send the message?

The omitted words are repetitive and add nothing to the meaning that the reader has not already gleaned. Because these added questions are considered part of the same sentence, they usually do not begin with capital letters.

Note: Oxford University Press, a major arbiter of British style, calls for capital letters for questions in a series.

Did you buy a car? When? Why?

Embedded Questions, in Parentheses

To set a question apart from the main idea, insert the question into the statement using parentheses:

Alan will bring the projector to the meeting (has he checked the condition of the screen?) and will be responsible for set up.

Naomi will gather the relevant data (which years?) and distribute them to all regional offices.

In the first example, the question in parentheses can stand alone as a separate sentence. Because it is tucked inside another sentence, no capital letter is used for the first word, *has.* In the second example, the words in the parentheses may not stand alone as a complete sentence but are acceptable since there is little chance that the reader will misunderstand that the writer wants Naomi to clarify which years she is studying.

Indirect Questions

Don't use a question mark for an indirect question, no matter where the question appears in the sentence.

Wrong: He wondered whether the blizzard would arrive before nightfall?

Why it is wrong: *Whether the blizzard would arrive before nightfall* is not really a question, though it does express doubt.

Right: He wondered whether the blizzard would arrive before nightfall.

Wrong: Where to put the cleaning supplies was our first decision?

Why it is wrong: *Where to put the cleaning supplies* is not a separate, independent question embedded in a sentence. Instead, it is a fundamental part of the statement in which it appears.

Right: Where to put the cleaning supplies was our first decision.

TO EXPRESS UNCERTAINTY

The question mark appears in scholarly writing whenever a date or other specific fact is the subject of dispute. Rather than indicating a request for information, a question mark reveals doubt or signals an educated guess. Some examples:

McFrench (1677?–1743) had little impact on the colony before his retirement in 1733.

The creator of this magnificent painting (Holbrook?) displays a muted color palette.

In the first sentence, the question mark tells the reader that McFrench's birth date is unknown. The author believes that 1677 is probable. Similarly, in the second sentence the artist's identity is uncertain, but the author's best guess is Holbrook.

Note: Oxford University Press calls for the question mark to precede the area of uncertainty.

> Lady Alice (?1403–1460) is burried in St. Mary's Cemetery.

The question mark tells the reader that Lady Alice was probably born in 1403, but the date of birth is uncertain.

TO MAKE A REQUEST

A question mark may follow a veiled or direct request. No question mark is necessary if a command, for the sake of politeness, is expressed as a question, but in such cases a question mark may soften the tone. Note the difference in these three sentences:

> May I count on your support? (direct request)
>
> Volunteers (Marty? Ellen?) will circulate a petition throughout the community. (indirect request)
>
> Will you please be quiet? (command)

In the first sentence, the reader knows exactly what is being asked and may decide how to respond. In the second example, Marty and Ellen are being pressed into service, though a polite refusal is still open to them. The writer is really asking whether these two volunteers are willing to take on the job of circulating the petition. The word order in the last example creates a question, but the meaning doesn't allow for such an interpretation. The audience for the last sentence knows that silence is required, not optional, and that the sentence is a command, not a question. A period is appropriate, but a question mark takes away some of the severity.

IN QUOTATIONS

Quotation marks, which the British call *inverted commas,* tell the reader that the exact words of a spoken or written source have been reproduced. When question marks and quotation marks intersect, strict rules ensure that they don't collide.

When the Quoted Words Ask a Question

In quoting spoken words, place a question mark inside the closing quotation mark if the quoted words are a question:

> "Does the recipe call for one or two lemons?" asked the chef.

> "When you graduate from college," inquired the loan officer, "will you have a steady job?"

> Our supervisor queried, "How long before the report is on my desk?"

In British style, single quotation marks are substituted for the double quotation marks, and double marks take the place of singles. (See Chapter 7 for more information on quotation marks in British and American style.) In both American and British English, however, it doesn't matter where the question appears. The speaker tag—the words identifying the source of the quotation—may be at the end of the sentence (as in the first example), in the middle of the sentence (the second example), or at the beginning of the sentence (the last example). Regardless of location, the quoted question ends with a question mark, which is placed inside the closing quotation mark in both British and American style.

In quoting written material, place a question mark inside the closing quotation mark only if the original source includes a question mark:

Washberg wrote, "Was the intervention of the Austrian army the deciding factor?"

Her question is still relevant today: "Does the artist's medium overpower the message?"

If the original source does not include a question mark, but the sentence that includes the quotation is a question, the question mark should be placed outside the closing quotation mark:

Why has the personnel department accepted her statement that the supervisor was "inappropriate"?

Quotation Marks and Ellipses

In quoting only parts of a long passage from a written source, you may omit unnecessary words and place an ellipsis (three dots) to show the reader where the gaps lie. If the omitted words are taken out of a question, you still need to place the question mark in the quotation, followed by an ellipsis:

Original: In discussing the causes of the war, several factors must be considered. Was the enemy's goal of complete domination realistic, given the strength of the opposition, the scarcity of supplies, and the severity of weather in that season? Most historians think that even the high command understood the futility of their efforts.

Shortened quotation: "In discussing the causes of the war, several factors must be considered. Was the enemy's goal of complete domination realistic? . . . Most historians think that even the high command understood the futility of their efforts."

The Proper Number of Endmarks

Except in comedy, no sentence ends with two endmarks. If a quoted question ends a sentence, the sentence does *not* end with a period because the question mark is already there.

Wrong: Agnes asked, "How should I title this report?".

Right: Agnes asked, "How should I title this report?"

If the entire sentence *and* the quoted words both ask questions, only one question mark is called for:

Wrong: Did Agnes ask, "How should I title this report?"?

Right: Did Agnes ask, "How should I title this report?"

When a Quoted Statement Appears Within a Question

If a quoted statement appears within a question, the question mark is placed outside the closing quotation mark:

> Did Yves ever say, "Your French is excellent"?

> Can any historian doubt that "the victor controls the historical record"?

> Is it any wonder that Helen always replies, "I choose not to run"?

Punctuation rules are not always logical, but this one makes perfect sense. The question mark belongs to the sentence as a whole, not to the quoted material.

Question Marks with Double and Single Quotation Marks

If the sentence calls for both single and double quotation marks, indicating a quotation embedded within another quotation, the rationale for placing the question mark is simple. The question mark is always associated with the part of the sentence that is asking a question. Place the question mark inside the closing quotation mark (either single or double) if the quoted material is a question and out-side the closing quotation mark if it is not. This sentence illustrates the rule:

> "What did Mary mean by her comment that 'no one is unscarred'?" asked Evelyn.

The sentence contains two different quotations: *no one is unscarred* and *What did Mary mean by her comment that no one is unscarred.* Following American custom (British custom is reversed), the embedded quotation is placed in single quotation marks and the larger quotation is placed within double quotation marks. The embedded quotation is not a question, so it would be wrong to place a question mark inside the closing quotation mark. The larger quotation *is* a question, so the question mark appropriately belongs inside the closing quotation mark.

Even if both quotations are questions, only one question mark appears, inside the closing quotation mark:

> "Why did Mary ask, 'Is no one unscarred?'" remarked Evelyn.

IN TITLES

A title in the form of a question should end with a question mark unless the writer wishes to omit the punctuation for the sake of literary effect. If the title is placed alone on a line (in a heading or title page), no quotation marks are used. In the text, the question mark is italicized if the title calls for italics. In a title surrounded by quotation marks, the question mark belongs inside the closing quotation mark. Examples:

> *Who Will See the Sunrise?*

> "Who Will See the Sunrise?"

For more information on whether a title should be itali-cized or placed in quotation marks, see Chapter 7.

3

The Exclamation Point

The exclamation point, which the British call the exclamation mark, is derived from the Latin word *io,* which expresses surprise and joy. The two Latin letters of that word, written one above the other, form the modern exclamation point.

The problem with exclamation points isn't understanding *how* to use them. It's understanding *when* an exclamation point is called for. The renowned American author F. Scott Fitzgerald once said that an exclamation point is "like laughing at your own joke." On the long-running television sitcom *Seinfeld,* one of the characters is nearly fired because she inserts exclamation points randomly throughout the text of a novel she is editing. American scientist and author Lewis Thomas said that encountering an exclamation point is like watching "someone else's small child jumping up and down crazily in the center of the living room shouting to attract attention." The message is clear: Don't overuse this punctuation mark.

But don't discount the exclamation point either. Human beings are emotional creatures, and the need to scream in print with more than word choice seems universal. The exclamation point does exactly what its name implies. It raises the level of emphasis and emotion of the sentence. In e-mails, for example, exclamation points often express excitement or warmth, emphasizing the good wishes and high spirits of the writer.

Using, Not Overusing, Exclamation Points

No one can maintain an intense pitch of emotion for very long before tuning out. If you place too many exclamation points in your writing, the reader will mentally discard them. Then when you truly want to emphasize an idea, you will have nothing at your disposal. Place these punctuation marks carefully and sparingly.

Mild exclamations may be indicated by commas, not exclamation points:

Well, I have looked for the macro file for an hour and not found it.

Oh, Paulina will return those encyclopedias to the shelf when she has a chance.

My goodness, a better alarm clock would certainly be helpful.

He is the best candidate, absolutely.

In the preceding examples, the words separated from the main idea of the sentence (*well, oh, my goodness, absolutely*) are exclamations, but the writer has chosen not to emphasize

AS AN ENDMARK

One of the three endmarks (the period and the question mark are the other two), an exclamation point signals the end of a complete sentence:

Don't leave me!

The auditorium is on fire!

No employee should leave before the end of the shift!

Clean up after yourself!

No one knows the trouble I've seen!

An exclamation point adds passion and intensity to a sentence. Perhaps because great emotion and logical follow-through don't always go together—or perhaps for no reason them. Each could certainly become a stronger statement with different punctuation:

Well! I have looked for the macro file for an hour and not found it.

Oh! Paulina will return those encyclopedias to the shelf when she has a chance.

My goodness! A better alarm clock would certainly be helpful.

He is the best candidate. Absolutely!

The choice between the comma of a mild exclamation and the intensity of a full-fledged exclamation point is nearly always a question of style, not grammar. One exception lies with the words *oh* and *O*. The first (*oh*) may be followed by either a comma or an exclamation point. The second (*O*) must always be written separately, capitalized and followed by an exclamation point:

Wrong: O, my joy is everlasting.

Right: O! My joy is everlasting.

at all—exclamation points have traditionally been allowed to mark off incomplete "sentences" as well. Note the exclamation points in these passages:

The wicked witch has cast a spell on the weary travelers. Alas! They have no idea what lies in wait for them.

Gentlemen! I will not tolerate any disrespect inside library grounds.

The instructions said to "enable macros." Well! That step would be easy if only I could find a macro that was disabled.

A map! Inez would donate an entire tank of gas if only she had a map of the area.

Alas, gentlemen, well, and *a map* are not complete sentences, but the rules of grammar allow their use as exclamations.

IN QUOTATIONS

The rules for placing an exclamation point in a quotation are similar to those governing the placement of question marks (described in Chapter 2). If the quoted material is an exclamation, the exclamation point goes inside the closing quotation mark. If the quoted material is not an exclamation but the sentence as a whole is, the exclamation point is placed outside the closing quotation mark. In quoting written material that includes an exclamation point, place the exclamation point inside the closing quotation mark. These sentences illustrate the proper placement of exclamation points:

> Sarah screamed, "You caught me!"

> As Nordstrom wrote in *The Complete Guide to Libraries*, "No library is ever completely silent!"

> I can't believe that Sarah said, "Wisconsin is my home"!

In the first sentence, the quoted words (*You caught me*) are an exclamation. Therefore the exclamation point precedes the quotation mark. In the second sentence, the original source contained an exclamation point, so the mark is place inside the closing quotation mark. In the third sentence the quoted words (*Wisconsin is my home*) are a fairly neutral statement, but the sentence as a whole is not. Thus the exclamation point comes at the end of the sentence, not at the end of the quotation.

When Both the Quotation and the Sentence Are Exclamations

If both the sentence and the quoted words are emphatic, place the exclamation point inside the closing quotation. Don't use two endmarks.

Wrong: I can't believe that Sarah screamed, "You caught me!"!

Right: I can't believe that Sarah screamed, "You caught me!"

IN TITLES

If a title is an exclamation, the author may choose to include an exclamation point or to omit this punctuation mark for literary effect. The choice is a matter of style and preference, not grammar. Once the author has made a decision, however, anyone referring to the title should abide by the author's choice. If the title ends in an exclamation point, italicize it (for titles in italics) or place the exclamation point before the closing quotation mark (for titles enclosed in quotation marks).

> *Strike Three!*

> "Strike Three!"

IN PARENTHESES

You may occasionally wish to include an exclamation inside another sentence, setting it off from the rest of the sentence by enclosing the exclamation in parentheses. The first word of the exclamation is generally not capitalized, and the exclamation point goes inside the closing mark, in this way:

> What he said (screamed!) was quite offensive.

> The track meet is coming soon (next week!) despite your lack of preparation.

> He accepted the proposal (O joy!) and will join us next week.

Note: The exclamation *O* is always capitalized.

Inappropriate Exclamation Points

Some writers have a habit of inserting exclamation points in parentheses, with no words at all, to show that they are surprised, offended, or amused by the quotation. Similarly, writers at times place several endmarks together to emphasize the craziness or intensity of a statement. Such punctuation is fine for comedy or informal notes or e-mails between friends. However, it is frowned upon in formal writing. The text surrounding the quotation may be a suitable spot for explaining how you feel about the quoted material.

Wrong: Scrivener wrote that he was "offended by the scene" (!) and wished to be excused from acting in it.

Right: I am stunned by Scrivener's comment that he was "offended by the scene" and wished to be excused from acting in it.

Wrong: Mavis ate an entire jar of cherries?!!

Right: Believe it or not, Mavis ate an entire jar of cherries!

4

The Comma

The comma is subject to so many rules that it wouldn't be surprising if the average writer preferred to ignore them and instead keep a salt shaker full of commas at hand, ready to sprinkle randomly over the text. Yet the rules governing the comma are actually quite simple, once you understand the purpose of this punctuation mark.

Commas create a pause for the reader. A comma pause isn't as long as the silence signaled by a period, a question mark, or an exclamation point. A comma pause is more of a half-breath, a tiny hesitation. In conversation, a change in tone or a bit of silence is the equivalent of a comma. Without these "verbal commas," it would be much more difficult to follow the onrush of words. Unfortunately, too many writers tend to insert a comma wherever they themselves would like to pause for a moment, perhaps to think about the next idea. Yet commas aren't meant to give the *writer* a brief rest. They exist only to serve the *reader*.

As with all punctuation, the most important reason to place a comma is to clarify the meaning of the sentence. There's a world of difference between sentences with and without commas:

> John tipped Mary because he appreciated good service.
>
> John tipped, Mary, because he appreciated good service.

In the first sentence John tipped someone named Mary. In the second, Mary is being addressed, and the reader doesn't know whom John tipped—a waiter, a taxi driver, or a house-cleaner. John may even have tipped Mary herself.

Because a comma creates a break in the flow of text, it separates one thought from another. The rules in this chapter often call for a word or phrase to be "set off" from the rest of the sentence by commas. The comma tells the reader where the separation lies and may signal the fact that the separated material is slightly different from the rest of the sentence. The text cut off by commas may be a comment on the rest of the sentence, some extra information, or, as in the preceding sentence about John and Mary, the name of the person being addressed. In the following sentences, the separation created by commas radically changes the meaning of the second sentence:

> Students who are obnoxious should be disciplined firmly.

> Students, who are obnoxious, should be disciplined firmly.

If you read this pair of sentences aloud, pausing at the commas in sentence two, you'll probably hear the difference in meaning. In the first sentence no commas set off *who are obnoxious* from the rest of the sentence. The main idea is the entire sentence: The students who are obnoxious—but not those who aren't—should be disciplined firmly. In the second sentence, which may have been written by a burned-out teacher, the separated material may be lifted out. The main idea of sentence two is what's left: *Students should be disciplined firmly.* In this version, *all* students should be disciplined firmly because *all* students are obnoxious.

Clarity isn't the only reason for inserting or omitting a comma. Commas are often governed by custom rather than by meaning. Those customs have changed through the years. Writers of previous generations used commas more generously than modern writers. The contemporary "open style" of writing emphasizes an uninterrupted flow of words—all the more reason to make every comma count.

Various style manuals differ on the placement of commas. If you are asked to follow a specific style manual for your writing task, be especially careful to note the variations listed here with some rules. If no variations are mentioned, the major style manuals agree.

Whether meaning or custom calls for a comma, this little punctuation mark is powerful. You should pay attention to its placement, though perhaps not as much as British writer Oscar Wilde, who once spent an entire morning deciding to take a comma out of one of his poems, only to put the comma back again in the afternoon. Nor should you be as carefree as another author, who wrote that commas have less and less importance for her because the reader can "catch his own breath." The rules in this chapter fall somewhere between these two schools of thought and will guide you in placing and deleting commas in your own writing.

TO CREATE A SERIES

A series is a list of three or more items inserted into a sentence. In speaking, short pauses distinguish each item from those before and after. In a freestanding list, each item appears on a separate line, with line breaks serving as punctuation. A comma takes the place of the line break or an oral pause when the list appears in a sentence. Here's an example:

> The tightrope walker leaned left, bent from the waist, slowly straightened up, and stepped forward confidently.

Four items—the actions of the tightrope walker—appear in this series:

1. leaned left
2. bent from the waist
3. slowly straightened up
4. stepped confidently forward

The commas separate these actions so that the reader knows that the tightrope walker *slowly straightened up,* not *bent from the waist slowly.*

The comma before *and* is optional because the word *and* signals the end of item three and the beginning of item four. Many writers include this last comma for the sake of symmetry or because they want an extra pause. Most major American style manuals—the *Modern Language Association Handbook, The Chicago Manual of Style,* and the *Publication Manual of the American Psychological Association*—call for this comma. In Britain, writers tend to omit the comma preceding *and.*

Take a look at these examples:

> Maude, Ellen, and I will compile the sales information you need.

> The best way to reach this student is to praise his best efforts, to scold him when he misbehaves, and to treat him with respect at all times.

> The initial plan is to hold a raffle, bake sale or dance in order to raise funds for the fire victims. (optional comma omitted)

If all items in a series are linked by *and,* no commas are needed:

> **Wrong:** She said that she wanted milk, and cookies, and candy.

> **Why it is wrong:** *And* takes the place of the comma between *milk* and *cookies* and between *cookies* and *candy.*

> **Right:** She said that she wanted milk and cookies and candy.

Sometimes commas are not enough to differentiate between the elements in a series. If even one item has a comma within it, the reader may become confused. Suppose that a guest list is made up names and titles:

Andrew Worth, President and Chief Executive

Gene Delowitz

union representative

Helen Herbert

Arthur Katetov, Vice-President in charge of sales

Molly Dell, Chief Operating Officer

If you were to insert this list into a sentence using only commas, the reader would not be sure where one item ends and the next begins. Questions would be inevitable: How many people are invited? Is Gene Delowitz a union representative? To clarify where the breaks between items occur, use a semicolon between every element, including the one that comes before the *and:*

Participants at today's meeting include Andrew Worth, President and Chief Executive; Gene Delowitz; a union representative; Helen Herbert; Arthur Katetov, Vice-President in charge of sales; and Molly Dell, Chief Operating Officer.

For more information on semicolons, see Chapter 5.

When a series separated by commas ends in *etc., and so forth, and so on,* or other such phrases, place a comma before the word or abbreviation indicating continuation:

He visited London, Madrid, Copenhagen, etc.

I would like you to give me the receipts, bills, order forms, and so forth.

Two Is Not a Series

Two items are not enough to make a series. Never separate two items with a comma, unless each of the two may stand alone as a separate sentence. (See "When Combining Two Complete Sentences" later in this chapter.)

Wrong: At his birthday party Herbert served milk, and cookies.

Why it is wrong: Only two items, *milk* and *cookies,* are on the list. The words after the comma—*and cookies*—do not form a complete sentence.

Right: At his birthday party Herbert served milk and cookies.

Wrong: The vice-president asked me to report on fourth quarter earnings, and to discuss our plans for a new manufacturing plant.

Why it is wrong: The vice-president's request includes only two tasks—*to report on fourth quarter earnings* and *to discuss our plans for a new manufacturing plant.* The words after the comma—*and to discuss our plans for a new manufacturing plant*—do not form a complete sentence.

Right: The vice-president asked me to report on fourth quarter earnings and to discuss our plans for a new manufacturing plant.

Wrong: Many Egyptian pharaohs planned elaborate tombs, and commanded their subjects to build them.

Why it is wrong: You are not joining two complete sentences. The sentence has one subject (*Egyptian pharaohs*) and two verbs (*planned, commanded*).

Right: Many Egyptian pharaohs planned elaborate tombs and commanded their subjects to build them.

IN A SET OF DESCRIPTIONS

Probably the most common form of description in English is an adjective—a descriptive word—placed in front of the person, place, or thing being described:

> Conscientious Molly bought crisp broccoli. (*Conscientious* describes *Molly* and *crisp* describes *broccoli.*)

> On television, blue shirts and dark ties work better than other color combinations. (*Blue* describes *shirts, dark* describes *ties,* and *color* describes *combinations.*)

When two or more descriptions of the same type and importance are strung together to describe a single person or thing, the descriptions are separated by commas. No comma ever separates the last descriptive word from the word it describes.

The key phrase in this rule is *of the same type and importance.* In grammar terminology, descriptions of the same type and importance are called coordinate. Here's an example of a sentence with coordinate descriptions:

> Mr. Inchworth selected an experienced, intelligent worker for that task.

In the preceding sentence, *experienced* and *intelligent* are coordinate. Therefore, they are separated by commas. When you include a set of descriptions in your writing, you must decide whether the descriptive words are coordinate, thus requiring commas, or not. A few guidelines may help you decide whether commas between descriptions are necessary:

1. You can determine whether the descriptions are coordinate by mentally inserting *and* between them. If the sentence still makes sense, the descriptions should be separated by commas. In this example, the sentence reads well:

> Mr. Inchworth selected an experienced and intelligent worker for that task.

2. Another way to check whether a set of descriptions is coordinate and requires commas is to reverse the order of the descriptions. If the sentence still makes sense, the descriptions are coordinate. In the example above, reversing the descriptions yields a perfectly fine sentence:

> Mr. Inchworth selected an intelligent, experienced worker for that task.

3. Numbers are never separated by commas from other descriptive words.

4. Words showing possession—*my, your, her, his, their* and the like—are never separated by commas from other descriptive words.

Take a look at these guidelines "in action" in the following examples:

> Marietta carefully placed the blank, pink, decorated sheet of paper in front of the judge.

Using guideline number one, you might say that the sheet was *blank* and *pink* and *decorated*. That statement makes sense; all three words give information about the sheet of paper. The descriptive words are equal and should be separated by commas. No comma appears between *decorated* and *sheet,* the word being described.

Note the difference in this sentence:

> Marietta carefully placed the three best pink sheets in front of the judge.

Now the descriptive words are *three, best,* and *pink.* Placing *and* between them doesn't work: The sheets were *three* and *best* and *pink.* Nor can you reverse the order of the descriptions—*best pink three.* This sentence sounds odd because the descriptive words don't function in the same way. One indicates a number (three). *Best* creates a comparison. *Pink* is the only straightforward description of the sheet. Because these three descriptions are all doing different jobs, they aren't coordinate (equal) and shouldn't be separated by commas.

Still another example:

Her carefully chosen comments sounded rehearsed.

No commas are appropriate in this sentence because *comments* is described by two words, *her* and *chosen*. As guideline three above states, words showing possession (in this sentence, *her*) are never set off by commas. *Chosen* and *carefully* aren't separated by commas because they describe different words: *carefully* describes *chosen,* and *chosen* describes *words.*

TO SET OFF NONESSENTIAL INFORMATION

Grammarians label some elements as either *essential* or *nonessential* to the meaning of the sentence. (The terms *restrictive* and *nonrestrictive* are also used at times to describe the same elements.) These elements are usually descriptive, explaining how or when something happened or giving information about a person or a thing. In grammar terminology, adjective and adverb clauses and phrases may be essential or nonessential. So may appositives. Don't worry about those terms. You can understand this rule without them, simply by reading the examples and explanations below. The primary principle here is simple: nonessential information is always set off by commas; essential information is not.

The preceding section of this chapter explains how to punctuate single-word descriptions (adjectives) that come before the person, place, or thing being described. The elements discussed in this section are generally longer and often appear after the word being described.

In deciding how to punctuate, you must first determine whether a particular expression is essential or nonessential. Several guidelines apply. Essential information can't be left out without changing the main idea you are trying to convey. Nonessential information, as the name implies, is interesting but not crucial to the reader's understanding of the sentence.

The sentence says more or less the same thing without the nonessential material. Another way to sort essential and nonessential elements is to decide whether the element is identifying the word it describes or simply providing an extra fact. Essential elements identify; without the essential element, you may not know which person, place, or thing is being discussed. Nonessential elements provide additional information that you might like to know but don't actually need in order to understand the sentence.

The first word of an element can sometimes help you differentiate between essential and nonessential descriptions. *That* often introduces an essential element, and *which* frequently signals a nonessential element. However, many essential and nonessential elements contain neither of those words.

Below are some pairs of sentences with essential and nonessential elements. By comparing them you can see the difference in meaning and punctuation.

Essential: I'm not going to the party unless you go.

Essential element: unless you go

Why it is essential: If you cut *unless you go* out of the sentence, the statement is absolute. I am not going to the party. But the writer may go to the party, if a certain condition is met.

Nonessential: I'm not going to the party, although I may attend the awards ceremony.

Nonessential element: although I may attend the awards ceremony

Why it is nonessential: The writer flatly states that he or she is not going to the party. The information about the awards ceremony is extra; it doesn't have anything to do with the narrator's attendance at the party.

Essential: The book on the bottom shelf needs a new cover.

Essential element: on the bottom shelf

Why it is essential: Without *on the bottom shelf* you don't know which book needs a new cover. The phrase *on the bottom shelf* is not simply descriptive but identifying information in this context.

Nonessential: Bess Truman's biography, which I read last winter, shows the demands of the First Lady's role.

Nonessential element: which I read last winter

Why it is nonessential: If those words are left out of the sentence, the main idea, that the biography describes the First Lady's role, is intact.

Essential: Shakespeare's play *Macbeth* is set in Scotland.

Essential element: *Macbeth*

Why it is essential: The term *Shakespeare's play* is vague. Which play? The title identifies which play is being discussed.

Nonessential: *Macbeth,* Shakespeare's play, is set in Scotland.

Nonessential element: Shakespeare's play

Why it is nonessential: This example reverses the order of the preceding sentence. Once the title of the play appears in the sentence, you know which play you are discussing. The information about the author, *Shakespeare's play,* is less important. True, there may be other plays with the same title written by other authors, but the point remains the same: once you know the title, you know that the main statement—that the play is set in Scotland—refers to *Macbeth,* and that is all you really need.

Essential: The question discussed at length during the last three meetings has still not been decided.

Essential element: discussed at length

Why it is essential: The sentence begins with a general term, *the question*. Therefore the expression *discussed at length during the last three meetings* serves to identify which question has not been decided.

Nonessential: The question of parking privileges, discussed at length during the last three meetings, has still not been decided.

Nonessential element: discussed at length during the last three meetings

Why it is nonessential: The sentence begins with *the question of parking privileges.* You know what has not been decided. The information about when the discussion took place is extra, not part of the main idea.

Two to Separate

If you're separating a nonessential element, be sure to do so completely. Don't place only one comma and let the beginning or the end of the element blend into the rest of the sentence.

Wrong: My oldest sister, Eileen plans to become an oral surgeon.

Why it is wrong: The nonessential element (*Eileen*) is preceded by a comma but not followed by one.

Right: My oldest sister, Eileen, plans to become an oral surgeon.

TO SET OFF INTERRUPTERS

An interrupter, as its name implies, may be left out of the sentence without changing the main idea. Interrupters resemble nonessential elements, discussed earlier in this chapter, in that they give the reader extra information. An interrupter may indicate a contrast, an example, or an extra comment. Like nonessential elements, interrupters are always set off by commas:

> This bowl of sugar, however, could add more than 4000 calories to one's diet. (*However* makes an extra comment.)

> Albertina did not, after all, run for office on an independent ticket. (*After all* comments on the main idea of the sentence.)

> The salt shaker, not the pepper mill, was carved from solid marble. (*Not the pepper mill* creates a contrast.)

> No newspaper is completely unbiased, in my expert opinion. (*In my expert opinion* is an extra comment.)

> Alice has been appointed to a position of some importance, but not Chester. (*But not Chester* creates a contrast.)

> Steam, for example, is just as damaging as acid for that material. (*For example* labels an example.)

In the preceding sentences the interrupter occurs within or at the end of the sentence. If one of these expressions occurs at the beginning of a sentence, you may not need to separate it from the rest of the sentence with a comma.

> In my expert opinion no newspaper is completely unbiased. (Comment occurs at the beginning of the sentence and doesn't need to be separated by a comma.)

See the section entitled "To Set Off Introductory Expressions" for more information.

Avoiding Choppiness

Don't place commas unnecessarily because excess punctuation makes your sentences sound choppy. Read the sentence to see whether it is more understandable if the words are cut away from the rest of the sentence by commas. Let common sense and the reader's convenience be your guide.

Wrong: Marylou loaded the computer program, into her laptop, and calculated the final grades.

Why it is wrong: The words set off by commas (*into her laptop*) are part of the main idea of the sentence, not an extra comment. Without *into her laptop* the sentence does not convey the same information.

Right: Marylou loaded the computer program into her laptop and calculated the final grades.

Wrong: Marylou prefers the laptop I think because she can work anywhere with it.

Why it is wrong: *I think* breaks the flow of the sentence, placing the speaker in a sentence about Marylou. Thus, *I think* is an additional comment, not a main idea.

Right: Marylou prefers the laptop, I think, because she can work anywhere with it.

WHEN COMBINING TWO COMPLETE SENTENCES

A complete sentence always contains at least one subject/verb pair and expresses an understandable, finished thought. (A *subject* is the person, place, or thing being talked about and the *verb* is the action or state of being of the subject.) When joining two complete sentences, you may use a semicolon (see Chapter 5) or a *conjunction*. A conjunction is a joining word. Conjunctions that connect ideas of equal importance include *and, but, or, nor, for,* and *yet.* Place a comma before each of these joining words when it is used to combine two complete sentences, as in this example:

> I reported on fourth quarter earnings, and I discussed plans for a new manufacturing plant.

Each of the two items may be a separate, complete sentence:

1. I reported on fourth quarter earnings.
2. I discussed plans for a new manufacturing plant.

The word that joins these equal, complete sentences, *and,* must be preceded by a comma. Here are some additional examples of correctly punctuated sentences:

> Do your homework today, or risk the teacher's anger tomorrow.

> Before the party Elena stirred the punch, yet it separated anyway.

Incorrectly Joined Sentence

Don't join two complete sentences with a comma unless you also insert a conjunction (*and, but, or,* and so on). This error is so common that it has its own name—a comma splice. If you don't want a conjunction, insert a semicolon instead.

Wrong: The snow was supposed to arrive at noon, school was dismissed early to avoid the danger of icy roads.

Why it is wrong: Two complete sentences (*The snow was supposed to arrive at noon* and *school was dismissed early to avoid the danger of icy roads*) are linked only by a comma. A comma may not link complete sentences.

Right: The snow was supposed to arrive at noon; school was dismissed early to avoid the danger of icy roads.

When No Comma Is Necessary

Don't automatically place a comma in front of every conjunction, or joining word. If the conjunction is linking anything other than two complete sentences, a comma isn't called for.

Wrong: Maxwell did not please the Internal Revenue agent, or his accountant.

Why it is wrong: The joining word, *or,* connects *agent* and *accountant,* not two complete sentences.

Right: Maxwell did not please the Internal Revenue agent or his accountant.

Wrong: Alex sipped the wine slowly, and eventually drank it all.

If you're linking three or more complete sentences, treat them as a series. (See "To Create a Series" earlier in this chapter for more information.) Place a comma after each sentence you are joining, as in this example:

> Archie drew an elaborate border for the program, Eleanor set the type, and Priscilla carried the finished product to the printer.

The comma before the *and* is optional, but most style manuals, including *The Chicago Manual of Style* and the *Publication Manual of the American Psychological Association,* and the *Modern Language Association Handbook,* prefer that the comma be inserted.

Extremely short sentences may sometimes be joined by a conjunction without a comma. In this sentence, the reader doesn't need a pause in order to grasp the meaning:

> Sidney washed and I dried the dishes.

Placing a comma in sentences this short and straightforward is a matter of style, not grammar. Let your ear by your guide.

Why it is wrong: The joining word, *and,* should not be preceded by a comma because *eventually drank it all* cannot stand alone as a complete thought.

Right: Alex sipped the wine slowly and eventually drank it all.

Wrong: The editor of the school newspaper, or the Student Body President will address the issue of unexcused absences at the next assembly.

Why it is wrong: The joining word *or* connects two titles (*editor of the school newspaper* and *Student Body President*), not two complete sentences. No comma is needed.

Right: The editor of the school newspaper or the Student Body President will address the issue of unexcused absences at the next assembly.

TO INDICATE DIRECT ADDRESS

Direct address refers to an intended audience that is named in the sentence—the person or people you are writing to. The direct-address expression should be set off from the rest of the sentence by commas. Note the "audience" in these sentences:

> Girls, please hand in your art projects now. (*Girls* = direct address)

> Don't go into the water after the lifeguard leaves, George. (*George* = direct address)

> The origin of this proverb, Mr. President, is not entirely clear. (*Mr. President* = direct address)

The commas pluck the name or title of the intended audience out of the sentence. You may read the sentence without the direct-address words, and the sentence still makes sense. In the first two examples, only one comma is needed because the direct-address words are at the beginning or the end of the sentence. In the last example, two commas set off a direct-address in the middle of a sentence.

Separating Direct-Address Expressions Completely

Many writers place only one comma instead of the two needed to separate a direct-address statement from the middle of a sentence.

Wrong: He explained, Alex that you should never cross the street against the light.

Why it is wrong: With only one comma, the word *Alex* is linked to the rest of the sentence. The reader tends to see *Alex that* and the words following as a unit. The meaning of the sentence, however, calls for *Alex* to be separate.

Right: He explained, Alex, that you should never cross the street against the light.

IN PERSONAL AND COMPANY TITLES

A title that appears at the end of a name of a person is often separated from the name by a comma. The designation *Inc.* and *Ltd.* (*Incorporated* and *Limited*) are also set off by commas, as in these examples:

> I've just mailed the package to John B. Duckworth, Jr.
>
> Send your legal inquiries to Karen Silja, Esq. (Esq. is the abbreviation for *Esquire*, a title given to an attorney.)
>
> I applied for a position with Declan Telecommunication, Inc.
>
> After the graduation ceremony, Helen was thrilled to hear the dean refer to her as "Helen Woo, PhD."

Some people prefer not to insert a comma in their own names. The Reverend Martin Luther King Jr., for example, did not separate the *Jr.* from his surname with a comma. Similarly, some companies place a comma before the *Inc.* or

Ltd. abbreviation (for *Incorporated* and *Limited*) and some do not. If you know the custom of the person or business you are writing about, you should honor that choice.

Once a comma is used before the title, it must be used after the title as well, if the sentence continues on:

> Declan Telecommunications, Inc., is my first choice.
>
> John B. Duckworth, Jr., is retiring tomorrow.

If the title is part of a possessive, omit the comma:

> Declan Telecommunications, Inc.'s benefits are appealing.
>
> John F. Kennedy, Jr.'s magazine was called *George.*

If the title comes before the name, do not separate it from the name with a comma.

> **Wrong:** Vice-President, Tabitha Fuller chaired the meeting.
>
> **Right:** Vice-President Tabitha Fuller chaired the meeting.

Don't place a comma before a roman numeral attached to a name.

> **Wrong:** The critics praised the commencement address given by John Jay Adams, III.
>
> **Right:** The critics praised the commencement address given by John Jay Adams III.

IN DATES

The rules for comma placement in dates are completely arbitrary. No one pretends that a reader will misread a date because of the presence or absence of a comma. Furthermore, the major style manuals each call for slightly different formats, and all diverge from the longstanding rules taught in many grammar books.

If you are writing for business or personal reasons, follow the traditional rules below. If you are writing a scientific or

Separating Months, Days, and Years

Do not place a comma between the month and the day.

Wrong: The bill is dated July, 15, 1972.

Right: The bill is dated July 15, 1972.

When a date is written on a separate line (as in a letter), do not place a comma after the year.

other academic report or for a publication that adheres to a specific style manual, check the style-manual section here or ask your editor about the comma rules for dates.

Regardless of the format you choose, be consistent throughout one piece of writing.

Traditional Rules

Most grammar books state that when a date occurs in a sentence, a comma separates the month and year. If the sentence continues, a comma follows the year as well. If the month, day, and year are included, a comma separates the day and the year but not the month and the day. These dates are punctuated correctly according to traditional rules:

In September, 1965, the sales revenue began to fall.

On March 30, 2004, Susanna Vargas was hired.

The cornerstone of this building was dedicated in January, 1805.

We celebrate my grandmother's birthday every July 4th.

Publication Manual of the American Psychological Association

The Publication Manual of the American Psychological Association omits the comma between the month and year if no day is included:

Wrong:

September 12, 2003,

Dear Oscar,

Right:

September 12, 2003

Dear Oscar,

For sample personal and business letters, see Chapters 13 and 14.

On April 12, 2005, twenty subjects were tested. (Includes commas because the day is specified.)

In April 2005 twenty subjects were tested. (Without the day, the commas are omitted.)

The Chicago Manual of Style

The Chicago Manual of Style allows a comma between the day and the year as well as after the year:

On April 12, 2003, the first hint of archaeological activity occurs.

However, when the day is not specified or when the day is placed before the month, the commas are omitted:

In April 2003 the first hint of archaeological activity occurs.

On 12 April 2003 the first hint of archaeological activity occurs.

The Modern Language Association Handbook

The Modern Language Association Handbook prefers that the day precede the month. In this format, or if only the month and year are given, commas are omitted.

President Truman gave that speech on 30 July 1949.

President Truman gave that speech in July 1949.

President Truman gave that speech in July 1949 to an appreciative audience.

IN ADDRESSES

When an address is inserted into a sentence, commas take the place of the line breaks that would ordinarily appear on an envelope. An address on an envelope or at the beginning of a business letter looks like this:

Marcia Stillman
309 West 339th Street
Pankville, New York 12090

If the same address is inserted into a sentence, commas separate the name, street, and city/state lines. Any commas that would normally appear within an address line on an envelope also appear in the sentence, as in this example:

When you have completed the registration form, please send it to Marcia Stillman, 309 West 339th Street, Pankville, New York 12090.

The comma after *Stillman* indicates the end of line one, and the comma after *Street* marks the end of line two. The comma between *Pankville* and *New York* remains as well.

If the sentence continues after the address, the last bit of the address (the zip code) is also separated from the rest of the sentence by a comma:

When you have completed the registration form, please send it to Marcia Stillman, 309 West 339th Street, Pankville, New York 12090, and enclose the application fee.

Here are a few more examples of addresses as they should be punctuated in sentences:

The annual meeting will be held at the Biltmore Hotel, 1515 Sycamore Avenue, Floral City, Vermont 05459, at 10:30

a.m. (Note the comma after the zip code, which separates the last part of the address from the rest of the sentence. No comma appears between the state and the zip code.)

If you need to reach me over the weekend, send a message in care of General Delivery, Athens, Greece. (Even though no street and house number appears, you still need commas after each element of the address.)

Only a few decades ago, commas were placed at the end of each line of an address on an envelope, except for the last line. In modern usage, however, no comma appears at the end of a line. Be sure to separate the city and state names with a comma.

IN LETTERS

Though much correspondence these days takes the form of e-mail or text messages, formal letters on paper still have not joined the dinosaurs in extinction. Commas in personal and professional letters follow different, but still strict, rules.

Personal Letters

In a personal letter, place a comma after the salutation, as you see here.

Dear Mary,

Dear Mr. Finn,

Dear Harold,

Also place a comma after the complimentary close:

Sincerely,

Your friend,

Yours truly,

Don't place a comma at the end of an address line or after the date.

Wrong:

1501 Broadway,
Washington, D.C. 20003
March 12, 2005,

Right:

1501 Broadway
Washington, D.C. 20003
March 12, 2005

For samples of personal letters, see Chapter 13.

Business Letters

Generally a colon follows the salutation of a business letter,
instead of a comma. If the sender and the recipient have
worked together for some time and have a friendly relationship or if the sender wishes to strike an informal tone, a
comma may substitute for the colon. In these examples,
sometimes the person receiving the letter is addressed by
name and sometimes by title. Business letters also allow
general, impersonal phrases such as "Sir" and "To Whom It
May Concern."

Dear Mr. Cobb:

To Whom It May Concern:

Dear Sir:

To the Billing Supervisor:

As in a personal letter, a comma follows the complimentary
close.

Yours sincerely,

Sincerely,

Very truly yours,

Similar to personal letters, the address and date lines of a business letter do not end in commas.

Chapter 14 of this book contains several sample business letters.

TO SET OFF INTRODUCTORY EXPRESSIONS

The basic structure of an English sentence is subject (who or what you are talking about), verb (what the subject is doing or a statement of being about the subject), and object (the receiver of the action, which may or may not appear in the sentence). This pattern is the workhorse of English expression. But variety is the spice of life, and an essay or a letter with only these bare bones quickly bores the reader, not to mention the writer. Introductory expressions vary the basic sentence pattern nicely, adding time, place, conditions, or reasons to the main idea of the sentence. Introductory expressions may also give more information about the actions of the subject. Unfortunately, punctuating the introductory expressions can be a bit tricky. The general guidelines are as follows:

1. Introductory expressions, especially if they run to some length, are generally separated from the main portion of the sentence by a comma.

2. Very short introductory statements don't always need commas.

3. Length is not the only factor in deciding whether or not to place a comma. More important is the reader's convenience. If the pause helps the reader understand more easily, insert a comma.

4. Consider how closely related the introductory words are to the main idea; the closer the relationship, the less need for a comma.

5. An introductory expression of time, unless it is extremely short, is followed by a comma.

6. An introductory verb form—a participle—is always followed by a comma.

7. Use a comma after an introductory expression that gives a reason or condition (expressions beginning with *although, though, despite the fact that,* and *because*).

As you may have guessed by now, a certain amount of judgment is called for when you're placing a comma after an introductory expression. Take a look at these examples and the rationale for placing or omitting commas:

> When the dance is over, the winners of the salsa contest will be announced.

When the dance is over adds a sense of time to the main idea—the announcement of the winners. An introductory expression of time, unless it is extremely short, is set off by a comma.

> Yesterday the winners of the salsa contest were announced.

Here the time expression, *yesterday,* is short and closely related to the main idea of the sentence. No comma is needed.

> In the closet behind the stairs leading to the attic, Henry discovered some architectural blueprints that had been missing for years.

In the closet behind the stairs leading to the attic is a fairly lengthy statement of place, so a comma is called for.

> Under the lion's paw the mouse wriggled frantically.

The punctuation of the above example is a judgment call: The comma isn't required but may be inserted. The decision is a matter of style, not grammar.

> Sitting in the rowboat, the Olympic champion proudly raised her medal for all to see.

Commas with Short Introductory Statements

Very short introductory statements may not need commas. If the meaning is clear and you have a choice, omit these commas. Otherwise your writing may sound choppy.

Wrong: Tomorrow, Harriet will attend her karate class.

Why it is wrong: No comma is needed because *tomorrow* is so short.

Right: Tomorrow Harriet will attend her karate class.

Sitting in the rowboat is an introductory participle—a verb form that gives extra information. Introductory participles are always followed by commas.

> Though he was tired, the senator insisted on continuing the filibuster.

Though he was tired explains the condition under which the main idea of the sentence took place. Introductory statements beginning with *though, although,* and *despite the fact that* should be separated by commas from the rest of the sentence.

> Because of rain, the picnic will be postponed until next month.

The introductory words in the above sentence give a reason. Introductory expressions beginning with *because* are set off by commas.

> Yes, the Halloween costumes have arrived.

Yes is set off by commas because it doesn't affect the main idea of the sentence. *Yes* and *no,* when they aren't part of the main statement of the sentence, are always followed by commas.

However, if *no* is part of the main idea of the sentence, don't place a comma after it. These two sentences have very different meanings and thus different punctuation:

So Easy to Make a Mistake

The word *so* is sometimes used to link two ideas in this way:

It was raining, so they cancelled the picnic.

Some writers place *so* at the beginning of a sentence, implying a link with an earlier sentence:

So they went to a movie instead.

No apples remain in the refrigerator. (Meaning: the refrigerator is bare of apples.)

No, apples remain in the refrigerator. (Meaning: Don't take the apples out of the refrigerator.)

Always place a comma after an introductory expression if there's a chance the reader may link ideas that should be separate. Take a look at this example, which is poorly punctuated:

Chanting the choir raised the volume as the celebrant intoned the prayer.

Without a comma the reader naturally reads *chanting the choir* and then lapses into confusion. The point of punctuation is to make the reader's task easier. Here's the same sentence, this time with a comma:

Chanting, the choir raised the volume as the celebrant intoned the prayer.

Now *chanting* is clearly introductory and the main idea of the sentence, *the choir raised the volume,* is more understandable.

If you move introductory words to the end of a sentence, you may often omit the comma.

Wrong: The teacher found a soiled handkerchief, under a stack of papers that she had graded last night.

Strictly speaking, *so* should not be used in this way because a joining word, by definition, should be linking two things in the same sentence. However, in informal writing, *so* may certainly start a sentence, just as *and* and *but* may. If you begin a sentence with *so*, don't follow it with a comma:

Wrong: So, they went to a movie.

Right: So they went to a movie.

More formal: Therefore, they went to a movie.

Why it is wrong: Placing a comma after *handkerchief* unnecessarily cuts the sentence in half. Without an introductory element, no comma is needed.

Right: Under a stack of papers that she had graded last night, the teacher found a soiled handkerchief.

Why it is right: *Under a stack of papers that she had graded last night* introduces the main idea and gives a sense of place.

WITH SHORT QUESTIONS

Most questions are stand-alone sentences ending in a question mark. Occasionally a short question is embedded in a statement. To clarify where the statement ends and the question begins, use a comma, as in these examples:

It is a lovely day, isn't it? (The statement is *It is a lovely day* and the question is *isn't it*. The comma separates the two and clarifies the meaning.)

The proceeds of the raffle may be, don't you agree, better this year than last. (A question—*don't you agree*—is embedded in a statement. The comma separates it from the main idea of the sentence.)

Don't place unnecessary commas in a question.

Wrong: Do you believe, that the ticket price is set too high?

Why it is wrong: The entire sentence forms one question. There is no reason to cut the question in half with a comma.

Right: Do you believe that the ticket price is set too high?

IN MILD INTERJECTIONS

The English language provides many ways to express strong emotion. One is the exclamation point, which adds emphasis and turns an ordinary statement into a shout. Yet writers often want to interject, or insert, comments into a sentence without the drama of a full-fledged exclamation. Those commentary words, also known as mild interjections, generally occur at the beginning of the sentence, though they may appear elsewhere. Like everything else that is not part of the main idea, mild interjections should be set off from the rest of the sentence by commas. In these examples, reading the sentence without the mild interjection does not change the meaning the writer is trying to convey:

Well, I'm not sure that I agree with you on that point. (*Well* is a mild interjection.)

My goodness, you have certainly done a great job. (*My goodness* is a mild interjection.)

Please don't leave before the clean up, for goodness sake. (*For goodness sake* is a mild interjection.)

Ah, we are alone at last. (*Ah* is a mild interjection.)

I'll go with you to the meeting, absolutely. (*Absolutely* is a mild interjection.)

Unbelievable, the planning commission has not yet approved your proposal. (*Unbelievable* is a mild interjection.)

Great, I'd like to chair the constitutional committee. (*Great* is a mild interjection.)

Oh, you're always joking when you should be serious. (*Oh* is a mild interjection.)

Note: *Oh* is a mild interjection, but *O,* which is found mostly in poetry, calls for an exclamation point.

> **Wrong:** O, my darling, why have you left me?
>
> **Why it is wrong:** *O,* by convention, should be followed by an exclamation point.
>
> **Right:** O! My darling, why have you left me?

To Be or Not to Be an Interjection

The same word may be an interjection in one sentence but not in another. The key is to determine whether the word is part of the main idea of the sentence or an extra comment on the main idea. If the word is part of the main idea, don't separate it from the rest of the sentence with commas.

> **Wrong:** A true Renaissance man, Andrew speaks five languages, well, and also plays a number of musical instruments.
>
> **Why it is wrong:** The word *well* describes how Andrew *speaks* and thus is part of the main idea. It should not be set off by commas.
>
> **Right:** A true Renaissance man, Andrew speaks five languages well and also plays a number of musical instruments.

IN QUOTATIONS

Whenever someone's exact words are reproduced, the words are enclosed in quotation marks. In standard American usage, commas at the end of a quotation are always placed inside the closing quotation mark. In Britain, where quotation marks are called "inverted commas," this custom is reversed: The comma is placed outside the quotation mark. If the sentence includes a quotation inside another quotation, the comma goes inside both sets of quotation marks (in America) and outside both (in Britain).

A comma at the end of a quoted statement takes the place of a period when the sentence continues on. The comma is a convenient way to show that the quotation is complete, but the sentence is not. (A period never appears within a sentence unless it signals an abbreviation.) If the quoted words would normally end with a period, the period appears only if the quotation ends the sentence. Take a look at these examples:

> "Helen boils those vegetables far too long." (A period ends both the sentence and the quotation.)

> "Helen boils those vegetables far too long," commented the chef. (Because the sentence continues, the period is replaced by a comma.)

Quoted questions or exclamations follow different rules. For more information on punctuating quotations, see Chapter 7.

Quotations with Speaker Tags

In the preceding example, *commented the chef* is a speaker tag—words identifying the person who said or wrote the quoted material. A speaker tag may appear before, after, or in the middle of a quotation.

Speaker Tag After the Quotation

If the speaker tag follows a quoted statement, the comma is placed inside the closing quotation mark (American English) or outside the closing quotation mark (British English).

> "I don't care for Helen's cooking at all," said the chef.

> "My family seems to like my recipes," replied Helen.

If the quotation ends with an exclamation point or a question mark, don't place a comma before the speaker tag:

> "Are you sure that Sri Lanka was once called Ceylon?" asked the attorney.

> "Of course I'm sure!" exclaimed the geographer.

For more information on punctuating quotations, see Chapter 7.

Speaker Tag Before the Quotation

An introductory speaker tag is separated from the quotation by a comma, as in these examples:

> The chef commented, "Helen boils those vegetables far too long."

> Helen argued, "The true flavor does not emerge immediately."

Speaker Tag Within the Quotation

A speaker tag placed inside a quotation is also separated from the quotation by commas, as in these examples:

> "Helen boils those vegetables far too long," explained the chef, "and nutrients are lost unnecessarily."

> "If you are worried about nutrition," retorted Helen, "take a vitamin."

Speaker Tag Without a Quotation

Sometimes speaker tags occur even when the sentence contains no directly quoted material. The speaker tag is generally set off from the rest of the sentence by commas:

> That song was recorded yesterday, Nuria claims.

Nuria claims is a speaker tag, even though the sentence doesn't give her exact words.

Quotations Without Speaker Tags

Some sentences quote only a bit of a speaker's remarks and introduce the quoted material with the word *that*. Other sentences identify the speaker only indirectly. In such cases, don't place commas around the speaker identification. Here are a few examples:

Helen reported that "raindrops and roses" are two of her least favorite things. (Because the quotation is introduced by *that,* omit the comma.)

Helen listed "raindrops and roses" as two of her least favorite things. (Clearly *Helen* is the implied speaker or writer of *raindrops and roses,* but the sentence has no true speaker tag and thus no comma.)

Whether or not you have a speaker tag, you may need a comma at the end of a quotation for other reasons—to set off an introductory expression, to mark an interrupter, or to serve other purposes in the sentence. Place the comma inside the quotation mark (in American English) or outside the quotation mark (in British English). Some examples:

Because the CD was "awesome," Jared had to buy it. (The comma after *awesome* is needed to set off the introductory expression *because the CD was "awesome"* and is placed inside the quotation mark, following standard American usage.)

The CD was "awesome," according to Jared, and he had to buy it. (The interrupter is *according to Jared.* It is set off from the rest of the sentence by commas. The comma is placed inside the quotation mark, following standard American usage.)

Other Comma Rules for Quotations

Never place an endmark and a comma at the end of the same quotation:

Wrong: "The art project drew several thousand extra visitors to the museum.", reported Mr. Monti.

Right: "The art project drew several thousand extra visitors to the museum," reported Mr. Monti.

Wrong: "The art project drew several thousand extra visitors to the museum,".

Right: "The art project drew several thousand extra visitors to the museum."

Run-On Quotations

When a speaker tag occurs within a quotation that is made up of two complete sentences, be sure to reflect two sentences in your choice of punctuation.

Wrong: "I walked for two hours in the park yesterday," explained Brad, "I would have liked to stay there all day."

Why it is wrong: The quotation includes two complete sentences: *I walked for two hours in the park yesterday* and *I would have liked to stay there all day.* With only one end-mark, the sentence is a run-on—an improper joining.

Right: "I walked for two hours in the park yesterday," explained Brad. "I would have liked to stay there all day." (Now the punctuation correctly indicates the two sentences that make up the quotation.)

Right: "I walked for two hours in the park yesterday." Explained Brad, "I would have liked to stay there all day." (Again, two sentences.)

Right: "I walked for two hours in the park yesterday," explained Brad; "I would have liked to stay there all day." (A semicolon joins the two sentences correctly.)

Right: "I walked for two hours in the park yesterday," explained Brad, "but I would have liked to stay there all day." (A conjunction, *but,* joins the two sentences correctly.)

WITH PARENTHESES

Parentheses interrupt the flow of the sentence and add extra information. (See Chapter 9 for more information on parentheses.) Punctuate the words inside the parentheses according to the usual comma rules described in this chapter. If you need to separate the portion of the sentence containing parenthetical material from the rest of the sentence, place a comma after the parentheses. One way to determine whether you need a comma after the parentheses is to read the sentence without the parenthetical material. If you would normally place a comma after the last word before the parentheses, you should have one after the parentheses. This example is punctuated correctly:

> Proudly hanging his diploma (he had graduated just that spring), Marshall declared his medical office open for business.

Applying the method described above, read the sentence without the parenthetical comment:

> Proudly hanging his diploma, Marshall declared his medical office open for business.

The comma after *diploma* is needed to separate the introductory expression from the rest of the sentence. Thus a comma is needed after the parenthesis.

No Commas Before Parentheses

Never place a comma before parentheses. The parentheses itself is enough to mark a separation between the preceding words and the words inside the parenthesis.

Wrong: If you wish to purchase a ticket, (each costs $10), send us a check.

Right: If you wish to purchase a ticket (each costs $10), send us a check.

Wrong: The dance will be held at 8:30 in Damascus Hall, (directions attached).

Right: The dance will be held at 8:30 in Damascus Hall (directions attached).

TO INDICATE OMITTED WORDS

A sort of verbal shorthand is common in speech, as in this exchange:

> Going to the store?
>
> Later, when I finish this letter.

In formal writing words are omitted much less frequently. Nevertheless, you may at times choose to omit some words in order to create a fluid or concise effect. The omitted words are sometimes replaced by a comma, as in these examples:

With words omitted: Give Ellen candy; Bob, cake.

With the omitted words replaced: Give Ellen candy; give Bob cake.

With words omitted: Shirley sold five books of raffle tickets; Alex, ten; and Arturo, three.

With the omitted words replaced: Shirley sold five books of raffle tickets, Alex sold ten, and Arturo sold three.

Clearly the first version of each sentence is better!

IN NUMBERS

Traditionally, a comma separates large numbers into group of three digits:

1,238,934   34,000   21,600

Four-digit numbers generally appear without a comma:

4500   9835   2010

TO AVOID MISREADINGS

The last rule in this chapter is the most important of all. No
matter what else you do with a comma, be sure to place one
where it is needed to avoid a misunderstanding. A good way
to place "clarity commas" is to read your sentences aloud. If
you stumble because you've linked ideas that should be separate, you know that you need a comma. Take a look at the
sentences below:

> After bathing, the dog splashed everyone in the room.

> To eat, children need smaller utensils.

> Having studied the provisions of City Law 221, 300 police
> officers prepared to enforce it.

> If I am dancing, dancing is the only thing I'm thinking
> about.

Without those commas, the reader imagines sentences
about *bathing the dog, eating children,* and more than 200,000
police officers. The last example comes across as a typographi-
cal error, with *dancing* repeated unnecessarily. Granted, even
in the absence of clarifying commas a careful reader will probably figure out the intended meaning at some point. But why
take the chance?

5

The Semicolon

The semicolon in one form or another has been in use since ancient Greece, when it was written as a dot placed low on a line. (A higher dot signaled a period.) The semicolon as we now know it was named by Aldus Mantius, an Italian scholar, during the Renaissance.

Scientist and author Dr. Lewis Thomas wrote that glimpsing a semicolon in a sentence was like "climbing a steep path through woods and seeing a wooden bench . . . where you can expect to sit for a moment, catching your breath." Not many people are as enthusiastic about this punctuation mark as Dr. Thomas. In fact, some writers see the semicolon as pretentious and dishonest because, as one commented, it allows you to link ideas without bothering to explain how the ideas are related to each other.

A semicolon is the punctuation equivalent of *and* or other joining words. It links one complete sentence to another, but with a semicolon the writer says, in effect, *I'm not finished yet.* The semicolon also separates complicated items when they are listed in a sentence.

TO JOIN SENTENCES

Use a semicolon between two complete sentences in place of a conjunction, or joining word. A semicolon is not the same as a period. When readers arrive at a semicolon, they know that more information is coming. The readers expect clarification, justification, or consequences after a semicolon.

Because a semicolon creates anticipation, the meaning of each of the sentences joined by a semicolon must be closely related; otherwise the reader will be thrown off the logical path, expecting a connection where none exists. Take a look at these sentence pairs, each containing one sentence with a conjunction and one sentence in which the conjunction has been replaced by a semicolon. Notice how the meaning of each part of the sentence relates logically to the rest of the sentence:

> **With a conjunction:** The movie received terrible reviews, and the critics agree that the quality of the acting is only slightly above that of the average school play.
>
> **With a semicolon:** The movie received terrible reviews; the critics agree that the quality of the acting is only slightly above that of the average school play.
>
> **With a conjunction:** The ice in the river broke last night, but the bay is still frozen.
>
> **With a semicolon:** The ice in the river broke last night; the bay is still frozen.
>
> **With a conjunction:** The speaker ran into the wings quickly because the spectators had begun to heave eggs, rotten fruit, and other objects at the stage.
>
> **With a semicolon:** The speaker ran into the wings quickly; the spectators had begun to heave eggs, rotten fruit, and other objects at the stage.

In the preceding pairs, the ideas in each of the sentences joined by the semicolon make sense when they are stated together. The negative reviews mentioned in the first pair presumably stem at least partly from the poor performances of the actors. In the second pair, the condition of the river and the bay are being compared. The last pair presents a cause and effect situation. Because the ideas belong together logically, a semicolon properly combines the two statements.

If the ideas are not logically related to each other, a semicolon is not appropriate:

Wrong: The gray-haired man paced furiously outside the emergency room; yesterday he had attended the school play.

Why it is wrong: Unless the man's attendance at the school play is related to his anger and his presence at a hospital, the two statements are too far apart to be linked by a semicolon. If the two events—the play and the hospital visit—are linked, the writer needs to explain how.

Better: The gray-haired man paced furiously outside the emergency room. He could hardly believe that only yesterday he had attended his daughter's school play; today she was in the hospital.

Why it is better: Now the connection between the emergency room and the play has been explained to the reader.

A semicolon may be grammatically correct in a particular sentence, as you see in the preceding examples, but logically flawed. Use this punctuation mark sparingly, only when the link between the two parts of the sentence will be clear to the reader without further explanation.

Comma Splices

Never join two complete sentences with a comma. This error, called a comma splice or run-on sentence, is very common. Take care to use a semicolon or a joining word (a conjunction) when each half of the material you are connecting can stand alone as a complete sentence.

Wrong: The fuzzy yellow duck was her favorite present, she kept it in a prominent place on her desk to remind her of the special friend who had given it to her.

Right: The fuzzy yellow duck was her favorite present; she kept it in a prominent place on her desk to remind her of the special friend who had given it to her.

WITH ADVERBS

Adverbs are words that explain how, when, where, or why something happened. (Adverbs have other functions too, not relevant here.) Some adverbs hint at connection. *Consequently, therefore,* and *thus* imply cause and effect. An addition to a previously stated idea is signaled by *besides, moreover, furthermore,* and *also. Then, next,* and *once* link two events chronologically or connect an action with a statement about time. *However* and *nevertheless* create a contrast between two ideas.

All these words add meaning to the sentence. They should be used whenever they express what you want to say. The point to remember when using such words is that while they hint at a connection, they do not actually create one. You cannot use them to join two sentences because they do not function as a proper grammatical connection. With a semicolon, however, you can join two statements, retaining the adverb that explains the nature of the connection.

These examples illustrate properly joined sentences:

> Margot slid on a banana peel and broke her arm; consequently, she became a dedicated member of the school's litter patrol.

> Freckles appear on my forehead after only the briefest time in the sun; nevertheless, I spend most of my vacations at the beach.

> First in the cafeteria line was George, hungry and tired; next was Amelia, who was simply keeping George company.

> I don't want to do any homework tonight; however, my mother will kill me if I fail history again.

Notice that in each of the above sentences, the semicolon may easily mark the breaking point between two separate sentences. With the addition of a capital letter, each half of the larger sentence can stand alone. The semicolon implies that the ideas are very closely related, and the adverb hints at the nature of the relationship between the two ideas. In the first sentence above, *consequently* suggests cause and effect. In the second sentence *nevertheless* add a hint of defiance to the beach vacation. In the third sentence above, *next* functions in both space and time. The reader knows where each stands in line, literally, and the expected order in which George and Amelia will be served. In the final sentence above, *however* explains the relationship between the idea in the first part of the sentence (*I don't want to do any homework tonight*) and the second (the consequences are so great that I will do the history homework anyway).

The most important point to remember is that these adverbs may not join two sentences. Use them for meaning, but add a semicolon to achieve a grammatically correct sentence.

These adverbs are often followed by commas. The comma is generally seen as a matter of style, not grammar. Notice the effect of the comma, which provides a short pause, in sentences one, two, and four on the previous page. In the third sentence no comma follows *next* because of the close relationship between that word and the following statement about Amelia. In general, your ear will guide you to the need to insert or to omit a comma.

IN COMPLICATED SENTENCES

The comma that precedes a conjunction (a joining word such as *and, or, but, nor, for*) occupies a special place in the reader's mind. That comma, along with the joining word that follows it, signals to the reader that another major idea is coming. But when you are linking sentences that themselves contain a comma or two, this special comma may be overlooked. Traditional grammarians, therefore, change the comma preceding the joining word to a semicolon—a punctuation mark that is more conspicuous than a simple comma.

In modern writing this rule is not always followed. You may ignore it and still achieve an educated, proper effect. In fact, sometimes following this rule causes trouble. Readers who don't understand the niceties of grammar frequently believe that the writer has made a mistake by placing a semicolon in front of a word such as *and, or, but,* and *nor.*

Unequal Partners

A semicolon should never link a complete sentence to a frag-
ment of an idea. This is a punctuation mark of equality, joining partners of the same rank.

Wrong: Alexander shouldered the heavy burden; although
he was reluctant to help his stepsister in her search.

Why it is wrong: The sentence is separated into two
halves, one on each side of the semicolon. The first half

Some examples of this rule in action include the following:

When confronted with the fact that she had lied, Elena simply smiled; but inside she was extremely embarrassed.

Oscar fervently hoped for a sunny day; and perhaps
because the odds favored him, he was rewarded with bril-
liant, clear weather when he awoke.

A prolific and fluent writer, Charles Dickens wrote thousands
of pages of incomparable prose; yet somehow he managed
to tour the English-speaking world, reading and performing
his work for an admiring public.

The three preceding sentences each contain a joining
word—*but, and, yet*—connecting two complete sentences. In
the first sample sentence above, the conjunction *but* links

When confronted with the fact that she had lied, Elena
simply smiled.

and

Inside she was extremely embarrassed.

The comma after *lied* does not function in the same way as
the comma before *but*. To emphasize the *but,* the comma that
precedes it may be "promoted" to a semicolon. Similarly, the
commas before *and* and *yet* in the second and third sentences
above may be changed to semicolons. Once again, a warning:
Following this rule shows that you understand the finest

of the sentence (*Alexander shouldered the heavy burden*) may function as a complete sentence. However, the second part of the sentence (*although he was reluctant to help his stepsister in her search*) may not stand alone as a complete sentence. The semicolon should link equals—specifically, two complete sentences that could conceivably stand alone and make sense.

Right: Alexander shouldered the heavy burden, although he was reluctant to help his stepsister in her search.

points of grammar, but only grammarians may appreciate your achievement!

TO SEPARATE ITEMS IN A SERIES

Items listed in a sentence are normally separated one from another with commas. But when one or more of the items contains a comma already, the reader may become confused about where one item ends and the next begins. To clarify the point of separation, place a semicolon between items. For example, suppose that you are inserting the following list of places into a sentence. Some are identified by the name of the town *and* the name of the county (to distinguish, perhaps, between two towns with the same name), and some are identified by the name of the town only:

Washingtonville, Collins

Manhattan, New York

Smithville, Sullivan

Ellesonville

Harpers Junction

Junction City, Ilesworth

In a list like the one above, the distinction between the name of the town and the name of the county is clear because line breaks tell you where one ends and another begins. When such a list is inserted into a sentence, however, the line breaks disappear. If a comma were the only punctuation mark, the reader would have no way to tell which name designates a town and which a county. Enter the semicolon. With a semicolon between items—including before the conjunction *and*—the distinction between one place and another is crystal clear:

> Tax revenue increased in Washingtonville, Collins; Manhattan, New York; Smithville, Sullivan; Ellesonville; Harpers Junction; and Junction City, Ilesworth.

The semicolons in the example above serve as line-breakers, helping the reader to identify each separate item in the series.

The example above contains several items with two parts (town and county). If a list contains even one item with two parts separated by a comma, semicolons are needed to distinguish between one item and another.

WITH PARENTHESES

When a semicolon joins two sentences, the first of which ends with parentheses, the semicolon is placed outside the parentheses, as in this example:

> He washed his hands thoroughly with antibacterial soap (he was phobic about germs); then he air-dried his hands to avoid what he called "towel contamination."

WITH QUOTATION MARKS

When a semicolon joins two sentences and one or both contain quotations, the semicolon is placed outside the quotation marks, as in these examples:

> He air-dried his hands to avoid what he called "towel contamination"; he was phobic about germs.

> He was phobic about germs; "towel contamination" was one of his great fears.

6

The Colon

The colon has an important role in business writing, crisply setting off the salutation (the *To Whom It May Concern* or *Dear Sir/Madam* portion of the letter) and punctuating the heading lines of a memo. But the colon appears less and less frequently in personal writing, perhaps because to many people this punctuation mark seems stiff and formal. The colon partly merits this reputation. In personal writing such as a friendly letter, the colon is often replaced by the comma, a much more ordinary punctuation mark. Despite the perception that it belongs only to business, the colon can be quite useful in all sorts of writing: It may introduce lists, separate two parts of a sentence (as it does in the sentence you're reading right now), and set up a long quotation.

These tasks are frequently performed by other punctuation marks, and at times the decision between a colon and a semi-colon or comma is a matter of preference and style, not grammar. As American humorist Mark Twain remarked, "Cast iron rules will not answer [because] what is one man's colon is another man's comma."

TO INTRODUCE A LIST

The colon is a punctuation mark that looks ahead. When the reader sees a colon, he or she understands that more is coming—more information, an explanation, or an example of what was stated before the colon. Perhaps the most common use of the colon is to introduce a list.

The traditional rule is that the material preceding the colon—the introductory statement—should be a sentence. That is, the colon follows a bit of writing that contains a subject and a verb and is a complete thought. This rule is not always followed, and, with a few exceptions, lists may be introduced perfectly well with only a few words (*for example, items needed,* and similar phrases). Below are several examples of lists introduced by colons.

> Those planning to run for chair of the prom committee must bring these items to next Wednesday's meeting: a signed permission slip from a parent or guardian, an excusal note from the homeroom teacher, a nominating petition signed by at least ten seniors, and a campaign budget statement describing the source of funds and planned expenditures.

> When Sullivan died, his rented room was nearly empty. The crime scene investigator reported finding only a few personal items:

> (1) a green wool shirt

> (2) a Bible

> (3) two pairs of trousers

> (4) $6 in coins

> To prepare the wall for Sanitaridex paper:
> - Wash the wall thoroughly.
> - Allow the wall to dry.
> - Patch any cracks with Sanicrac putty and sand smooth.
> - Prime the wall with Saniprime.

The first two examples above introduce the list with a complete sentence (*Those planning to run for chair of the prom committee must bring these items to next Wednesday's meeting* and *The crime scene investigator reported finding only a few personal items.*) The last example shows a list that is set up only by a phrase (*to prepare the wall for Sanitaridex paper*). All of these introductions are fine, though the first two are more formal.

Note: Oxford University Press, a major British style-setter, calls for no punctuation at all after an introductory statement that is not a complete sentence. The bulleted items are considered part of the sentence and punctuated as if they were not in a list. Thus the *Sanitaridex* example on the previous page would appear this way in British style:

To prepare the wall for Sanitaridex paper

- wash the wall thoroughly,

- allow the wall to dry,

- patch any cracks with Sanicrac putty and sand smooth, and

- prime the wall with Saniprime.

Introducing a List Properly

Grammarians agree that you should take care not to introduce a list with an expression ending in a preposition. A preposition is a relationship word such as *of, by, for, to, after,* and so forth. Neither should you introduce a list with an expression ending with a form of the verb *to be.* A colon should not be preceded by expressions such as *the guests are* or *the marketing director will try to.* These two rules proceed from custom, rather than from logic, but you should follow them anyway in formal writing.

Wrong: Monday's meeting is:

Why it is wrong: The colon should not be preceded by a form of the verb *to be,* such as *is, am, are, was, were,* or *will be.*

Right: Monday's meeting is scheduled to include these issues:

Wrong: The cake consists of:

Why it is wrong: The last word of a list introduction should not be a preposition (*of, by, for, in,* and so forth).

Right: The cake consists of these ingredients:

TO INTRODUCE A QUOTATION

Quotations may be introduced by a comma or a colon, depending upon the length and formality of the quotation. Follow these guidelines:

1. A short quotation may be tucked into a sentence without being introduced by any punctuation at all.

2. Many slightly longer quotations may be properly introduced by a comma.

3. Long quotations are frequently preceded by a colon.

4. Blocked quotations (three or more lines of text) always call for a colon. A blocked quotation is placed in an indented block of text and introduced on separate line. A colon must follow the introductory matter.

5. The more formal the writing and quotation, the more likely you are to need a colon instead of a comma after the introductory expression.

6. To make the quotation more emphatic, regardless of length, introduce it with a colon.

For a complete explanation of quotations, see Chapter 7. Below are examples of several quotations, properly punctuated.

Quotation Not Introduced by a Colon

Snelling claims that the ruling party "never had an honest agenda."

Finster remarked, "Bribery, secret deals, and assassination were tactics the ruling party employed without hesitation."

These two quotations are quite short. The first needs neither a comma nor a colon before the quoted words because the quotation flows smoothly, without a pause, from the words preceding it. In fact, the quotation is a seamless part of the sentence. In the second example above, the quotation is short and the verb *remarked* is relatively informal. A comma preserves the informality.

Quotation Within a Sentence, Introduced by a Colon

Snelling describes a society in turmoil, with opportunists desperately striving for power: "Not even one day passed without a rally in Central Square, complete with placards, bullhorns, emphatic speakers and passionate dissent."

Arbeck declared: "I am the authority here."

In the first example the quotation is a bit longer, and the tone of the writing is scholarly. A colon fits both tone and length. The second example, while extremely short, may be preceded by a colon because *declared* is emphatic. However, this same sentence would be fine with a comma instead of a colon. The writer may choose either, depending upon the degree of emphasis desired.

Blocked Quotation, Introduced by a Colon

Loblein believes that the council deliberations were never conducted in earnest:

> The Royalists had decided in their October meeting to ban all forms of political demonstration. In the opening session, the Chair of the Governing Council pretended to place the question of demonstrations under discussion, but in reality the outcome was never in doubt. What the Royalists wanted, the Royalists got, and they wanted no protest at all.

Colons Following a Quotation

As explained in the section below, a colon may occasionally
function as a link between two complete sentences. If the first
sentence to be joined ends with a quotation, the colon is
placed outside the closing quotation mark, as in this example:

> Frank called the decision "unfair": To spend ten months in
> jail for simple littering seemed excessive.

TO JOIN TWO THOUGHTS

Two complete sentences may be joined by a word expressing
the relationship between each part (*and, but, because, since,
although,* and so forth). The same sentences may be linked by
a semicolon, provided that the link between each part is obvious to the reader without any additional words. Finally, and
more rarely, two sentences may be connected by a colon. A
colon may be used in this way only under one of these circumstances:

1. The words after the colon explain further the meaning of
    the part of the sentence preceding the colon.

    > Terry had much to do before the party: She had to con-
    > firm the number of guests with the caterer, check that
    > the hall had been cleaned, and order the flowers.

    > No one could achieve that spectacular design with the
    > ease of the architect who was finally awarded the com-
    > mission: Samuel Clark dazzled the owners with his inven-
    > tiveness and left his competitors far behind.

2. The words after the colon summarize the part of the sen-
    tence preceding the colon.

    > Writing the place cards and deciding on the seating plan
    > took hours: Party planning is extremely time-consuming.

This use of the colon has fallen out of favor in recent years. Writers are much more likely to create two separate sentences or to use a semicolon for this function. Nevertheless, you shouldn't hesitate to employ a colon to join sentences fitting the patterns described in this section if you want a formal effect, with a pause slightly longer than that created by a semicolon and slightly shorter than the one achieved by a period.

Sometimes a colon may also link a complete sentence to something less than a complete sentence—a few words or a phrase. The material preceding the colon must be a complete sentence, and the material following the colon must fit the criteria explained above, as in these examples:

> She had only one goal for her Saturday: to get a haircut.

> Lanscomb attributes the success of his production to one factor: his decision to hire a publicity agent.

In example 1, *to get a haircut* defines her *goal*. In the second sentence above, *his decision to hire a publicity agent* explains the factor to which *Lanscombe attributes the success of his production*.

The first word following the colon need not be capitalized if the material after the colon is not a complete sentence.

TO DESIGNATE TIME AND TITLES

In the United States a colon separates the hour from the minutes and the minutes from seconds when time is written with numerals:

> 10:00 a.m. (ten a.m.)

> 3:15 (fifteen minutes past three)

> 4:02:58 (two minutes and fifty-eight seconds past four)

In Britain, periods replace the colon:

10.00 a.m. (ten a.m.)

3.15 (fifteen minutes past three)

4.02.58 (two minutes and fifty-eight seconds past four)

A colon also separates a title from a subtitle:

Putting One's House in Order: The Art of Housecleaning
(title = *Putting One's House in Order,* subtitle = *The Art of Housecleaning*)

"In Search of Mark Twain: A Tour of the Mississippi"
(title = "In Search of Mark Twain" and subtitle = "A Tour of the Mississippi")

A colon also separates chapter and verse in the Bible:

Luke 2:15 (Chapter 2 of the book of Luke, verse 15)

IN BUSINESS WRITING

The colon's main function in business communications is to punctuate the introductory information of a letter or memo and to prepare the reader for a list or, less frequently, a quotation.

Business Letters

The traditional business letter includes a formal greeting—a salutation—such as the following:

Dear Sir or Madam:

To Whom It May Concern:

To the Director of Marketing:

Dear Ms. Magil:

Dear Mr. Evans:

The colon ends the line on which the salutation appears.

Memos

Most word processing programs provide templates for memos. Typically the heading contains some variation of the following:

To: Purchasing

From: E. B. Caslin

Date: 12 March 2006

Re: Office Supply Invoices

CC: Accounts Payable

Each of the lines in the preceding example contain a general designation (*To, From,* etc.) that applies to every memo and a specific piece of information about this particular memo (*Purchasing, E.B. Caslin,* and so forth). The general designation is always separated from the specific information by a colon.

E-Mails and Faxes

The heading of an e-mail is standard to whatever program or Internet service provider you're using, so punctuation is not an issue there. In the body of the e-mail, use a colon to introduce a list or to separate two parts of a sentence, as described earlier in this chapter.

Many companies provide standard cover sheets for faxes as well, leaving the writer only the task of filling in the blanks. If you are creating your own cover sheet, use a colon to separate the general designations from the specific, as in this example:

To: Mr. Edward Solomon, Leasing Agent

Fax number: 800-555-0598

From: Genia Wentworth, Sanford Properties

Date: 2/5/04

Re: Rental Fee Agreement

Number of pages: 2

Business Presentations

Slide presentations and other reports or proposals that give a great deal of information in shortened form often employ colons to introduce numbered lists or bullet points. These examples illustrate the proper form.

Key points of the new organizational structure include the following:

- two student body presidents, sharing power equally
- five representatives from each grade
- six faculty representatives

New shipping options have been added:

(1) Express overnight—$15.95

(2) Two-day air, domestic—$12.00

(3) Two-day air, foreign—$17.99

For examples of the most common business formats, turn to Chapter 14 (business letters), Chapter 15 (memos), Chapter 16 (e-mails and faxes), and Chapter 17 (presentations and resumes).

7

Quotation Marks

The primary goal of what Americans call *quotation marks,* and the British *inverted commas,* is integrity. Quotation marks allow writers to be honest: to give credit to the original speaker or writer when his or her words are reproduced. Quotation marks also permit fiction writers to designate lines of dialogue. Finally, these punctuation marks set off titles of some works and distance writers from any slang or jargon they may employ.

Because British and American traditions are almost directly opposite when it comes to quotation marks, each section in this chapter contains two explanations. The first describes the American rule, and the second discusses the British rule. In brief, the double quotation marks of the American system are single in Britain; similarly, the single quotation marks of the American system are nearly always doubled in Britain. (British newspapers sometimes use double quotation marks.) The placement of most commas and periods is reversed as well. Take note of the custom of your own side of the Atlantic as you read this chapter and as you write.

DIRECT QUOTATIONS IN SENTENCES

Quotation marks indicate that the words you are writing are not your own; in nonfiction they indicate that you are repeating exactly what someone else wrote or spoke. In fiction, quotation marks indicate the words spoken or written by a character. The material inside quotation marks may stand alone as separate sentences or may be tucked inside a sentence. A "speaker tag"—a little label that tells the reader the source of the quoted material—is attached to some quotations, and not to others.

Quoting with a Speaker Tag

A speaker tag identifies the person who said or wrote the material inside the quotation marks. The speaker tag may appear before, after, or in the middle of the quotation. These examples all follow the American custom of double quotation marks:

> Gilwell replied, "I am not interested in political poetry."
> (speaker tag = *Gilwell replied*)
>
> "I much prefer to read romantic poems," he added.
> (speaker tag = *he added*)
>
> "To see the force of human emotion," continued Gilwell, "is my motivation in reading any poetry at all."
> (speaker tag = *continued Gilwell*)

In the British system, these same sentences would be punctuated differently:

> Gilwell replied, 'I am not interested in political poetry'.
>
> 'I much prefer to read romantic poems', he added.
>
> 'To see the force of human emotion', continued Gilwell, 'is my motivation in reading any poetry at all'.

You may notice that the location of the commas and period in the British and American sentences also varies. The rules for comma and period placement are explained in the sections that follow.

Speaker Tag at the Beginning

In the American system a speaker tag preceding a quotation is followed by a comma, and the first word of the quotation is capitalized. If the quotation concludes the sentence and makes a statement or issues a command, the period goes inside the closing quotation mark. An example:

> She muttered, "This test is impossible."

If the sentence continues on and a comma is needed to separate parts of the sentence, the comma appears inside the closing quotation mark:

> She muttered, "This test is impossible," but her voice was so soft that the teacher couldn't hear her.

In the British system, the period or comma is placed outside the quotation:

> She muttered, 'This test is impossible'.

> She muttered,'This test is impossible', but her voice was so soft that the teacher couldn't hear her.

If a parenthetical source citation is included, the citation is placed within the sentence but not within the quotation. Both American and British styles are alike in this placement. These examples follow American style:

> As Oliver wrote, "No single organism can survive that sort of assault" (56).

> Oliver wrote, "No single organism can survive that sort of assault" (56), but this microbe proved him wrong.

If the quotation or sentence is a question or exclamation, the rules are slightly different. Questions and exclamations are addressed a little later in this section.

Speaker Tag at the End
In the American system, the speaker tag at the end of a sentence is followed by a period. A quotation that makes a statement or issues a command is separated from the speaker tag by a comma, which is placed inside the closing quotation mark.

In the British system, the comma goes outside the closing quotation mark. If the quotation asks a question or makes an exclamation, the question mark or exclamation point is

placed inside the closing quotation mark (both systems).
Some examples in American style:

> "The antibacterial soap is no help when it comes to viruses,"
> stated the doctor firmly.
>
> "Is the antibacterial soap a waste?" asked the patient.
>
> "That sort of soap will not help you!" declared the doctor
> with some annoyance.

Examples in British style:

> 'The antibacterial soap is helpful in this outbreak', explained
> the public health officer.
>
> 'Is the antiviral soap available?' asked the nurse.
>
> 'I told you to buy some last week!' exclaimed the nursing
> supervisor.

Speaker Tag in the Middle

Following the American system, the first half of a split quotation concludes with a comma, which is placed inside the closing quotation mark. The speaker tag is followed by a comma,
unless the second half of the quotation is a new sentence, in
which case the speaker tag is followed by a period:

> "I need to visit the mall," said Aunt Emma, "to pick up
> some party supplies."
>
> "I need to visit the mall," said Aunt Emma. "The party is
> tomorrow, but I have no balloons."

The British system moves the comma and the concluding
period to the outside:

> 'I need to visit the mall', said Aunt Emma, 'to pick up some
> party supplies'.
>
> 'I need to visit the mall', said Aunt Emma. 'The party is
> tomorrow, but I have no balloons'.

Comma Splice Quotations

The fact that material is quoted is no excuse for ignoring the normal punctuation rules on comma splices—two complete sentences joined only by a comma. Two complete sentences may be joined only by a conjunction (*and, or, but, nor,* etc.) or a semicolon. If the quotation runs for more than one sentence, the punctuation must reflect that fact. The examples below follow American style.

Wrong: "I have no change for the bus," stated Will, "I will take a cab home instead."

Why it is wrong: The quoted material includes two complete sentences: *I have no change for the bus* and *I will take a cab home instead.* These two sentences cannot be joined by a comma, such as the one after *Will.*

Right: "I have no change for the bus," stated Will. "I will take a cab home instead."

Quotations Without Speaker Tags

Quotations are often tucked into a sentence without an identifying tag. In this sort of sentence the word *that* frequently leads into the quotation. In quotations without speaker tags, no comma precedes the quotation. No punctuation is placed at the end of the quotation unless the sentence needs an endmark or some other punctuation. These sentences in American style illustrate how to punctuate a quotation without a speaker tag:

Descas declared that "liberty and death" were the only options.

The novel, which the critics said was "enlightening," is now a bestseller. (Comma needed to set off *which the critics said was "enlightening"*—not because "enlightening" is in quotation marks)

"Overrated" is what he called the novel his sister sent him.

> The novel his sister sent him was deemed "overrated."
>
> Alistair thinks "peanuts, popcorn, and fly balls" are part of every baseball game.

Notice that the preceding sentences do identify the speaker, but the identification is woven into the sentence, not separated in an expression such as "he said" or "Oliver declared."

Sometimes a proverb or well known statement appears in a sentence as an appositive—an equivalent term placed next to another. The quoted proverb is set off by commas if it appears as *extra* information. It is not set off by commas if it acts as an essential identification. See the examples below.

> **Extra:** Benjamin Franklin's famous proverb about foresight and planning, "a stitch in time saves nine," is good advice.
>
> **Essential:** The saying "a stitch in time saves nine" offers good advice.

In the first example above the proverb is identified by the author (*Franklin*) and the subject (*foresight and planning*), so the proverb itself is not essential to the meaning of the sentence. Hence it is set off by commas. In the second example, *saying* is vague, and the quotation serves as an essential identifier. As such it is set off by commas.

Questions and Exclamations

If the quoted material or the sentence in which the quotation appears is a question or an exclamation, special rules apply. Fortunately, the British and American systems mostly match in this regard, though the British custom of using single quotation marks still differs from the American double quotation marks.

The general rule here is quite logical. If the quotation is a question or an exclamation, the question mark or exclamation point is placed inside the quotation marks. If the quotation is *not* a question or an exclamation, but the sentence in which the quotation appears *is,* the endmark goes outside. Some examples, all with American double quotation marks:

> "Have you had lunch?" inquired the chef. (quotation is a question)

> Did the chef really say, "No one eats in my restaurant unless I say so"? (quotation not a question)

> "I can't eat a thing!" shouted the dieter. (quotation is an exclamation)

> I can't believe the dieter said that the food was "carbohydrate-free"! (quotation not an exclamation)

If both the sentence and the quotation are questions, place the question mark inside. Treat exclamations the same way. Don't use two endmarks for the same sentence. (Both British and American styles agree on this point.) For example:

> **Wrong:** Did the chef really ask, "Have you had lunch?"?

> **Right:** Did the chef really ask, "Have you had lunch?"

> **Wrong:** I can't believe the chef screamed, "Fire!"!

> **Right:** I can't believe the chef screamed, "Fire!"

Semicolons and Colons with Quotations

If the part of a sentence containing quoted material is followed by a semicolon or colon, those punctuation marks appear outside the quotation in both the British and American systems:

> Maria deemed the lemon "large enough"; I thought it was a bit too small for that recipe. (American)

> Maria told us all about her "culinary vacation": She spent two months in a French cooking school. (American)

> Maria thought the mince pie was 'top notch'; I threw mine away. (British)

Maria says that my ideas about food are 'strange': She thinks mince pie goes perfectly well with soda pop, and I don't. (British)

If the quoted material contains a semicolon or a colon, keep the punctuation mark where it is, with one exception. If the material you are quoting *ends* with a colon or a semi-colon, replace those marks with a period. For example:

Original: The festival of Tiwala was held in the mountains; that setting relieved some of the effects of the summer heat.

Quoted in a sentence: Hember thinks that Tiwala festivals took place "in the mountains." (period replaces the semicolon)

Single Quotation Marks

In the American system, double quotation marks are always the first choice, and single quotation marks enclose quotations embedded in other quotations. (The British, in general, reverse this practice.) A common misconception is that the size of the quotation determines the type of quotation mark used; many writers think that short quotations need single marks and longer quotations double marks. Not true! The location, not the length, is key. Note this example, in American style:

Wrong: He sighed and replied, 'Yes, I will.'

Why it is wrong: The quotation is not embedded in another quotation so single quotation marks are not called for.

Right: He sighed and replied, "Yes, I will."

Quotation Within a Quotation

The punctuation of quotations becomes even more compli-cated when one quotation is nested inside another. Two sets of quotation marks are called for. In the American system, a single mark designates the embedded quotation, contrasting with the double marks for the larger quotation. The British system is reversed: Double quotations reside within the single marks. Here are some examples:

> "I think that he said, 'Go now,' but I may be wrong," mused Elizabeth. (American system, embedded quotation = *Go now*)

> Spencer replied, "No, what he really said was, 'Stay for an hour if you can.'" (American system, embedded quotation = *Stay for an hour if you can*)

> 'The Queen's comment that "war is never less than tragic" was widely reported', commented Adler. (British system, embedded quotation = *war is never less than tragic*)

> Adler commented that he detested stories about 'tragedy, or what the citizens called "misfortune"'. (British system, embedded quotation = *misfortune*)

Notice that the rules described earlier in this chapter on placement of commas and periods apply here as well. In the American system the comma or period is placed inside both sets of quotation marks if they fall in the same place. In the British system the reverse is true.

Quoting Poetry

If you quote a substantial amount from a poem, block the quotation according to the rules described later in this chapter. If you quote only a few lines, tuck the quotation into the text as if it were any other type of quotation. The only special aspect of quoting poetry is line breaks. To show the reader where the lines of the original poem end, insert a forward slash with a space before and after. For example:

> Shakespeare asks whether he should "compare thee to a summer's day / Thou art more lovely and more temperate."

Quotations of Several Sentences or Paragraphs

The closing punctuation mark follows the last bit of quoted material in a quotation of more than one sentence. Take a look at these examples:

> According to Oliver, "This year's newest color is red with a hint of orange in it. The skirts will drop almost to the floor, and pencil skirts will make a comeback. The wise buyer will invest in satin knits." (American)

> According to Oliver, 'This year's newest color is red with a hint of orange in it. The skirts will drop almost to the floor, and pencil skirts will make a comeback'. (British)

> Alice responded, "I have come to work. I will not waste your time. Where is the workroom?" (American)

> Alice responded, 'I have come to work. I will not waste your time. Where is the workroom?' (British)

> "No one is in the workroom. How are we supposed to finish on time?" asked Ben. (American)

> 'No one is in the workroom. How are we supposed to finish on time?' asked Ben. (British)

If the quotation extends over more than one paragraph, each new paragraph begins with an opening quotation mark, but only the last paragraph ends with a closing quotation mark:

> Carmen related her story. "I was born in a farmhouse in Western Spain. When I was only a child, I was enrolled in a boarding school in the United States. Though I saw my family only during school holidays, I remained close to my mother.

> "The summers were especially joyous. I learned to cook courtesy of Miguelina, the family's housekeeper. Miguelina started me on flan, and soon I graduated to tortillas and other main courses.

"Miguelina's husband, Jose, taught me how to ride. He would saddle up my pony and take me around the barn, leading the pony until I could manage her by myself. It was an idyllic time."

BLOCKED QUOTATIONS

If a quotation is lengthy, approximately 40 or more words, it appears in a block of text, indented from the normal margin. Such quotations are fairly common in academic writing, but you may see them in business writing as well, perhaps when a testimonial or critical comment is quoted.

The blocking functions as a signal that the material is quoted. Thus you do not need to insert quotation marks around blocked material. If the quoted material itself contains a quotation, the quotation marks from the original remain. If the source of the blocked material is cited, the number of the footnote or endnote or the parenthetical citation is placed at the end of the block.

The block is indented about an inch (7–10 extra spaces) from the left margin. A colon generally introduces the blocked quotation, though an introductory line ending with *that* has no punctuation. The introduction to a blocked quotation may also be a complete sentence ending with a period (not a colon) as long as the sentence does not end with "the following," "as follows," and the like, which naturally leave the reader in suspense. In such cases a colon is better because it implies continuation.

Below are examples of blocked quotations.

Blocked Quotation, Prose

This example deals with science, but the same style may be employed for all sorts of writing. If the manuscript is double-spaced, the blocked quotation should be double-spaced as well.

Harcourt dissected the specimen over the course of three days, but he found no abnormality until he subjected his sample to microscopic examination. He later wrote:

> I found abnormal cells throughout the sample, with nuclei that were twisted and distorted. The stain I applied was concentrated in the nuclei to an unheard of degree. I simply could not understand what I was seeing, but I was determined nonetheless to understand its significance. (12)

Note the colon after the last word of the sentence introducing the quotation, *wrote*. Also notice that the blocked quotation is not placed inside quotation marks.

Blocked Quotation, Poetry

If you are quoting only a small number of words from a poem, the quotation may be woven into your sentences in the usual manner and with the usual punctuation, described earlier in this chapter. The only addition is a forward slash to mark where each line of the poem ends. To block a quotation from a poem, indent 7–10 spaces from the left margin and end each line of the block where the verse lines end in the original. (If a line is too long, break to a new line and indent an additional five spaces.) Thus the reader sees the poet's line breaks as they were written. No quotation marks appear unless they are in the original poem.

> In his poems Wishinhouse often employs nature imagery, which he once explained was a consequence of his frequent walks around Central Park. In one poem, "Central Park Duet," Wishinhouse compared the bicycle riders to birds, writing that
>
>> I went for a ten-mile walk at least once
>> or twice a week, weaving between the bikes
>> zooming like pigeons beside me,
>> "Hear the birds, and see the clouds,"
>> I said to Margaret, just as three bikes

> skimmed past us, a plague as any that
> ever darkened the skies,
> and nearly as noisy. (42)

This blocked quotation is not placed inside quotation marks, but the embedded quotation (*Hear the birds, and see the clouds*) is surrounded by quotation marks. The introductory expression (*Wishinhouse compared the bicycle riders to birds, writing that*) is not followed by a colon because the introduction ends with *that*.

Both British and American writers block quotations in essentially the same way. The only difference occurs when an embedded quotation appears. In Britain the embedded quotation would be placed inside single quotation marks, following the rules explained earlier in this chapter. In America double marks are used, as in the example above.

QUOTATIONS WITH WORDS OMITTED

In making a point in an essay or report, you may not need to quote every word of an original. Yet you should show the reader where your quotation differs from the original. A handy punctuation mark, the ellipsis, saves the day by taking the place of missing material. (The ellipsis, three spaced dots, is covered in detail in Chapter 10. This section explains only the most common use of the ellipsis in quotations.)

Some changes in a quotation are accepted without any special mark. You may capitalize the first word of a quotation that begins a sentence, even if the original was not capitalized. You need not place an ellipsis at the beginning of a quotation, provided, of course, that the reader will not misunderstand the meaning intended by the original writer. You normally do not need to place an ellipsis at the end of a quotation either, because the reader assumes that you have not quoted the last words of the original source. If you cut words from within a quotation, add an ellipsis:

Original: The growth of the Chinese American community has resulted in a rich variety of food stores and restaurants in that neighborhood. Originally catering only to Chinese-speaking customers, the business owners quickly learned that they could increase their profit margin and diversify their customer base in an interesting way by having at least one English-speaking employee on the premises.

Quotation with words omitted, embedded in text: Adapting to the customer is all important. As Yowling wrote in his economic analysis of New York's Chinatown, non-Chinese customers created a need and "business owners quickly learned that they could increase their profit margin . . . by having at least one English-speaking employee on the premises" (444).

If the omitted words include the end of a sentence or an entire sentence, the three dots of the ellipsis are joined by one more—the period. Notice the four dots in the example below:

Original: The bus route in that area moves from the financial district through a shopping center and then into a residential area. High rise office buildings give way to malls and then to single-family houses. The riders represent every walk of life and every income level.

Quotation with sentence omitted: The transit report notes that the "bus route in that area moves from the financial district through a shopping center and then into a residential area. . . . The riders represent every walk of life and every income level."

If the omitted words fall at the end of a question or an exclamation, the question mark or exclamation point is moved up to the last quoted word, and the ellipsis is placed after the endmark:

Original: Should he attend the ball, with all its trappings of wealth and power? Undoubtedly he would have an awful time, and the other guests would sense his discomfort. He was torn between the desire to please his aunt, to whom he owed so much, and his distaste for elaborate social occasions.

Quotation with words omitted, embedded in text:
Corning created a character who agonizes about every decision, as in "Wandler's Way," when the protagonists muses,
"Should he attend the ball? . . . He was torn between the
desire to please his aunt, to whom he owed so much, and
his distaste for elaborate social occasions" (55).

To omit a line of poetry that you are quoting in blocked
form, insert a line of spaced dots:

I met a man

. . . .

and he was me.

QUOTATIONS WITH WORDS ADDED

To add a word or phrase to a quotation, perhaps to clarify the
meaning for the reader, use brackets:

Collins considers the music of that region "primitive,
though they [the original inhabitants] are capable of sophis-
ticated phrasing and melodic lines" (33).

Notice that the pronoun *they* is explained by the writer's
addition, *the original inhabitants.* The brackets indicate that
Collins did not write those words in the original.

INDIRECT QUOTATIONS

Comments from oral or written sources often find their way
into a sentence without being quoted directly. The information
may be summarized or referred to, but the actual words of the
speaker or writer are not duplicated. Such indirect quotations
are *not* placed inside quotation marks. Some examples:

She told me that she had only six more months on the job
before becoming eligible for retirement.

Lisa inquired whether it was likely to become chilly during
the tour.

I'm not sure whether George said blue or pink when I asked him about baby clothes.

Eleanor asked why I wanted popcorn.

What Wyatt called unacceptable was perfectly fine with me.

In these sentences, the reader knows what *she, Lisa, George, Eleanor* and *Wyatt* said but does not "hear" their actual words. No quotation marks are needed in this sort of sentence.

DEFINITIONS AND TRANSLATIONS

When an unusual term is defined in your text, you may italicize the term or place it in quotation marks the first time it appears. Thereafter, no italics or quotation marks are needed. For example:

The "predicate nominative," or the word completing the meaning of an expression containing a linking verb, is always in the same case as the subject. The predicate nominative in each of the following sentences is a proper noun.

The *bicameral* or two-house legislature is the most common form, though single-house systems may be found in some countries. The United States has a bicameral legislative branch.

If a foreign word or phrase appears with its translation in your writing, quotation marks generally enclose the translation. The foreign expression may be italicized or underlined:

The *picadors* or "those who carry spears" appear during the next stage of the bullfight.

In Spain one with free time will *dar un paseo,* literally "give a stroll," until it is time to resume the workday.

If the word "so-called" precedes a word or phrase, italics or quotation marks are omitted, as in this example:

Her so-called school phobia was really laziness.

SPECIAL TERMS

A few philosophical terms such as *being, nonbeing,* and *the divine* may be placed in single quotation marks, according to *The Chicago Manual of Style.* When such terms are punctuated this way, any punctuation mark following the term is placed outside the closing quotation mark. An example:

> He deals with 'nonbeing' as a variation of the state of 'being'.

TITLES

The title of a section of a longer work—a poem from a collection of poems, a song from an album, a particular episode of a television series, for example—is placed in quotation marks when it is referred to in the text. When it is centered on a line as a title, no quotation marks are needed. Longer works (titles of books, plays, operas, television series, and so forth) are not placed in quotation marks. These titles are italicized or underlined except when they appear alone on a line, as on a title page or in a heading. The punctuation before or after titles in quotation marks follows the rules described earlier in this chapter. Take a look at these examples, which all follow American style:

> My favorite poem is "The Raven" by Edgar Allan Poe.
>
> Have you read "The Raven"?
>
> My aunt visits us every Halloween and reads Poe's "The Raven."

In British style, these titles would appear this way:

> My favorite poem is 'The Raven' by Edgar Allan Poe.
>
> Have you read 'The Raven'?
>
> My aunt visits us every Halloween and reads Poe's 'The Raven'.

Not all titles of literary works are placed in quotation marks. The names of sacred texts such as the Koran and the Bible need no marks; nor do the smaller divisions of these works, such as the books of the Bible.

PUNCTUATING TITLES

Segments of larger works are placed in quotation marks, but full-length works are italicized or underlined (not both).

Quotation Marks

"Lilacs" (poem)

"Anything You Want" (short story)

"If I Love You" (song)

"The Reformation" (chapter title)

"On Being Fifty" (essay)

"Nicaragua" (encyclopedia article)

"Your Child's Health" (magazine article)

"Explosive Growth Challenges Planners" (newspaper article)

"The Bizarre World" (episode of television series)

Italics or Underlining

The Odyssey (book-length poem)

To the Shore (novel)

The Geography of Africa (non-fiction book)

Writers on the Block (collection of essays)

Don Giovanni (opera)

Anything Goes (musical)

The Collected Works of John Allister (poetry collection)

The White Album (musical album)

World Encyclopedia (encyclopedia)

Ladies Home Reporter (magazine)

The Record (newspaper)

Late Night Review (television series)

Note: Ship titles should be italicized, though not the preceding abbreviations "USS" or "HMS" (*United States Ship* or *Her Majesty's Ship*), as in the USS *Endeavor*.

DISTANCING QUOTATION MARKS

Occasionally writers insert a bit of slang or jargon into their work and place quotation marks around the inserted phrase. These quotation marks distance the writer from the expression, saying, in effect, I know that this expression is a bit off, but I will use it anyway for effect. Here are some examples:

> He signed up for an "ocean liner" of fried fish but received a "rowboat" instead. (slang for large and small sizes)
>
> Some of the "prols" were actually quite wealthy. (slang)

Similarly, writers may place quotation marks around a word or phrase expressing a value judgment that does not match their own views. Finally, distancing quotation marks may indicate a word that is purposely misused. Some samples:

> Did you hear the "music" emanating from her guitar? (sounds too discordant to qualify as music)
>
> The "sounds" of that painting positively scream at the viewer. (word purposely misused)

The above examples all employ American double quotation marks. In Britain, those marks would be replaced by single quotation marks, as in this example:

> Have you enjoyed watching her 'progress' through the maze? (not really progress, in the writer's view)

Distancing Can Go Too Far

Distancing quotation marks wear out their welcome extremely quickly. If you find yourself using more than one in a piece of writing, you should probably reword.

With distancing quotation marks: Columbus "discovered" America.

Implied meaning: Columbus is said to have discovered America, but in fact he did not do so.

Better sentence: Though Columbus is hailed as the explorer who discovered America, in reality the land he encountered was already populated.

If you're quoting something that is misspelled or erroneous, the best way to distance yourself is to insert the word "sic" in brackets next to the offending expression:

Rita wrote that her "speling [sic] is excellent."

Sic, derived from the Latin word for "so, thus" indicates that the writer knows that the quotation contains an error.

8

The Dash and the Hyphen

The dash and the hyphen are punctuation marks in a hurry. These small straight lines at mid-letter height rush the reader forward, from the word preceding them to the word after. Like the hundred-meter race with which it shares a name, the dash catches attention. It is a showy punctuation mark, one that won't fade into the background. With the invention of word processing and automatic wraparound text, the hyphen has lost its main function. Before computers, the hyphen was used mainly as a mark of separation, dividing words that were too long to fit at the end of a line of text. People who write by hand or on a typewriter still need hyphens for that purpose, but the hyphen now serves primarily to link two words in a compound form.

The rules governing the dash are fairly simple; deciding when to use a dash is a question of style rather than grammar. Placing the hyphen, on the other hand, can be extremely confusing. Complicating the decision whether or not to insert a hyphen is the fact that the major style manuals disagree on certain points.

Fortunately, most writers don't need to worry about the niceties of hyphenation required by various publishers or academic disciplines. In everyday communication, most of us need only use common sense and be consistent. To help you in placing hyphens and dashes, this chapter provides some generally accepted guidelines. This chapter also explains when the major style manuals differ on hyphen use.

THE DASH

This section should actually be entitled "the dashes" because this punctuation mark comes in a few different sizes, the *em dash,* the *en dash,* and the *two-* or *three-em dash.* These names are printing terms that refer to the length of the dash. An em dash—about two characters wide as shown here—is twice as long as an en dash (–). A two- or three-em dash, as the names imply, are four or six times as long as an en dash; they used only rarely. The other two marks have different functions, but most writers (those who are not publishing their work) don't need to worry too much about the difference in en and em dashes. Just knowing when a dash is appropriate is enough to take you through nearly every writing task.

If you are working on an academic paper or an article for publication and you must differentiate between the two dashes, a word processing program will help. Most programs allow you to place an en or em dash with the "insert symbol" command. The symbol menu labels each type of dash so you know which one you are inserting. Most word processing programs also automatically convert two hyphens into an em dash, so long as the hyphens are not separated from the words before and after by spaces.

The Em Dash

This is the punctuation mark most people think of when they hear the word *dash.* The em dash overlaps with some of the functions of the comma, but the dash is much more dramatic. It serves to set off interrupting remarks, to indicate summaries or definitions, to emphasize a point, and to show an abruptly curtailed comment. The em dash is always placed without any spaces surrounding it.

To Set Off Interrupters

Commas are the most common means of setting off interrupters from the rest of the sentence. However, commas are not appropriate if the interrupter is a complete sentence; to tuck one complete sentence inside another, only parentheses or dashes will do. The dash, even when setting off just one or two words, is much more emphatic than a comma. With a dash the sentence switches gears, sending readers off in a new direction and then bringing them back to the main point again. Notice how the meaning is interrupted in these examples:

> We arrive in St. Louis shortly before lunch—the plane is a great way to travel—and plan to go directly to the meeting.

> Marcia baked sugar cookies—I don't know how she finds the time—and will soon deliver them to every secretary in that division.

> Tom's graduation—do you believe that he has already finished high school?—should be a gala event.

> The dash is easier to understand than the hyphen—more fun too!

> Place that weapon—now, please!—on the ground in front of you.

As you see in the above sentences, the material between dashes may be safely omitted from the sentence without compromising either meaning or clarity. In the first example, *the plane is a great way to travel* is a side comment on the fact that the writer will be in St. Louis in time for lunch, presumably because air travel is so swift. The first word of the embedded sentence is not capitalized because technically there's only one long sentence. The material between dashes is a part of the larger sentence. No period is placed at the end of the embedded sentence for the same reason: There is actually only one true sentence here.

In sentence two, the writer offers a comment on Marcia in the midst of explaining what she is doing. This time the embedded material begins with a capital letter, but only because *I* is always capitalized. Once again the period is omitted; periods never occur inside a sentence unless one is needed to form an abbreviation. (For more information on the correct use of periods, see Chapter 1.)

The third example places a question inside a statement. The question mark remains to alert the reader to the shift from statement to question, but the first word is not capitalized, highlighting the fact that the material between dashes is part of the larger sentence.

In the last two examples, the interrupters may not stand alone as complete sentences. In the second to last sentence, a comma may replace the dash without loss of meaning, though the dash has a stronger effect. In the last sentence above, the interrupter is appropriately set off by a dash rather than by commas. Since the interrupter itself contains a comma, it cannot be separated from the rest of the sentence by the same punctuation mark. Only dashes or parentheses will do the job:

Wrong: Place that weapon, now, please, on the ground in front of you.

Why it is wrong: The three commas blend together, and the sentence is too choppy.

Right: Place that weapon—now, please—on the ground in front of you.

Also right but less emphatic: Place that weapon (now, please) on the ground in front of you.

Dashes Don't Connect Sentences

In very informal writing (notes between friends, perhaps) dashes may substitute for periods. In formal writing, however, you may not connect two complete sentences with a dash. A dash may *embed* one sentence inside another but not link two sentences one after the other.

Wrong: Johnny just came home—he plans to play golf.

Why it is wrong: Each half of the above example is a complete sentence and must be linked by a semicolon or a conjunction.

Right: Johnny just came home, and he plans to play golf.

Also right: Johnny just came home; he plans to play golf.

Also right: Johnny just came home. He plans to play golf.

The bottom line: Don't send a dash to do the work of a semicolon, period, or conjunction.

To Summarize or Define

Summary statements or definitions may also be set off by dashes, as in these examples:

> We gave her everything a child needs—a home, food, education, love.

> A home, food, education, love—we gave her everything a child needs.

> Pink, purple, rose, ecru, and olive green—this spring's colors—appear in everything from appliances to nail polish.

> How could anyone know that this little girl—the orphan found on the church steps—would one day lead a worldwide movement?

> The leader of the rebellion—none other than the Thane of Cawdor—is executed by the king.

In each of the above sentences the material separated by a dash defines or summarizes something in the sentence. In the first and second examples, the information set off by the dash specifies the meaning of *everything a child needs*. In the third example, *this spring's colors* summarizes the list of colors at the beginning of the sentence. In sentence four, *this little girl* is also defined as *the orphan found on the church steps*. Similarly, the last sentence equates *The leader of the rebellion* with *the Thane of Cawdor*.

The material set off by a dash may be a complete sentence or a portion of a sentence. In some sentences the dash may be replaced by another punctuation mark without causing misunderstanding:

> We gave her everything a child needs: a home, food, education, love. (colon replaces dash)

> Pink, purple, rose, ecru, and olive green (this spring's colors) appear in everything from appliances to nail polish. (parentheses replace dash)

> How could anyone know that this little girl, the orphan found on the church steps, would one day lead a worldwide movement? (commas replace dash)

The leader of the rebellion (none other than the Thane of Cawdor) is executed by the king. (parentheses replace dash)

The dash, as you see, adds a note of drama, but it is not absolutely necessary.

Drama May Be Overdone

The dash is a dramatic punctuation mark, and drama, by definition, should be something special. If dashes occur too frequently in a piece of writing, the reader may feel overpowered or worse, annoyed with the abrupt changes in pace. Use dashes where they make a strong effect, but see them as a contrast to your normal choice of punctuation, not as your first option.

Wrong: I went to the store to buy provisions for the company dinner—twenty pounds of sirloin, a few bushels of potatoes, and a pail of salad. The store clerk—a pimply fellow—carried the bags to my truck. I was parked on a side street—in what I thought was a legal parking zone. Imagine my surprise—a police officer approached and told me that I had to pay—fifty dollars!—a hefty fine.

Why it is wrong: With so many dashes, the paragraph above becomes almost unreadable.

Better: I went to the store to buy provisions for the company dinner: twenty pounds of sirloin, a few bushels of potatoes, and a pail of salad. The store clerk, a pimply fellow, carried the bags to my truck. I was parked on a side street in what I thought was a legal parking zone. Imagine my surprise when a police officer approached and told me that I had to pay—fifty dollars!—a hefty fine.

Why it is better: Now a single set of dashes surrounds the amount of the fine, which is the point the writer wants to emphasize. When other dashes appear in the same story, the amount of the fine blends in and loses its dramatic effect.

To Emphasize

Em dashes take up two spaces, so it is not surprising that they attract the attention of the reader in a strong way. This ability goes hand in hand with another function of the dash, emphasis. While the same point may often be made with commas, colons, or parentheses, the dash appears literally to slice an idea away from what is around it and thus place the idea in a position of importance:

> I would like to introduce to you the new champion of the table tennis tournament—Mark Safflen.
>
> Only one remedy remained, and it was a drastic one—amputation.
>
> Louisa placed her head on the desk—finished at last!—and sighed.
>
> Herbert said, "I have thought about you endlessly—and I want you to go to the dance with me."

How much more emphatic could a punctuation mark be? You can imagine an actor reading these words, pausing at each dash to increase the reader's anticipation. Even a drum roll seems possible because the material set off by the dash jumps out at the reader. Note the difference between the above sentences and these, which are written without dashes:

> I would like to introduce to you the new champion of the table tennis tournament, Mark Safflen.
>
> Only one remedy remained, and it was a drastic one: amputation.
>
> Louisa placed her head on the desk, finished at last, and sighed.
>
> Herbert said, "I have thought about you endlessly, and I want you to go to the dance with me."

In each of the above sentences, the material that had once been singled out is now much more seamlessly woven into the fabric of the sentence. The reader gets the point without a dramatic pause and theatrical continuation.

To Show a Curtailed Comment

On rare occasions, dashes may also indicate silence or absence. In such cases they do not set off a word or phrase from the rest of the sentence, but instead show that the sentence has been cut short. Take a look at these examples:

"He is coming—," screamed Lenny.

Just then he opened the door and—.

Notice that the normal punctuation (the comma and quotation mark in the first sentence and the period in the second) follow the dash. Normally no punctuation marks precede a dash. (For more detail on quotation marks and dashes, see the next section, "Dashes and Other Punctuation.")

When a sentence is cut short by a dash, the effect is more abrupt than a sentence ending in an ellipsis (three spaced dots), which has more of a sense of an idea trailing off or of the speaker or writer sputtering to a stop:

I was just wondering . . .

(For more information on ellipses, see Chapter 10.)

Dashes and Other Punctuation

Dashes generally don't mingle with other punctuation marks, with the exception of quotation marks, exclamation points, and question marks. If the material set off by dashes is an exclamation or question, those marks are included before the second of the pair of dashes:

His job—we all know that he likes to keep busy!—was to tend the children while their parents attended church.

Her goal—did she send you the memo?—was to raise money for a new childcare center.

Since the dash replaces the comma, no comma is ever necessary before a dash. A comma is placed after a dash only if the dash ends a quotation and is followed by a speaker tag.

Material that is set off by a dash may have one or more commas within.

> Oscar came home from work—he was a blacksmith—and turned on the air conditioner. (no comma)
>
> "Is everyone—," said Olivia, choking with emotion. (comma before the closing quotation mark)

In British style the last example would be punctuated differently, with single quotation marks (which the British call *inverted commas*) and the comma placed outside the quotation:

> 'Is everyone—', said Olivia, choking with emotion.

Dates and Cross References

Dates and cross references are generally set off from the rest of the sentence by parentheses, not by dashes.

Wrong: Arthur Copeland—1788–1812—is the primary source of information about that era.

Why it is wrong: The dashes around the date range clash with the dash between dates.

Right: Arthur Copeland (1788–1812) is the primary source of information about that era.

Wrong: The equilateral triangle has three equal sides—see figure 3—and three equal angles.

Why it is wrong: The cross reference should not be set apart by dashes.

Right: The equilateral triangle has three equal sides (see figure 3) and three equal angles.

The En Dash

Unless you are writing for a particularly fussy editor, don't worry about the length of an en dash as opposed to an em dash or a hyphen. (The en dash is shorter than an em dash but a bit longer than a hyphen.) An en dash is used to show a range, as in these examples:

> The library is open from 1–6 p.m. every day but Sunday.
>
> From Monday–Thursday only, overdue books will not be fined.
>
> The library was constructed over the course of several years (1934–41) because the site presented so many problems.
>
> Poet Marie Seta (1978–) will read from her works tomorrow.

In the first three sentences above, the en dash fits snugly between the elements that define the range without any intervening spaces. In the last sentence, there is no ending date because the poet is still alive. An open-ended expression such as this reaches beyond the present and into the future.

In the third example above, you may write *1934–1941* if you wish, though the major style manuals prefer the shortened form (*1934–41*).

The en dash may also connect two words when *to* or *and* is implied. The two words connected in this way form a single expression that precedes and describes another word. The same function is often performed by a hyphen, but the en dash is used when the two elements are equal in importance and may be reversed without altering the meaning. Some examples:

> The teacher–student relationship is crucial.
>
> The Portland–Yarmouth ferry is privately owned.
>
> The New York–Boston match resulted in sadness for Yankee fans.

An en dash connects two names (again, of equal importance) when two people are referred to. The en dash contrasts with the hyphen, which may separate parts of one name:

> The Jeter–Rodriguez controversy was fanned by the press.
>
> Are you attending the Barbes–Foster wedding?

I don't believe the Alexan–Smith exercise method achieves lasting results.

The en dash may also replace missing letters, primarily in fiction when the author wants to give the impression that the "true" name may not be disclosed:

The regiment traveled to B– – shire.

Two- and Three-Em Dashes

These punctuation marks have extremely limited usage. In 18th and 19th century fiction, a doubled em dash often replaced the en dash to represent missing letters, giving the reader the impression that the author wanted to protect the identity of a person or place. Similarly, the double em dash is sometimes used to represent the missing letters of an obscenity that the author does not care to spell out in its entirety.

A three-em dash indicates that an entire word is missing. An author may use it to hide someone's identity in a sentence such as this one:

The district attorney questioned ——— for about an hour.

The three-em dash also has a place in bibliographies (for more information, see Part III) when more than one work by a single author is cited.

THE HYPHEN

Older writers, who began their work before the invention of the word processor, remember all too well coming to the end of a line with a word that was too large to fit inside the margin. The task of splitting the word was given to the hyphen. Nowadays computer programs automatically move the word to a new line, and hyphenation has crept closer to the ranks of dial telephones, slide rules, and phonographs.

Even today, however, some writers work with pen and ink or typewriters. Also, some writers using word processors still prefer to split a word rather than to leave a long gap at the end of a line. The hyphen comes in handy in these cases. If you are working with a word processing program and place a hyphen manually to separate a word, proofread your work very carefully to avoid a common pitfall. Sometimes the computer moves the entire word to a new line, but the hyphen remains, incorrectly creating a compound word.

Hyphens also form one description from two words, link names, and separate some prefixes from the root words. Finally, hyphens occasionally serve writers of fiction as they create an impression of hesitation or reluctance.

Recommended hyphen usage varies between one style manual and another. This section explains the generally accepted rules as well as those specified by the major manuals.

To Divide Words

To divide a word at the end of a line, break the word between syllables and place a hyphen at the end of the last syllable before the break:

> Examining the stock portfolio, we were surprised to see diversi-
> fied holdings and not the single stock we had expected.

> The architects conferred for hours about struc-
> ture, labor costs, and materials.

> All applicants aspiring to join the honors pro-
> gram at the university were directed to the dean.

If you unsure about dividing a particular word, turn to the dictionary for help. The dictionary, in addition to definitions, shows the syllable breaks where a word may be properly split.

In Britain, words are sometimes split and hyphenated not by sound but by structure. The root may be divided from the prefix or suffix, even if the syllable divisions fall elsewhere. Even in Britain, however, syllable division is accepted.

> **British:** eight-een, demo-cracy

> **American:** eigh-teen, democ-racy

Some Words Can't Be Divided

Single syllable words, no matter how many letters they contain, should not be divided.

Wrong: Gloria, in the interest of saving time, drove through the nature preserve.

Why it is wrong: *Through* is one syllable and cannot be split.

Right: Gloria, in the interest of saving time, drove through the nature preserve.

Nor should you break a multisyllable word so that only one or two letters remain on a line.

Wrong: The proctor for this final math exam is especially concerned about cheating.

Right: The proctor for this final math exam is especially concerned about cheating.

Wrong: She was renowned throughout the land for beauty and kindness.

Right: She was renowned throughout the land for beauty and kindness.

In Linked Descriptions

Imagine that a reader is trying to decode this sentence:

The fans were dismayed at the second base error.

What does the reader envision? Two errors by infielders? Or one error at second base? Look at this sentence again, this time with a hyphen in place:

The fans were dismayed at the second-base error.

Now the reader is able to decode the meaning correctly: one error took place at second base. The hyphen has connected *second* and *base,* and the new combination word describes *error.* The general rule may be stated this way: Hyphenate two

Descriptions Following the Word Described

If a multi-word description follows the word it describes, hyphens are not inserted:

Wrong: Tickets are now at bargain-prices.

Why it is wrong: *Bargain* describes *prices*. They are not joined together to form one description.

Right: Tickets are now at bargain prices.

Wrong: Language requirements for the third-year include a passing grade on an oral exam.

or more words which, when combined, form one description that precedes the word being described. Some examples:

The bargain-priced tickets go on sale at noon.

Third-year language requirements include a passing grade on an oral exam.

The brown-eyed child had curly red hair.

The best-dressed list caused shock and outrage in Hollywood.

The sentences above illustrate the hyphenation rule in action. In sentence one, the *tickets* are not *priced* and *bargain*. The two descriptors don't make sense unless they are combined. In sentence two, *language* describes *requirements*. But *third* and *year* don't describe *language* separately; these two words are meaningful only as a unit. Thus, they should be joined by a hyphen. Similar reasons explain why *brown* and *eyed* and *best* and *dressed* must be linked. In the end, common sense tells you when a description of two or more words should be hyphenated.

Note: Description pairs are not hyphenated if the first word in the description describes the second word. A *recently enacted* law breaks down this way:

- *recently* describes *enacted* (*enacted* when? *recently*)

- *enacted* describes *law* (What kind of *law*? An *enacted* law)

Why it is wrong: *Third* describes *year.* They don't form a unit.

Right: Language requirements for the third year include a passing grade on an oral exam.

Wrong: The child with brown-eyes has curly red hair.

Why it is wrong: *Brown* describes *eyes.* They don't form a unit.

Right: The child with brown eyes has curly red hair.

Here's a helpful tip: Following the logic above, -ly adverbs such as *recently* are never joined by a hyphen to another descriptive word because these adverbs always describe the second description.

The guidelines in this section are all the ordinary writer needs to know about hyphenating descriptions. These general guidelines also apply to scholarly writing. If you are writing for publication, however, you must follow some additional specific rules set forth by style manuals.

The American Psychological Association
Various scientific magazines and journals have their own rules, but the best general reference for science and social science is the *Publication Manual of the American Psychological Association.* The APA manual offers these guidelines:

- Two-word descriptions in which the second word is a verb form (*food-deprived, tension-producing,* and so on) should always be hyphenated when they precede the word being described.

- Two-word descriptions in which the first word is a number (*three-year, sixth-grade,* and so on) are always hyphenated when they precede the word being described.

- A two-part description that includes a number or letter as the second element (*Plan B, group 2,* and so on) should not be hyphenated.

- Chemical terms are not usually hyphenated.

- Foreign phrases are not usually hypenated.

- A two-word description that makes a comparison (*better understood, less valid,* and so on) should not be hyphenated.

The Modern Language Association

The Modern Language Association (MLA) sets standards for papers and articles in the humanities. Their guidelines on hyphenation are somewhat different from those favored by the sciences and social sciences.

- Two-word descriptions that make a comparison or evaluate quality (*best-known, well-prepared, least-involved,* etc.) should be hyphenated when they precede the word being described.

- Two-word descriptions in which the second word is a verb form (*sleep-induced, nature-loving,* and so on) should always be hyphenated when they precede the word being described.

- Two-word descriptions in which the first word is a number (*three-volume, seven-year,* etc.) are always hyphenated when they precede the word being described.

- Familiar two-word terms (*elementary school, book review,* etc.) are not hyphenated, even when they precede the word being described.

The Chicago Manual of Style

The Chicago Manual of Style (CMS), widely used in all academic fields, is much more open to hyphen use than the other major style manuals. Two words joined together to form one description may nearly always be hyphenated according to the *CMS* rules, even if the description follows the word being described, though in such cases the hyphen is not strictly necessary. The general guidelines earlier and later in this section are appropriate for anyone asked to write according to this style manual. A few specifics from the CMS include the following:

- A hyphen is always inserted when the reader may misunderstand the meaning without one.

- The CMS follows *Webster's* preference, so if you are in doubt, consult that dictionary.

- Compounds are never formed with an –ly adverb. Thus the CMS prescribes *newly formed committees,* not *newly-formed committees.*

- Colors and chemical forms are not hyphenated, nor are ethnic designations such as *Asian American.*

In Compound Words

Language, like everything else in life, changes over time. New technology breeds new terms, for example, and slang rises and falls in popularity as fast as current fashion. Even formal grammar evolves, despite the fact that it appears set in stone and bound by unchangeable rules. Punctuation is no exception. New compound words (two or more separate words permanently linked together and conveying one meaning) tend to appear first as hyphenated forms. After they have been in use for a while, they tend to drop the hyphen and appear as two separate words or even as one word.

If you are trying to decide whether *email* or *e-mail* is correct, the best guide is the dictionary. Computer programs that check grammar and spelling often miss errors in hyphenated terms, though they do catch the most common mistakes.

With Prefixes and Suffixes

Prefixes are word parts attached to the beginning of a word, changing the meaning of the original. Common prefixes include *pre-, anti-, un-, non-, dis-, tele-, trans-, re-,* and many others. Suffixes are word parts that follow the root word. Common suffixes include *–ed, -tion, -ly,* and many more.

As you may have noticed in the first paragraph of this section, hyphens are included when a prefix or suffix is written without being attached to a word. In the context of a complete word, prefixes are seldom separated nowadays from the root word by a hyphen, though you may see many hyphenated forms in older printed works. Only a very small number of expressions call for a suffix to be separated by a hyphen.

Some guidelines to hyphen use with prefixes and suffixes are as follows:

1. If the word may be misread without a hyphen, insert one. For example, to distinguish between *re-creation* (creating again) and *recreation* (relaxation activity), a hyphen is crucial.

2. Prefixes attached to a capitalized word should be separated by a hyphen from the base: *post-Elizabethan, anti-UN,* and so on.

3. When the prefix ends with the same letter that begins the root, resulting in a doubled letter, a hyphen is frequently inserted: *re-election, anti-insurance.* Some very common words, such as *cooperation,* do not use a hyphen, even though they contain a doubled letter. If you are unsure about a particular word, check the dictionary.

4. A hyphen is frequently inserted after the prefix *self,* as in *self-motivated, self-destructive,* and so forth.

5. British style calls for more hyphens between the prefix and root word than does American style. In Britain, for example, a point that is *non-negotiable* is likely to be *nonnegotiable* in America. Again, a dictionary is the ultimate authority on this point.

6. Some suffixes that arise from slang or current trends are separated from the root by a hyphen. The suffix *–gate,* a reference to the Watergate scandal, may appear in expressions such as *Monica-gate.* These words are coined by journalists and seldom correct in formal English.

7. The suffix *like* is sometimes separated from the root by a hyphen, unless the resulting word is in common use. A statue may be *lifelike* (common word, no hyphen) and *goddess-like* (unusual combination, hyphenated).

With Two Prefixes and the Same Root

Repetition is seldom attractive, so if you have a sentence that includes, for example, *two-minute* and *three-minute sprints,* you may want to take advantage of a shortened version:

> The team ran two- and three-minute sprints.

The hyphen after the *two* indicates that the word has not been completed and that the form combines with the same root word as the next prefix. You may string together as many hyphenated prefixes as you wish, so long as they all attach to the same root.

Hyphenated Names and Identity

With the goal of equality, many couples today have chosen to hyphenate their surnames or to give their children a hyphenated surname. Other couples choose to use two names without a hyphen. This custom is evolving as society's ideas change, and there is currently no set rule. If you know the preference of the person involved, honor it. Otherwise, the choice is yours.

Similarly, some people choose to insert a hyphen in such terms as *Asian-American* and *African-American.* The hyphen implies that both segments of the expression are equal in importance. Other people omit the hyphen on the grounds that the primary identity is *American.* This choice is obviously a reflection of personal values. Whichever form you use, remember to be consistent.

Note: The CMS and the APA prefer not to hyphenate ethnic designations.

For Literary Effect

Hyphens may indicate hesitation or place emphasis within a word:

> She screamed, "No-o-o-!" (word *no* drawn out)
>
> "B-b-but I can't," he explained. (hesitation)

These effects are best left to literary fiction or very informal writing.

Understanding Fractions

Many writers confuse hyphenated and unhyphenated fractions. Yet the rule is quite simple. If the fraction stands alone as a quantity (in grammatical terms, the fraction is a noun), no hyphen is needed. If the fraction describes something else), a hyphen should be inserted:

Wrong: I arrived at the answer, which was two-thirds.

Why it is wrong: The fraction is not describing something else. It stands alone.

Right: I arrived at the answer, which was two thirds.

Wrong: The bottle is two thirds full.

Why it is wrong: *Two-thirds* describes *full.*

Right: The bottle is two-thirds full.

9

Parentheses and Brackets

Not many writers would agree with D.H. Lawrence, the English novelist, who believed that parentheses were "by far the most important parts of a non-business letter." *Parentheses* is an American term; the British refer to these marks as *rounded brackets* or, more simply, *brackets*. The terms refer to both the curved symbols and the material inside. Parentheses interrupt the flow of meaning, but they are quite helpful to the writer, so long as they are used with care. Too many parentheses confuse the reader and indicate that the writing lacks a logical structure. Parentheses also enclose citations in academic papers and appear in bibliographic entries.

What Americans call *brackets,* which resemble flattened-out parentheses, are called *squared brackets* in Britain. Brackets have important but limited usage. Material inserted into a quotation is enclosed in brackets to differentiate it from the words of the original source. Brackets also appear in bibliographies.

PARENTHESES

Parentheses inject something extra into a sentence: additional information, a remark on the content of the sentence, a cross reference, or a source citation. Parentheses may also enclose several sentences or paragraphs, signaling a digression from the main topic. They may also enclose numbers when a list appears in a sentence.

Note: The word *parentheses* is plural. The singular, *parenthesis*, is less frequently used these days. Both words are more or less interchangeable. The adjective form is *parenthetical.*

To Insert Additional Information

In a general sentence, parentheses are an efficient way to insert specifics, as in these examples:

> The theme we've chosen for the banquet (Springtime in Paris) is sure to be a success.

> The Ticket Committee (Eleanor Slovik, chair) has already sent out a mass mailing.

> We expect increased sales because of the new three-tiered pricing structure ($45, $55, $70).

> Inge is on a visit to Spain (did you know that she's visiting Madrid?) but is expected back next week.

> Has anyone seen Meg (she said she'd attend) or Janet?

> No one is happy with today's weather forecast (they said it would be cloudy with a chance of showers!), but we're going ahead anyway.

Notice that the material inside the parentheses varies in completeness and in grammatical structure. In the first three examples above, the parenthetical information is just a few words or numbers, not a complete thought. In the last three examples above, the parentheses contain full sentences—a question, a statement, and an exclamation.

Note: Parenthetical material tucked inside another sentence does not begin with a capital letter unless one is needed for a proper noun or the pronoun *I*. The logic underlying this practice is that there is only one sentence, which the parenthesis is part of.

Parentheses are optional in that they may be replaced in specific situations by other punctuation marks, the dash and the comma.

If the additional information is not a complete sentence, commas or dashes may set it off from the rest of the sentence:

> The theme we've chosen for the banquet, Springtime in Paris, is sure to be a success.

The Ticket Committee—Eleanor Slovik, chair—has already sent out a mass mailing.

We expect increased sales because of the new three-tiered pricing structure—$45, $55, $70.

Too Many Commas May Confuse the Reader

Commas are not a good substitute for parentheses if the information to be set off itself contains a comma.

Wrong: The colors we've chosen to highlight for the for the fall fashion show, green, yellow, and blue, must be worn by at least 50% of the models.

Why it is wrong: The information about the *colors* is set off by commas, but those commas blend it with the commas between the colors.

Right: The colors we've chosen to highlight for the for the fall fashion show (green, yellow, and blue) must be worn by at least 50% of the models.

Note: Dashes may also set off inserted material containing commas, as in this sentence:

The colors we've chosen to highlight for the for the fall fashion show—green, yellow, and blue—must be worn by at least 50% of the models.

If the additional information is a complete sentence, a dash (but not commas) may substitute for the parentheses:

Inge is on a visit to Spain—did you know that she's visiting Madrid?—but is expected back next week.

Has anyone seen Meg—she said she'd attend—or Janet?

No one is happy with today's weather forecast—they said it would be cloudy with a chance of showers!—but we're going ahead anyway.

Note that the material set off by dashes does not begin with a capital letter, even if the material could itself form a complete

What Does Not Belong in Parentheses

The only thing that may *not* be inserted in parentheses is a totally unrelated idea.

Wrong: The public relations staff is going out for lunch today (tonight's film begins at eight) and will not answer requests for information after 11:30 a.m.

Why it is wrong: The parenthetical information—*tonight's film begins at eight*—bears no clear relationship

---

sentence. The obvious exception to this rule is parenthetical material beginning with a proper noun or the pronoun *I*.

To Add Remarks or Comments to the Sentence

Parentheses, especially in humorous or informal writing, give the author a space in which to comment ironically or seriously on the ideas expressed in the rest of the sentence. Some examples:

Louise and Barry (we all know how efficient they are!) lost the keys to the closet containing the paper supplies.

When summer begins (and I certainly look forward to that day), I will put my books away and begin a much-needed rest.

The late Mr. Olson (sincerely missed) will be the subject of a documentary produced by the Alexis Company.

Though I belong to the older generation (pre-dinosaur era), I love teen romance films.

My mother asked if I had time to take out the garbage (and I had better make time, judging by her tone of voice).

As the sentences above show, the words inside the parentheses may be complete thoughts (as in the first sentence) or not. Writers may substitute dashes for parentheses whenever a stronger, more emphatic tone is required. Commas may replace parentheses only when the parenthetical material is not a complete sentence.

to the rest of the sentence. The reader is left confused. Why is the writer telling me about a movie?

Right: The public relations staff is going out for lunch today and will not answer requests for information after 11:30 a.m. They would like everyone to know that the film that was recently shot on company grounds will air at 8 p.m. tonight.

Why this version is better: Now the relationship between the film and the lunch is made clear.

To Insert a Cross Reference

Many nonfiction works cross reference information, sending the reader to a different paragraph or section for explanations, illustrations, and the like. The cross references may be placed in parentheses so that they do not distract the reader from the main ideas of the sentence or paragraph they appear in.

> Insert tab B into slot A (fig. 12) and staple securely.

> Nouns are words that name people, places, things, or ideas. (Chapter 3 contains more information on nouns.)

> "Man of Sorrow" is his favorite poem. (For more information on this poem, consult the American Poets Association website.)

Notice that the information in parentheses may be a complete, separate sentence or may be only a brief phrase. If the parentheses enclose a separate sentence, the first word is capitalized. If the parenthesis is tucked into another sentence, the first word is not capitalized unless a capital is needed for a proper noun or for the pronoun *I*.

To Cite Sources

Citing sources was once solely a matter of footnotes and endnotes. However, modern writers may use parentheses to indicate the author, title, and/or page that a particular idea or quotation was drawn from. Part III of this book explains parenthetical citation in detail. In brief, the text may give the title and/or author of the material. In such cases, the parentheses contain only the page number. If the text does not mention the title or author, the parentheses give enough information to identify the source and page. The bibliography, appended to the end of the piece, provides all the rest of the information on the source.

Notice that the parenthetical citation is part of the sentence but not part of any quotation being cited. The format for science papers or articles is slightly different from that favored by the humanities. Some examples follow.

Humanities Citation

> Miller claims that "the inflation rate was a primary factor in the president's defeat" (99).

> Inflation led to the defeat of the president in the general election (Miller 99).

Notice that in the first example the page number alone is sufficient to identify the work cited because the author's name is in the sentence. In the second example the author's name does not appear in the text, so it is placed in the parentheses along with the page number. The bibliography (not shown here) gives all the information missing in this sentence, including the title, publisher, date, and so forth.

Science Citation

Because the date of a source is more important in science and social science than it may be in the humanities, the parenthetical citation always includes a date. Some examples:

> Miller (1999) identified the bacterium.

> The bacterium was identified after an outbreak of disease in Philadelphia (Miller, 1999).

> The bacterium "is deadly only to those whose immune systems are compromised" (Miller, 1999, 12).

The parenthetical information in the first sentence above follows the name of the author and includes the date of Miller's publication. The second sentence identifies the author and date, as Miller's name does not appear in the text. In the last sentence above, the page number of the quotation is added to the author's name and date. As with all parenthetical citations, enough information is given so that the reader can turn to the bibliography and find full identification of the source.

To Signal a Digression

Occasionally writers place a paragraph or even a few paragraphs inside parentheses to mark a digression from the main point they are writing about. Needless to say, such a practice is risky because, as a British writer Sir Richard Burton once remarked, too long a parenthesis results in a reader who "forgot the sense that went before."

If you use parentheses in this way, place the opening mark before the first word of the digression and the closing mark after the last word and the endmark (period, exclamation point, question mark) or quotation mark, if there is one. The punctuation of the material within the parentheses follows all the normal rules. An example follows.

> Augustine slipped quietly into the back of the courtroom. How tired Alice looked, he mused. She liked to pretend that the grueling schedule had no effect on her health, but the reality was quite different.
>
> (September in Majorca! What a difference then in Alice's demeanor. She sparkled on the dance floor, glowed in the little café under the arch, and literally jumped up the few stairs to their room at the inn. "Catch me!" she had cried as she leapt into his arms.)
>
> The judge looked sternly at the jury.

Instead of parentheses, long digressions are often indicated in modern writing with a different font or with italics. These effects are more common in literature than in nonfiction essays or letters. The wise writer should consider long parenthetical interruptions very carefully. Chances are the reader will prefer a straightforward, logical structure. Note this example:

> Augustine slipped quietly into the back of the courtroom. How tired Alice looked, he mused. She liked to pretend that the grueling schedule had no effect on her health, but the reality was quite different.

September in Majorca! What a difference then in Alice's demeanor. She sparkled on the dance floor, glowed in the little café under the arch, and literally jumped up the few stairs to their room at the inn. "Catch me!" she had cried as she leapt into his arms.

The judge looked sternly at the jury.

To Number a List

Parentheses may enclose numbers when a numbered list appears in a sentence, as in this example:

When closing the store, follow these steps: (1) count the cash; on hand; (2) record the sales and returns; (3) straighten stock; and (4) alert security.

Notice that each item in the list above is followed by a semicolon, including the last item before the *and*. If the list is free-standing, you may omit the parentheses and simply place a period after each number:

When closing the store, follow these steps:

1. Count the cash.

2. Record the sales and returns.

3. Straighten stock.

4. Alert security.

If the numbers in a free-standing list are enclosed in parentheses, do not insert periods after the numbers.

Parentheses and Other Punctuation

Other punctuation marks sometimes appear inside or after parentheses, but not before. Take a look at these sentences and explanations:

Albertina sat down at the piano. (She had been taking lessons, paid for by her father, for years.) We awaited her performance eagerly.

In the first example, an entire sentence has been inserted into the parentheses. Any punctuation the sentence requires—in this example only commas and a period—goes inside the parentheses as well.

> Albertina sat down at the piano (she had been taking lessons, paid for by her father, for years) as we awaited her performance eagerly.

Now the parenthetical material is part of a larger sentence. No period appears inside the parentheses because technically the sentence isn't finished yet. The true end of the sentence occurs after *eagerly,* and that's where the endmark appears. Any commas needed in the parenthetical material, such as the ones that enclose *paid for by her father,* are included.

> Albertina sat down at the piano (she never took a lesson in her life!) and began to play.

> Albertina sat down at the piano (do you know that she never took a lesson?) and began to play.

In the above examples the exclamation point and the question mark are placed inside the parentheses. These endmarks are allowed inside the sentence because the emotion or tone they indicate is helpful to the reader. Note the absence of a capital letter; the lowercase letter is an indication that the parenthetical material is not a true sentence, but part of another, longer sentence.

> When Albertina returned (she had been in France for a week), she gave a concert.

The comma after the parentheses is necessary because of the introductory material preceding the parentheses. Commas may appear after but not before parentheses.

> Albertina played a long piece (*Etude in B Major*).

A period follows the parentheses in the above sentence because the parentheses end the sentence. No period belongs inside the parentheses because the expression inside is not a complete, stand-alone sentence.

BRACKETS

Brackets resemble parentheses, but the side of a bracket is straight instead of curved. Brackets appear only rarely and serve primarily to insert material into a quotation or to differentiate material inside parentheses.

To Insert Material into a Quotation

The most important issue in quoting a written or oral source is accuracy. The reader should know which words come from the source, which do not, and whether any words were omitted. Ellipses, or three spaced dots, take care of omissions. Brackets signal insertions. Sometimes the insertion is necessary to clarify the meaning of the quotation. Because writers seldom quote something in its entirety, the reader may be confused about the context of the quotation. A name or place may be referred to only as *she* or *there*. The brackets allow the writer to clear up any ambiguity. Take a look at these examples:

> "She [Elisabeth] entered counseling in May and was discharged in September," stated the doctor.

> The doctor went on to explain, "After arriving [at the hospital], Elisabeth was interviewed by the intake counselor."

> The standard practice, according to the hospital confidentiality policy, is to "follow federal regulations [the Privacy Act of 1992] in conveying information only with the patient's consent."

The bracketed information in the preceding sentences would probably not be necessary if the reader were able to read the doctor's entire statement or the paragraphs surrounding the last sentence. Since these quotations are excerpted, they lack the context that the brackets provide.

Bracketed information is usually brief. If much more information is needed, the writer should address the issues in the text, not inside the quotation.

To Identify Errors in Quotations

An extremely useful little word is *sic,* derived from the Latin term for *so* or *thus.* If you are quoting a source that contains a misspelled word or another error, the word *sic* in brackets distances you from the mistake. It indicates that you know what is wrong but cannot change the original quotation:

> "Dan peeled a potatoe [sic] for lunch."

The spelling of *potato* is a problem in the quotation above, as the writer knows and communicates to the reader with the bracketed *sic.*

To Alter Legal and Scholarly Quotations

Capitalizing the first word of a quotation, even if the original source is lowercased, is fine for everyday writing. The reverse is also true; you may usually change a capital to a lowercase letter without alerting the reader. The reader assumes that the quotation may be altered in this way without notification and seldom cares about such a trivial issue. However, in scholarly or legal writing, exactness is an important. Placing a capital letter in brackets indicates that the original source has been changed from upper to lower case:

> "[S]pecific instructions were never issued."

> The defendant replied that he was "[e]xasperated."

To Insert Material into a Parentheses

Parentheses separate the material inside from the rest of the sentence or paragraph. If you want to insert material into parentheses, use brackets:

> (Additional parts are available [see catalogue] for a small fee.)

As you may imagine, you should try to avoid brackets inside parentheses. The reader is too likely to wonder why you haven't simply reworded the sentence:

> (The catalogue lists additional parts that are available for a small fee.)

Sometimes commas are enough to set off an expression within parentheses. These two sets of sentences convey the same information, but the second sentence of each pair is cleaner:

(Mr. Phelps [Director of Overseas Operations] asks that you call for further information.)

(Mr. Phelps, Director of Overseas Operations, asks that you call for further information.)

(Insert the tabs into the matching slots [see figure B] and staple.)

(Insert the tabs into the matching slots, as shown in figure B, and staple.)

10

Ellipses

What a glorious punctuation mark is the ellipsis! Three spaced dots, the ellipsis takes the place of words that are cut out of a quotation. The possibilities, especially to the unscrupulous writer, are endless. "You may take the car keys . . . tonight" is a handy transformation of "You may take the car keys over my dead body tonight." Poet and cynical social observer Alexander Pope commented on the ability of this punctuation mark to hide reality: "The ellipsis, or speech by half-words [is the peculiar talent] of ministers and politicians." Obviously, Pope was not a fan of government leaders.

The ellipsis (plural, *ellipses*) should of course *not* be used to change the sense of a quotation. Writers—or at least honest writers—must remain faithful to the intention of the original. But ellipses come in handy when a given quotation is simply too long to be effective in the report, paper, or letter you are writing. This punctuation mark permits the deletion of words that are irrelevant to the purpose of the overall quotation. So that the reader always understands the nature of the quotation presented in your text, you must take care to observe certain conventions, especially when you combine an ellipsis with another punctuation mark. Ellipses are also used in literary works to indicate a fading tone of voice or a trailing thought, to imply that a series continues on, and to demonstrate where an original manuscript is damaged or illegible.

TO REPLACE OMITTED WORDS IN QUOTATIONS

In quoting only a portion of a written work or a speech, insert ellipses at the spot where words are omitted. The placement of punctuation differs slightly depending upon what is cut— a part of a sentence or a whole sentence or even several sentences and paragraphs. Where the deleted words appear in the original is also important. The deleted words may be from the end of a sentence, the beginning, or the middle. Each of these cases is handled somewhat differently. Blocked quotations, which are indented and separated from the rest of the text, follow slightly different rules, too. Furthermore, excerpting words or lines from poetry and drama requires different placement of ellipses and other punctuation marks. Each of these cases is discussed in turn in this section.

Quoting Consecutive Words

A habit of good writers is to select only the portion of the original text that relates to the thesis of the essay or paper. You do not normally need to place an ellipsis at the end of a sentence that quotes only a few consecutive words of an original source. If the quoted material is only a phrase or, indeed, anything less than a complete sentence, the reader understands that the original continues on. Imagine, for example, that you are working from this original text by a writer named Sheldron:

> **Original:** The marketplace was crowded with fruit sellers, basket-toting shoppers, and every conceivable variety of transport; but the militants were able to slip through the mob with ease.

In your writing you include this sentence:

> **Excerpted:** Although Sheldron observed the "basket-toting shoppers," he did not describe the many undercover agents who mingled with the other customers.

The reader of the above sentence knows that Sheldron wrote or said more than "basket-toting shoppers." No further explanation in the form of ellipses is necessary.

Words Omitted from the Middle of a Quotation

Sometimes you may want to cut words from within a quotation. Take a look at this paragraph, printed here in its entirety, from Charles Dickens' novel *Great Expectations:*

Original: Home had never been a very pleasant place to me, because of my sister's temper. But Joe had sanctified it, and I believed in it. I had believed in the best parlour as a most elegant saloon; I had believed in the front door as a mysterious portal of the Temple of State whose solemn opening was attended with a sacrifice of roast fowls; I had believed in the kitchen as a chaste though not magnificent apartment; I had believed in the forge as the flowing road to manhood and independence. Within a single year all this was changed. Now, it was all coarse and common, and I would not have had Miss Havisham and Estella see it on any account.

The sentence below, which might appear in a literary essay, quotes only the middle portion of the extremely long third sentence of Dickens' passage:

Excerpted: Pip becomes aware of his status in society only after visiting Miss Havisham's house. He explains, "I had believed in the best parlour as a most elegant saloon . . . I had believed in the forge as the flowing road to manhood and independence."

The three spaced dots indicate that this part of the sentence has been removed:

I had believed in the front door as a mysterious portal of the Temple of State whose solemn opening was attended with a sacrifice of roast fowls; I had believed in the kitchen as a chaste though not magnificent apartment;

Notice that the punctuation within the deleted section (in this case, two semicolons) does not appear before or after the ellipsis. If the words cut from a quotation are all from the middle of one sentence, the punctuation within the deleted portion is generally omitted as well. Any punctuation mark immediately preceding the ellipsis may be retained, if doing so will help the reader better understand the quotation. In common practice, commas and semicolons are seldom kept, but endmarks do appear. The next section, "Words Omitted from the End of a Quotation," contains a more complete discussion of the way endmarks interact with ellipses.

Words Omitted from the End of a Quotation

If you shorten a sentence in the original and give the reader the impression that you have quoted the entire sentence, an ellipsis is appropriate. Take a look at this sentence, which is drawn from this original text:

Original: The marketplace was crowded with fruit sellers, basket-toting shoppers, and every conceivable variety of transport; but the militants were able to slip through the mob with ease.

Excerpted (some punctuation missing): Sheldron observed, "The marketplace was crowded with fruit sellers, basket-toting shoppers, and every conceivable variety of transport."

A reader of the above passage may assume that Sheldon's sentence is quoted in its entirety because the quotation could stand alone as a complete sentence. To avoid confusion, you must signal that only a part of the sentence has been reproduced. In such cases, a period follows the last quoted word and an ellipsis is placed at the end of the quotation, for a total of four spaced dots:

Excerpted (punctuated correctly): Sheldron observed, "The marketplace was crowded with fruit sellers, basket-toting shoppers, and every conceivable variety of transport. . . ."

Now the writer has made the nature of the deletion clearer to the reader.

If the deleted section includes a question or an exclamation or quoted dialogue, the question mark, exclamation mark, or closing quotation mark is also retained to help the reader grasp the tone and meaning of the original. These punctuation marks are moved up so that they are flush with the end of the last quoted word. For example, suppose that you are working from this original:

Original: Dodge was revered by all who met him, regardless of political beliefs, because he truly cared about the poor.

How could anyone ignore his selfless devotion, even in the face of harsh treatment? No one could overlook this hero.

You include this sentence in an essay:

Excerpted: As a role model the students chose Dodge, about whom they wrote, "Dodge was revered by all who met him, regardless of political beliefs, because he truly cared about the poor. How could anyone ignore his selfless devotion? . . . No one could overlook this hero."

The question mark follows *treatment* in the original but has moved next to *devotion* in the excerpt. The ellipsis signals a gap.

Ellipses and Parenthetical Citations

Parenthetical citations, which are placed at the end of quotations, tell the reader the page number from which the quoted material has been drawn and may also indicate the author or title of the work. (Complete details on citation styles are included in Part III of this book.)

When a parenthetical citation interacts with an ellipsis, the three dots of the ellipsis precede the closing quotation mark. Then come the parentheses and the period at the end of the sentence:

Howarth states, "Binary systems were not particularly common in that era . . ." (12).

One or More Sentences Omitted

Cutting one or more complete sentences from an original is done following the same rules used for deleting material at the end of a sentence. (Indeed, this custom sometimes presents a problem to the reader, who is left to wonder whether the writer has omitted just the end of one sentence or much more material.) The endmark remains and is followed by an ellipsis. This punctuation gives the reader some sense of what is missing from the original. Here is another passage from Charles Dickens' novel *Great Expectations:*

> **Original:** "Laws of the game!" said he. Here, he skipped from his left leg on to his right. "Regular rules!" Here, he skipped from his right leg on to his left. "Come to the ground, and go through the preliminaries!" Here, he dodged backwards and forwards, and did all sorts of things while I looked helplessly at him.

Now look at a passage from a literary essay quoting part of the above passage:

> **Excerpted:** The young boy whom Pip fights is given to quick but ineffective boxing maneuvers: "Here, he skipped from his left leg on to his right. . . . he dodged backwards and forwards."

The first dot in the passage above represents the period at the end of the sentence. It is followed by three spaced dots—the ellipsis, which signals the deletion.

Too Many Ellipses . . .

If you find yourself needing more than one or two ellipses in the same sentence, you may want to reword. Few readers enjoy decoding a patchwork quilt.

> **Too many:** "Herbert slept . . .the fireworks boomed around him. . . . It was the Fourth of July. . . . The day was all hotdogs and baseball and barbecues."

> **Better:** On the Fourth of July, Herbert did not wake despite the fact that "the fireworks boomed around him." He later said that "the day was all hotdogs and baseball and barbecues."

> **Why it is better:** Quoting the original in two sections, with text joining them, eliminates the choppy effect of the first excerpt.

Purposely Incomplete Sentences

If words are cut from an original source and a sentence is left incomplete on purpose, only three dots (the ellipsis) are inserted, not four. An example:

> Lincoln began, "Four score and seven years ago . . ."
> Now that we are much further removed from the event, we still appreciate the battle that he commemorated.

If the last part of the quoted sentence plus some or all of the following sentence or sentences are deleted, the endmark (the period, question mark, or exclamation point) "moves up" flush with the last quoted word, even though the sentence is still technically incomplete. (Some words are missing.) Any quotation marks that appear in the original also move up. Take a look at this example, excerpted from the original text of *Great Expectations:*

> **Original:** "Laws of the game!" said he. Here, he skipped from his left leg on to his right. "Regular rules!" Here, he skipped from his right leg on to his left. "Come to the ground, and go through the preliminaries!" Here, he dodged backwards and forwards, and did all sorts of things while I looked helplessly at him.

> **Excerpted:** Pip fights the mysterious boy, who astonishes his opponent with his lively dialogue and erratic movements: "'Laws of the game!' said he. Here, he skipped from his left leg on to his right. 'Regular rules!' Here, he skipped from his right leg on to his left. 'Come to the ground!' . . . I looked helplessly at him."

Notice that the exclamation point and closing quotation mark appear before the ellipsis, even though in the original the quotation continues for on a few more words. Both marks are retained because they help the reader grasp the meaning.

Word Omitted from the Beginning of a Sentence or Paragraph

It is not usually necessary to replace words removed from the beginning of a quotation with an ellipsis. The reader understands that the writer has not included all the material that precedes the quotation. In certain circumstances—legal documents, for example—when exactness is required, three dots may be placed at the beginning of a quotation to show that words have been omitted.

An ellipsis is also necessary if a blocked quotation begins with a partial sentence that is not part of the same sentence as the introductory expression. More information on blocked quotations may be found in the next section.

Ellipses and Complete Sentences

The words before and after an ellipsis and a period (in other words, four dots) should be able to function as a complete sentence.

Wrong: Michaels writes that it is "very important. . . . No one may use a cell phone where the noise will disturb others."

Why it is wrong: The words before the four dots (the period plus the ellipsis) do not constitute a complete sentence.

Right: Michaels writes, "Courtesy is very important. . . . No one may use a cell phone where the noise will disturb others."

Why it is right: Now the quoted material before and after the ellipsis and period (*Courtesy is very important* and *No one may use a cell phone where the noise will disturb others*) are complete sentences.

Asterisks Are Not Ellipses

Some writers imagine that asterisks (*) may replace ellipses. Not so! The asterisk signals a note, usually located at the bottom of the page of text. It does not function as a marker for deleted material:

Wrong: "He went home and *** we walked for about an hour."

Why it is wrong: The asterisks are used improperly.

Right: "He went home and . . . we walked for about an hour."

In Blocked Quotations

Blocked quotations are long passages (more than 40 words) that are shaped like a separate "block" that is indented a little further from the left margin. A blocked quotation begins on a separate line and is not "run into" the text. Because a blocked quotation stands out, no quotation marks are necessary.

Quotation Begins with a Complete Sentence

An ellipsis is not necessary at the beginning of a block so long as the quotation starts with a complete sentence. In that case, the reader does not assume that these are the first words in the piece. Take a look at this example:

Winstron explains that the fees are nominal:

At fifty pounds per year, no one is likely to suffer from this fee. It represents only a fraction of the average amount spent on cable television service or high-speed Internet access. Yet the populace continues to complain about the entertainment tax.

The first words of the block (*At fifty pounds per year, no one is likely to suffer from this fee*) are a complete sentence, so no ellipsis is required.

Quotation Begins with a Partial Sentence

If the blocked quotation begins with a partial sentence that completes the introductory expression, no ellipsis is necessary. This passage illustrates:

> Winstron explains that the fees
>
>> are nominal. At fifty pounds per year, no one is likely to suffer from this fee. It represents only a fraction of the average amount spent on cable television service or high-speed Internet access. Yet the populace contin- ues to complain about the entertainment tax.

The introductory expression, added to the first quoted words in the block, forms a complete sentence: *Winstron explains that the fees are nominal.* No ellipsis is needed.

If a blocked quotation does not fulfill either of these requirements (doesn't begin with a complete sentence or fin- ish the thought of the introduction), use an ellipsis. Bracketed insertions can clear up any confusion for the reader, as in this example:

> According to Winstron
>
>> [the tax is] . . . a fraction of the average amount spent on cable television service or high-speed Internet access. Yet the populace continues to complain about the entertainment tax.

Quotation Ends with a Partial Sentence

No ellipsis is needed at the end of a blocked quotation unless the quotation stops in the middle of a sentence. In that case the period and ellipsis are appended. Below is an example.

> **Original:** At fifty pounds per year, no one is likely to suffer from this fee. It represents only a fraction of the average amount spent on cable television service or high-speed Internet access. Yet the populace continues to complain about the entertainment tax, completely without justification.

Excerpted:

Winstron deals with public attitudes about the tax:

> It represents only a fraction of the average amount spent on cable television service or high-speed Internet access. Yet the populace continues to complain about the entertainment tax. . . .

Quotation of More than One Paragraph

If you are quoting more than one paragraph, you may wish to cut words from one spot or another. The ellipsis moves around depending upon the location of the omitted words. Below are samples of several possible situations.

Original Source:

> Towards the front marched legions of soldiers from all parts of the empire. They were tired and hungry but determined to defend their homeland against the invaders.
>
> Preceding each regiment was an armored vehicle carrying communications equipment, and the messages flew back and forth all day. Headquarters and the field commanders consulted. To strike first or to wait for the enemy's offensive was the crucial decision.

Quoted with Words Missing from Paragraph Two   If you omit words from the beginning of a paragraph other than the first, place an ellipsis where the words have been cut:

Megans describes the battle in detail:

> Towards the front marched legions of soldiers from all parts of the empire. They were tired and hungry but determined to defend their homeland against the invaders.
>
> . . . [T]he messages flew back and forth all day between headquarters and the field commanders. To strike first or to wait for the enemy's offensive was the crucial decision.

The ellipsis preceding *[T]he messages* (first words of paragraph two) is indented, just as the missing text would be. The bracket shows that the lowercase *t* of the original has been capitalized.

Quoted with Words Missing from Both Paragraphs   Suppose you wish to trim the end of paragraph one and the beginning of paragraph two. Now you need two ellipses, one at each place that words are missing:

> Megans describes the battle in detail:
>
> > Towards the front marched legions of soldiers from all parts of the empire. They were tired and hungry but determined. . . .
> >
> > . . . [T]he messages flew back and forth all day between headquarters and the field commanders. To strike first or to wait for the enemy's offensive was the crucial decision.

Once again the ellipsis preceding *[T]he messages* is indented. At the end of paragraph one, *determined* is followed by four dots: one period and three for the ellipsis.

Entire Paragraph Missing from the Quotation   If an entire paragraph is deleted but the preceding and following paragraphs are quoted, the paragraph before the deletion ends with three dots (the ellipsis). An example follows.

> **Original Source:**
>
> Towards the front marched legions of soldiers from all parts of the empire. They were tired and hungry but determined to defend their homeland against the invaders.
>
> Preceding each regiment was an armored vehicle carrying communications equipment, and the messages flew back and forth all day. Headquarters and the field commanders consulted. To strike first or to wait for the enemy's offensive was the crucial decision.
>
> As the day wore on, nerves frayed. Finally, the decision was reached. The first strike belonged to the allies.

Excerpted:

Megans describes the battle in detail:

> Towards the front marched legions of soldiers from all parts of the empire. They were tired and hungry but determined. . . .
>
> As the day wore on, nerves frayed. Finally, the decision was reached. The first strike belonged to the allies.

In Poetry

Poetry quotations that run into the text follow all the same rules as prose quotations, with one exception: the line breaks are represented by slash marks. Missing words are represented by an ellipsis. If an entire line is omitted, the lines from the poem should be blocked, with the deleted line or lines represented by a line of spaced dots, extending more or less the same length as the line of poetry. The line of spaced dots, strictly speaking, is not an ellipsis, but close enough to do the job. To illustrate, here is a selection from a Shakespearean sonnet:

> Shall I compare thee to a summer's day?
>
> Thou art more lovely and more temperate.
>
> . . . .
>
> So long as men can breathe and eyes can see,
>
> So long lives this, and this gives life to thee.

The poem in its entirely is 14 lines long. The missing lines follow *temperate* and precede *So long as men can breathe.*

If lines from a poem are blocked and the last line or lines are omitted, insert a line of dots to indicate to the reader that the poem continues after the quotation.

In Drama

Short quotations from drama may be inserted into the text without varying from the general rules of ellipses explained earlier in this chapter. Longer, blocked quotations of several lines, with at least one whole line missing, are treated like poetry, as explained in the preceding section. A line of spaced dots, extending from margin to margin, replaces the deleted lines. This line is not actually an ellipsis, but it functions in the same way as that punctuation mark:

> FRANKLIN: This is the last time I send you to court.
>
> ESTHER: You're always saying that! I will go. I will!
>
> . . . .
>
> ESTHER: I knew you wouldn't hold me to it. You coward.

In Damaged Manuscripts

Ellipses are particularly useful to scholars working with damaged or illegible manuscripts. The dots indicate where a portion of the original cannot be decoded and reproduced.

TO SHOW A TRAILING THOUGHT

Fiction writers at times show a character's emotions—hesitancy, uncertainty, shyness, second thoughts and the like—by "quoting" their words. That is, they insert dialogue into a story. Ellipses aid character development by signally a fading tone of voice, a hesitation or speech problem, or a trailing thought. Ellipses used in this way are effective but should not be overused.

> He muttered, "Why can't I. . . . "

The above quotation is written in American style, with one dot for the period and three for the ellipsis. To present this quotation in British style, place the period outside the quotation marks and the ellipsis inside:

> He muttered, 'Why can't I . . . '.

The above example adheres to the usual British style of single quotation marks (inverted commas). For more information on quotation marks, see Chapter 7.

Dialogue ending in question marks or exclamation points keeps these endmarks, which are moved up to follow the last quoted word if the quotation continues after the ellipsis:

> **Original:** Why can't I go to court again to argue this case? I love litigation and despite what you say, I'm good at it!
>
> **Quoted:** He muttered, "Why can't I? . . . I'm good at it!"
>
> **Quoted:** He muttered, "Why can't I . . .?"
>
> **Quoted:** He muttered, "I love litigation and . . . I'm good at it!"

Building Suspense with an Ellipsis

A favorite of mystery writers, an ellipsis may be used to leave the reader in suspense:

> Archie slowly eased the door open and . . .

Not many readers have the patience for this sort of sentence more than once in a long while. Writers, beware.

IN SERIES

An ellipsis may indicate that the reader should continue the series, following the pattern laid down with the previous terms:

> He studied the piano, the harpsichord, the lute, . . . and finally decided that music was not for him.

In this example the reader can easily imagine the missing terms. Do not use this device if the reader may misunderstand or must work overly hard to decode your meaning.

11

The Slash

Despite its name, which may lead you to believe that this punctuation mark belongs in a teen horror movie, the slash is perfectly respectable. It has few duties, but those that it has may be important to your writing. The slash indicates alternatives; links word pairs; punctuates Web addresses and some abbreviations; and separates the day, month, and year in dates. A slash may also show the line breaks in quoted lines of poetry.

The slash actually has several names, including *solidus, virgule, diagonal, separatrix,* and *shilling.* Computer users often refer to this punctuation mark as a *forward slash,* to differentiate it from the *backward slash* (\). Whatever you call it, you should learn to place this mark correctly, because an errant slash can imply the exact opposite of what you mean.

TO INDICATE ALTERNATIVES

The primary function of the slash is to substitute for the word *or.* Working as a kind of shorthand, the slash helps the hurried writer to jot down sentences such as these:

> Please help yourself to milk and/or cookies from the refreshment table.

> Every student is expected to bring his/her gymsuit to class.

> The personnel department asks that you phone/e-mail your decision as soon as possible.

> His chances for an Oscar/Emmy/Tony were slim.

> Ellen will travel to the conference by air/rail.

Though the slash appears more and more frequently these days, traditional grammarians do not consider the preceding sentences appropriate for formal writing. The more accepted forms of these sentences are as follows:

Milk and cookies are available from the refreshment table. Please help yourself.

Every student is expected to bring his or her gymsuit to class.

The personnel department asks that you phone or e-mail your decision as soon as possible.

His chances for an Oscar, an Emmy, or a Tony were slim.

Ellen will travel to the conference by air or rail.

Which form should you choose? The decision hinges upon the writer's relationship with the reader. If your reader is unlikely to worry about the niceties of English grammar, the first set of sentences is fine. To be perfectly safe, avoid the slash and substitute alternatives, such as *or* and similar words.

TO LINK ELEMENTS

Paradoxically, another function of the slash is to link two terms, rather than to separate them as alternatives. (The preceding section, "To Indicate Alternatives," explains this concept.) The slash is sometimes used to show that two roles are joined together:

The secretary/treasurer will now distribute the minutes and collect this month's dues.

The winner/champion of that match, Muhammed Ali, is a legend in the boxing world.

The corrected proofs should be sent to printing/engraving for final processing.

The star's agent/accountant collects all his appearance fees.

Avoiding Sexism

Years ago the so-called *masculine universal* was popular. A masculine term such as *he, him, mankind, chairman,* and the like was supposed to represent everyone, including females. In the early 1970s the modern feminist movement turned a spotlight on this practice and pointed out the injustice of writing, for instance, *he* or *his* when the word was intended to refer to either a male or a female.

Many nouns with a masculine reference have been replaced by more truly universal terms (*chair* or *leader* instead of *chairman,* for example). But English has no singular pronoun for a person of either sex (*it* is not appropriate for people). To be more inclusive, many writers now use *his or her* and similar expressions when they need a singular pronoun. The slash is helpful in this situation, allowing writers to specify *he/she* and *his/her.* This usage, however, grates on some readers, who see it as graceless, especially in sentences calling for a number of pronouns:

If anyone calls, please ask him/her for his/her phone number and say that I will call him/her back.

Whether you insert a slash or the word *or* in all those pairs, the sentence is awkward. The better alternative is to reword the sentence, thus avoiding the need for the pairs:

Please ask all callers for their phone numbers and say that I will call back.

If you are dealing with only one pair, however, most readers today will accept expressions such as *his/her* or *his or her.* The latter is slightly more formal and therefore more appropriate for business or academic writing.

In the first sentence, one person holds the post of both secretary and treasurer. In the second, Ali wins one bout and also the title of champion. The third sentence indicates that the same department handles printing and engraving. Similarly, in the last sentence, one person performs the duties of agent and accountant.

Linked or Separated?

The problem for a writer inserting a slash is that since this punctuation mark serves two opposite functions (indicating alternatives or links), the reader may become confused. In this sentence, for example, the reader may wonder whether the job involves two states or one:

We are now hiring sales representatives for Maryland/Virginia.

Clarity is the most important quality of good writing, so if there is any chance the reader may not grasp what you are trying to say, the slash is not a good idea. Reword to express your message unambiguously:

We are now hiring sales representatives for the territory encompassing Maryland and Virginia.

or

We are now hiring sales representatives to work in either Maryland or Virginia.

TO LINK WORD PAIRS

Certain words appear frequently in pairs. In writing about such pairs, a slash commonly connects the words, which are then discussed as a unit:

In *either/or* sentences, match the verb to the closest subject.

Conjunctions such as *not only/but also* frequently present problems.

IN ABBREVIATIONS

A few abbreviations customarily contain slashes:

c/o (in care of, courtesy of)

N/A (not applicable)

A/C (air conditioning)

w/o (without)

w/ (with)

s/b (should be)

The last three abbreviations above are best reserved for very informal writing as many grammarians consider them nonstandard.

The slash is also used to represent the word *per,* as in these examples:

They traveled about 50 km/hr only on paved roads; on other surfaces their speed dropped to 20 km/hr. (*km/hr = kilometers per hour*)

The fuel economy (30 m/gal) was not what they had hoped. (*m/gal = miles per gallon*)

Water dripped into the tube at a rate of 5 ml/min. (*ml/min = milliliters per minute*)

As with all abbreviations, take care to ensure that the reader is likely to understand your meaning. If there is any doubt, spell out the word:

The fuel economy (30 miles per gallon) was not what they had hoped.

IN WEB ADDRESSES

The World Wide Web has become an indispensable part of modern life, facilitating research and commerce. The Web address, or *URL* (an acronym of *Universal Resource Locater*), is now a fixture of all types of business and personal writing. Web addresses rely on the period (dot) to separate the main components, but the slash indicates divisions within one website:

www.havad.edu/admissions

No spaces are inserted before or after a slash in a Web address.

Dividing Web Addresses

Web addresses are notorious for their complexity. Periods (dots) and slash marks may separate ten or more units of one address. Because of length, an address may not fit on one line. Take care in dividing a Web address to break it at a dot or a slash, never in between:

Wrong: To download this form, go to www.az.org/reimbur-sment.

Right: To download this form, go to www.az.org/reimbursement.

IN DATES

A slash may separate the month, day, and year in a date written solely with numerals:

10/2/2005

This style may be used informally, though the writer should be aware of one potential problem: Readers may interpret the above date as either October 2, 2005, or February 10, 2005, depending upon the custom in their country of residence.

Slashes may also indicate a range of time. (The en dash also functions this way; see Chapter 8 for more information.) These examples illustrate the slash:

The 2005/2006 yearbook covers all the extracurricular activities in depth.

The taxes he paid for November/December are much higher than the amount he paid in March/April.

IN QUOTING POETRY

Line breaks are part of the art of poetry; their placement enhances the effect intended by the poet. In quoting poetry, you should alert the reader to a line break by inserting a slash, with a space before and after:

> Shakespeare frequently employs nature imagery in his sonnets: "Shall I compare thee to a summer's day? / Thou art more lovely and more temperate."

The slash shows the reader that in the original sonnet, the lines were arranged in this fashion:

> Shall I compare thee to a summer's day?
>
> Thou art more lovely and more temperate.

If a quotation from a poem is blocked, no slashes are needed because the line breaks are reproduced:

> Shakespeare's nature imagery frequently appears in his sonnets:
>
> > Shall I compare thee to a summer's day?
> >
> > Thou art more lovely and more temperate.

In Britain the line breaks of a quoted poem are more commonly indicated by a straight line (a vertical), rather than by a slash:

> Shakespeare frequently employs nature imagery in his sonnets: "Shall I compare thee to a summer's day? | Thou art more lovely and more temperate."

IN CITATIONS

If a work has been reprinted, a slash separates the two publication dates in some citation styles:

> Miller (1805/2005)

In the above example, a work by Miller, originally published in 1805, was reissued in 2005.

For more information on bibliographic styles, see Part III.

12

The Apostrophe

Pity the poor apostrophe. It was once considered the easiest punctuation mark. Grammarians used to devote only a few lines to its placement, assuming that its function was self-evident. These days, however, a two-minute walk down an average city street is enough to supply the alert observer with several examples of misplaced apostrophes. Far from being easily understood, the apostrophe seems to have become a baffling puzzle.

This punctuation mark has also starred in a number of battles through the years. Gertrude Stein, an American author with strong views on apostrophes, wrote, "I do not like it and leaving it out I feel no regret." Her opinion was that "perhaps it does appeal by its weakness to your weakness." At the other end of the spectrum is the Apostrophe Protection Society, a British group.

The word *apostrophe* comes from the Greek. Its original meaning, "a turning away," relates to the apostrophe's function in contractions, where the writer "turns away" from some letters. The apostrophe also indicates possession and has a place in expressions of time and monetary value. In addition, an apostrophe may sometimes be used to form the plural of numbers, symbols, and letters.

TO SHOW POSSESSION

Some languages show possession only by words, not by punctuation. In Spanish, for example, the writing instrument belonging to an offspring may be referred to as *la pluma de mi hija*, "the pen of my daughter" but not *mi hija's pluma*. English, until the 17th century, did not have possessive apostrophes, though the mark was employed to create contractions. Now, standard English allows an apostrophe to function as an indicator of ownership.

Singular Possessive Forms

Most singular possessives follow a simple rule: To the name of the possessor, add an apostrophe and the letter *s*. A few special cases vary from this rule.

Simple Forms

To create a singular possessive form, add an apostrophe and the letter *s* to the "owner"—the person or thing possessing the object named:

> my daughter's pen (my daughter owns the pen)
>
> George's tree (George owns the tree)
>
> the plant's leaves (the leaves belong to the plant)
>
> Captain Morgan's idea (the idea belongs to Captain Morgan)
>
> the book's cover (the cover belongs to the book)

Hyphenated Forms

If the "owner" is hyphenated, the apostrophe and letter *s* are attached to the last word:

> the vice-president's bodyguard
>
> the editor-in-chief's responsibility
>
> the Secretary-General's clerical staff
>
> Sergeant-Major's order
>
> mother-in-law's recipe

Nouns Ending with an s Sound

If the name of the "owner" or possessor already ends with the sound of the letter *s* (but not necessarily with the letter itself), adding an apostrophe and another *s* creates a hissing sound:

> Ms. Liss's English text
>
> the kiss's sweetness

> Mr. Marx's exam
>
> the bass's stripe
>
> Puss's boots

A writer can, of course, avoid this unpleasant sound by rewording the sentence:

> the text that Ms. Liss uses
>
> the sweetness of the kiss
>
> the exam written by Mr. Marx
>
> the stripe on the side of the bass
>
> the boots that Puss wore

However, you may still wish to form the possessive of these words with an apostrophe. Two schools of thought prevail. According to one view, the apostrophe and *s* are added to the base word. Another method is to add only an apostrophe. The list above then becomes simpler:

> Ms. Liss' English text
>
> the kiss' sweetness
>
> Mr. Marx' exam
>
> the bass' stripe
>
> Puss' boots

In ordinary writing (not for publication or for academia), either form will do. *Ms. Woods's punctuation handbook* is correct, and so is *Ms. Woods' punctuation handbook*. The only prohibited form is one with an apostrophe inserted within the name. The book belonging to Ms. Woods may not be referred to as *Ms. Wood's book*. That last expression designates a book belonging to someone named *Wood,* not *Woods*.

Writing for publication or for a professor generally means that you must follow a specific style manual, and one may call for *'s* while another asks only for an apostrophe. The

Publication Manual of the American Psychological Association takes no position on the subject, so science writers may decide for themselves. Here is a guide to the other important style manuals.

The Modern Language Association   The Modern Language Association, which governs the humanities, calls for the addition of an apostrophe and the letter *s:*

> Dickens's novels
>
> Yeats's poems
>
> Lochness's monster

The Chicago Manual of Style   A general style guide for many disciplines, *The Chicago Manual of Style* (CMS) calls for an apostrophe and the letter *s* for most words:

> Ross's apartment
>
> the bus's wheels
>
> Queen Bess's realm

The CMS allows the addition of just the apostrophe to common nouns (but not to most names) ending with an *s* sound. The CMS states that custom and a more pleasant sound may make a simple apostrophe the better choice:

> for appearance' sake
>
> the conscience' reasons
>
> illness' symptoms

The CMS further states that *Jesus, Moses,* and classical names ending in the sound "eez" should be made possessive only by an apostrophe, not an added *s:*

> in Jesus' name
>
> Moses' journey in the desert

Sophocles' plays

Xerxes' throne

Pericles' oration

In general, the CMS acknowledges that the author should have some leeway in deciding whether or not to append an *s*.

Oxford University Press   The major British style guide published by Oxford University Press (OUP) calls for the writer to decide whether to add an apostrophe and an *s* or just an apostrophe. The most important concern, according to the OUP, is sound. The apostrophe alone is preferred if the word following the possessive also begins with an *s:*

for goodness' sake

a lass' seat

Mr. Ness' sacrifice

The OUP specifies that most classical names be made possessive only by an apostrophe, without an added *s:*

Venus' arms

Augustus' empire

Erasmus' philosophy

An exception is a lengthy classical name that is not accented on the last or second-to-last syllable. Such names may be made possessive by attaching an apostrophe and an *s,* or an apostrophe alone may be attached. The choice belongs to the writer.

Plurals Do Not Need Apostrophes

Probably the most common apostrophe mistake is to insert this punctuation mark in a simple plural, where an apostrophe definitely does not belong.

Wrong: Arrow's are sharpened here.

Why it is wrong: The *arrow* does not possess anything. You are not referring to, for example, *an arrow's point.* Plurals should not include an apostrophe.

Right: Arrows are sharpened here.

Wrong: For sale: melon's, three for a dollar

Why it is wrong: The *melon* possesses nothing. As a plural, it should not have an apostrophe.

Right: For sale: melons, three for a dollar

Wrong: The Collins's live next door.

Why it is wrong: The name of the family is Collins. The plural is Collinses. No apostrophe is needed for a plural.

Right: The Collinses live next door.

Plural Possessive Forms

Apostrophes may create an expression of ownership by a group. Where and how the apostrophe is placed depends upon the spelling of the simple plural form.

Plurals Ending in s

To form the possessive of a regular plural—a plural ending in *s*—simply attach an apostrophe:

> boys' physical education class (the class "belongs" to more than one boy)
>
> statues' pedestals (the pedestals support more than one statue)
>
> workers' uprising (more than one worker is rebelling)

ducks' feathers (feathers belonging to more than one duck)

papers' advertisements (advertisement in more than one paper)

This rule is quite straightforward and is a great help to the reader, who may sometimes care whether the books below to one girl (girl's books) or to several (girls' books).

Irregular Plurals

If the plural form does not end in the letter *s*, an apostrophe and the letter *s* is attached in order to form a possessive:

children's books (plural of *child = children*)

geese's migration (plural of *goose = geese*)

sisters-in-law's birthday (plural of *sister-in-law = sisters-in-law*)

oxen's yoke (plural of *ox = oxen*)

women's rights (plural of *woman = women*)

deer's ticks (*Deer* expresses both the singular and plural.)

These forms show possession and may not be used without an apostrophe to express a simple plural, non-possessive idea. These words do not exist: *womens, mens, childrens, deers, sisters-in-laws,* and so forth. If you are unsure about the proper plural, check the dictionary.

Compound Possessives

Joint ownership is expressed differently from separate ownership. If two people own two separate things, add an apostrophe to the name of each possessor:

Jean's and John's toothbrushes (Jean has her toothbrush, John his.)

Dan's and David's x-rays (Dan has one x-ray, David another.)

the boys' and girls' locker rooms (two separate rooms, one for each sex)

The Possessor, Not the Possessed, Counts

In punctuating possessives, ignore the possession and concentrate on the owner. If the owner is singular, follow the rules for singular possession, whether or not the owner has one or a million of the item or quality possessed. If there is more than one owner, go with a plural possessive. A special case is compound ownership, addressed in the section entitled "Compound Possessives."

Wrong: The boy's locker room was crowded.

Why it is wrong: The locker room belongs to all the boys.

Right: The boys' locker room was crowded.

Wrong: The students' grades were higher this semester than last, and she received a reward for this achievement.

Why it is wrong: Though the sentence refers to *grades,* a plural, the important word is *student,* because the context makes clear that the word is singular. The possessive form in this sentence should not be plural.

Right: The student's grades were higher this semester than last, and she received a reward for this achievement.

---

the lions' and tigers' cages (separate cages for each group of animals)

the umpire's and the player's points of view (They see the situation differently.)

If two people jointly possess something, an apostrophe and the letter *s* are added only to the second name:

George and Jenna's hobby (They share a hobby.)

the freshmen and sophomores' savings account (The account belongs to both groups.)

the student and teacher's basketball game (one game, two teams)

Penn and Teller's magic act (two men, one act)

Gene and Mary's theater tickets (The couple bought the ticket with joint funds.)

Possessive Pronouns

One group of words indicates possession without an apostrophe. In fact, inserting an apostrophe is definitely against the rules. These possessive personal pronouns never have an apostrophe:

my

mine

our

ours

your

yours

their

theirs

his

her

hers

its

whose

Names Belong to Their Owners

Naming a company is a privilege granted to the owners, who may choose to insert or omit an apostrophe, regardless of grammar rules. Thus *Lloyds of London* has no apostrophe, but *Bloomingdale's* (of New York and other American cities) does. You should follow the wishes of the company or enterprise, if you know it.

These pronouns, on the other hand, show ownership with an apostrophe:

everyone's

no one's

someone's

other's

others'

another's

everybody's

nobody's

somebody's

Apostrophes also take the place of missing letters in contractions, shortened forms of two or more words. (The next section explains contractions in detail.) A few of the possessive pronouns listed above may also function as contractions. For example, *everyone's* may also mean *everyone is* or *everyone has,* and *somebody's* may also mean *somebody is* or *somebody has.* The context of the sentence should make the meaning perfectly clear.

IN CONTRACTIONS

The first function given to the apostrophe, creating contractions, remains an important task of this punctuation mark. To create a contraction, delete some letters and replace them with an apostrophe:

that's (*that is,* apostrophe replaces *i*)

should've (*should have,* apostrophe replaces *ha*)

I'm (*I am,* apostrophe replaces *a*)

e'er (*ever,* apostrophe replaces *v*)

o'clock (*of the clock,* apostrophe replaces *f the*)

he'd (*he would,* apostrophe replaces *woul*)

'til (*until,* apostrophe replaces *un*)

she's (*she is* or *she has,* apostrophe replaces *i* or *ha*)

you'll (*you will,* apostrophe replaces *wi*)

The list of common contractions is long. A few vary from the simple letter-out-apostrophe-in pattern described above, largely because they come from outdated forms. The contraction *won't,* for example, is short for *will not,* even though no *o* appears in *will.*

'N Is Not a Contraction

The apostrophe may properly replace letters in standard English, but not every letter and not in every situation. A trend these days is to insert *'n* as a shortened form of *and* in names such as *Linens 'n Things, Bagels 'n Lox,* and so forth. While this custom may be fine for informal English, it is inappropriate for standard, formal writing.

Wrong: For dinner I had rice 'n beans.

Why it is wrong: There is no contraction for *and.*

Right: For dinner I had rice and beans.

Contractions create a breezy, conversational atmosphere. Take care, in formal writing, to use only the most accepted forms. A great many contractions in a single piece of writing relax the tone a bit too much, especially if you would like to sound businesslike or professional. On the other hand, if your goal is to sound like a friend chatting casually, contractions are helpful.

Commonly Confused Contractions

A few sets of words confuse many writers:

✦   *its* indicates possession (*it* owns something)

✦   *it's* means *it is*

✦   *there* designates a place

✦   *they're* means *they are*

✦   *their* indicates possession (*they* own something)

✦   *whose* indicates possession (*who* is the owner)

✦   who's means who is

IN EXPRESSIONS OF TIME AND VALUE

An apostrophe is sometimes used to express the relationship "of" or "for" in reference to time and money, as in these expressions:

> an hour's work (the work of an hour)
>
> two weeks' wages (the wages of two weeks)
>
> ten dollars' worth (the value of ten dollars)
>
> a month's notice (notice of one month)
>
> a day's pay (the pay for one day)

The apostrophe is added to these words following the same rules as for possession:

1. If the word is singular, add an apostrophe and the letter *s: one day's, a week's,* etc.

2. If the word is plural and ends in the letter *s,* just add an apostrophe: *two weeks', three months', six dollars',* etc.

3. If the word is plural and does not end in the letter *s,* add an apostrophe and the letter *s: two millennia's changes.*

TO FORM SOME PLURALS

To form the plural of a word that is used as a word, not as a unit of meaning, add an apostrophe and the letter *s.* The word-used-as-a-word is generally placed in italics or quotation marks as an aid to the reader:

> She has a tendency to include five or six *furthermore's* in everything she writes.

> His *missile's* are frequently misspelled.

> *Then's* are a poor beginning for your sentences.

Similarly, letters may be made plural with an apostrophe and an *s,* with italics added:

> There are five capital "T's" in that title.

> Can you count the *i's* in team?

> In the puzzle thus far I have placed three *e's.*

To talk about symbols (in the plural), not to use them for their meaning, italicize or insert quotation marks and add an apostrophe and the letter *s:*

> I would rather not see many "&'s" in formal work.

> The %'s are crooked on that sign.

Note: In the past the plural of numbers was also created with an apostrophe. Now, however, the trend is to simply add the letter *s:*

1960s

20s

1650s

Too Many Apostrophes

Apostrophes are useful little marks, but too many, particularly when placed consecutively, make for an awkward sentence.

Awkward: My secretary's mother's birthday was yesterday.

Better: Yesterday was the birthday of my secretary's mother.

Awkward: I've got *p's* and *q's* that I'd like to delete.

Better: I would like to delete some of my *p's* and *q's*.

Part II

PUNCTUATION IN COMMON WRITING FORMATS

13

Personal Letters

With cell phones playing their annoying little songs in every public place, it's hard to believe that anyone ever sits down with pen or keyboard to write a personal letter. Yet billions of dollars are spent on stationery each year, and at least some of the money goes towards personal-letter supplies.

A personal letter may accomplish any of a number of tasks:

- excuse an absence from school or work
- offer thanks for a present or a good deed
- invite friends and colleagues to festive occasions
- offer complaints or opinions to public officials

You may believe that how you present yourself in a personal letter is less important than the image you project in business communication. Indeed, those who know you very well are unlikely to be influenced by the quality (or lack of quality) of your writing. But many personal letters go to people you know only slightly or not at all, and in such circumstances, your words serve as an introduction. Most of us subscribe to the old saying about the need to "put your best foot forward." And even in letters to old friends, you can bestow care and attention on your writing.

Whether you write on a notecard with pen and ink or print your letter from a computer (and both are fine), you should pay attention to the conventions of personal letters. Your letters should be neat and legible. The paper should be clean and, if necessary, folded neatly to fit the envelope.

The conventions of personal letters also include the placement of commas, abbreviations, and the like. This chapter includes samples of the most common types of personal letters, each accompanied by an explanation of the punctuation. Where variations are acceptable in standard English, these options are explained as well. Keep in mind that more complete explanations of each separate punctuation mark may be found in Part I of this book.

A few general guidelines apply to all personal letters:

- If you are writing on stationery that includes your address in a decorative heading, you need only write the date at the top of the letter. On plain paper, you may include the address at the top of the page as a courtesy to your correspondents. Any recipients who wish to respond to your letter do not have to look up your address before composing a reply.

- In the address, a comma separates the city from the state, but no comma separates the state from the zip code.

- No punctuation follows any line of the address unless the lines ends with an abbreviation that requires a period.

- The two-letter state abbreviations preferred by the postal service (NY, IA, AL, OH, and so forth) do not take periods.

- In a date written in traditional style, a comma separates the day from the year (May 13, 2005).

- Dates written in day-month-year format do not take commas.

- The salutation (Dear May) is followed by a comma in a personal letter instead of the more formal colon (:) that is used in a business letter.

- The abbreviations *Mr., Mrs.,* and *Ms.* traditionally end with periods. However, in modern writing they may also be written without periods. Whichever you prefer, be consistent.

- The closing (Sincerely, Yours truly) is followed by a comma.

- If the letter is typewritten, the name of the writer appears twice—in print and in writing. If the entire letter is handwritten, the signature appears only once.

ABSENCE NOTE

A   B

455 S. 6th Street
Malacky, IA 40498 ⊢ D
April 18, 2005

C

E   F

Dear Mr. Dobbs,

Please excuse the absence of my older daughter, Susan ⊢ G
Deveranti, from school last week. She did not attend classes on
Tuesday, April 12, 2005, and Wednesday, April 13, 2005, ── H
because of a stomach virus. The doctor has assured me that she is
not contagious now.   I

I would appreciate Ms. Cliff's giving her a list of assignments
to make up. Thank you.

J

K

Sincerely,

Helen Deveranti

Helen Deveranti

L

Punctuation in an Absence Note

A. The abbreviation for *South* (S) is followed by a period. Compass points, when abbreviated, are generally followed by periods. The choice to abbreviate or to write the full form of compass points and street designations (Avenue, Street, Road, etc.) is the writer's.

B–F. See page 186 for an explanation of these points.

G. The name of the daughter (Susan Deveranti) is surrounded by commas because her identity (my older daughter) has already been established. Extra information in a sentence should be set off by commas.

H. Commas set off dates from the rest of the sentence. The month and day should not be separated by a comma. Had the date been written in day-month-year format (12 April 2005), only the year would be followed by a comma.

I. An apostrophe and the letter *s* turns a name, *Ms. Cliff,* into a possessive, *Ms. Cliff's.* The possessive is appropriate because the writer does not appreciate *Ms. Cliff* but rather the *giving* of *a list of assignments.* The possessive shifts the focus from the name to the task.

J. *Thank you* is not technically a complete sentence, but it is often punctuated as one, ending with a period.

K. A comma follows the closing (Sincerely).

L. In this letter the writer's name is presented without a title. Another, more traditional option is to place the title (*Mrs., Dr.,* etc.) in parentheses before the typewritten name.

THANK-YOU NOTE

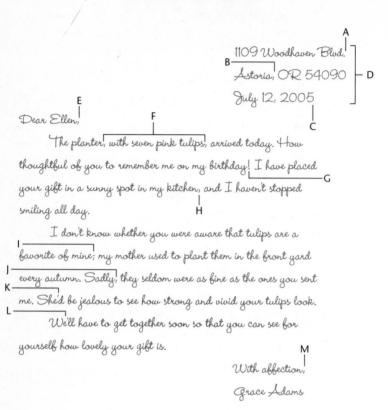

A

1109 Woodhaven Blvd.

B

Astoria, OR 54090 ⊣ D

July 12, 2005

C

E

Dear Ellen,

F

The planter, with seven pink tulips, arrived today. How thoughtful of you to remember me on my birthday! I have placed your gift in a sunny spot in my kitchen, and I haven't stopped smiling all day.

G

H

I don't know whether you were aware that tulips are a favorite of mine; my mother used to plant them in the front yard every autumn. Sadly, they seldom were as fine as the ones you sent me. She'd be jealous to see how strong and vivid your tulips look.

I

J

K

L

We'll have to get together soon so that you can see for yourself how lovely your gift is.

M

With affection,

Grace Adams

Punctuation in a Thank-You Note

A. The abbreviation for *Boulevard* (Blvd.) is followed by a period. Abbreviations ending in lowercase letters are generally followed by periods.

B–E. See page 186 for an explanation of these points.

F. The phrase *with seven pink tulips* is surrounded by commas because it adds extra description and is not essential to the meaning of the sentence. Extra information in a sentence should be set off by commas. Essential, identifying information should not be surrounded by commas. No commas separate *seven* and *pink* because they are different types of descriptions (a number and a color). In grammatical terms, they are not coordinate.

G. An exclamation point is appropriate for this sentence, in which the word order signals strong emotion.

H. A comma precedes the joining word *and*. When *and* unites two complete sentences, it should be preceded by a comma.

I. Here two complete sentences are linked by a semicolon. The semicolon is necessary because there is no joining word (*and, but, or, nor,* etc.).

J. *Sadly* is an introductory expression and as such is set off by a comma.

K. The apostrophe takes the place of the missing letters in this contraction (she'd), which is short for *she would*.

L. The apostrophe takes the place of the missing letters in this contraction (we'll), which is short for *we will*.

M. The closing (With affection) is followed by a comma. The closing and inside address in this letter are indented but may be written flush with the left margin if you wish.

INVITATION

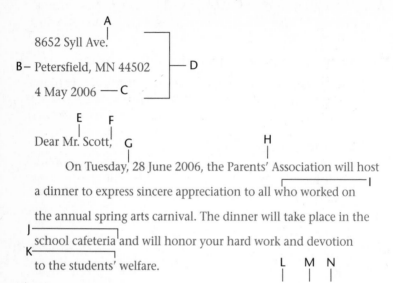

A

8652 Syll Ave.

B— Petersfield, MN 44502   — D

4 May 2006 — C

E   F

Dear Mr. Scott, G

On Tuesday, 28 June 2006, the Parents' Association will host H

a dinner to express sincere appreciation to all who worked on ⌐——————⌐ I

the annual spring arts carnival. The dinner will take place in the

J ⌐——————————⌐

school cafeteria and will honor your hard work and devotion

K ⌐——————————⌐

to the students' welfare.   L   M   N

We will serve hot and cold appetizers at 6:45 p.m. (cash bar

available) and dinner shortly thereafter. The chamber chorus will

perform. Highlights from the spring theater production, *Anything* ⌐——————O

Goes, will also be presented.

Please use the enclosed card to let us know whether you can

attend.

P

Sincerely,

Patricia Vogel

Patricia Vogel

Dinner Committee Chair

Punctuation in an Invitation

A. The abbreviation for *Avenue* (Ave.) ends with a period. Abbreviations ending in lowercase letters are usually followed by a period.

B–F. See page 186 for an explanation of these points.

G. Commas usually follow each part of a date when the date is inserted in a sentence. You may omit commas when only a month and year are specified (*May 2006,* for example).

H. *Parents'* is a plural possessive, so the apostrophe follows the *s*.

I. No comma precedes *who* because *who* begins an identifying expression (*who worked on the annual spring arts carnival*). Identifiers are not set off by commas.

J. No comma precedes the *and* because in this sentence *and* links two actions (*will take place* and *will honor*), not two complete thoughts.

K. Adding an apostrophe after the *s* in *students* creates a plural possessive.

L. The colon separates the hour and minutes. (In Britain, the colon is replaced by a period.)

M. The abbreviations for morning and afternoon may be written in lowercase with periods (*a.m., p.m.*) or in capitals without periods (*AM, PM*).

N. Parentheses surround extra information inserted into a sentence.

O. Commas set off the title of the play (which, as a full-length work, is italicized and not placed in quotation marks) because *the spring theater production* identifies what you are discussing and the title simply adds more information.

P. The closing (Sincerely) is followed by a comma.

LETTER OF COMPLAINT

A —

499 Mercer Square

Apt. 111

Tompkins, OH 50290 — B

9 December 2005 — C

— D

E

To the Superintendent,

For the past three days the heat in my apartment has not
functioned properly. Although the radiator does warm up slightly,
the apartment remains extremely cold. A thermometer in my
apartment indicates that the temperature in my living room
hovers around 50° during the day, and it drops even lower at
night. According to city ordinance 1251, from October–May the
landlord must supply enough heat in winter so that the interior
temperature reaches a minimum of 65° during the day and 55°
at night.

F

G

H

I

I expect that you will take care of this problem promptly.
Should you need to check my radiators, I will be home tomorrow
until 2 PM. —— K

J

Thank you for your attention to this matter.

Sincerely, —— L

Oscar Sewall

Oscar Sewall, Esq.   —— M

Punctuation in a Letter of Complaint

A. The abbreviation for *Apartment* (Apt.) is followed by a period because it ends with a lowercase letter. The apartment number may be placed on a separate line or following the street address. If it is on the same line as the street address, it is not preceded or followed by a comma.

B–D. See page 186 for an explanation of these points.

E. In a personal letter a comma usually follows the *salutation* (To the superintendent). In a business letter a colon, a more formal punctuation mark, generally follows the salutation. This letter of complaint falls somewhere between the two forms, because the superintendent is not a friend. Thus, either a comma or a colon would be fine.

F. A comma follows *Although the radiator does warm up slightly.* Expressions beginning with *although* and *though* should be set off from the rest of the sentence by commas.

G. A comma precedes *and* when that word links two complete sentences, as it does in this case.

H. The comma follows an introductory expression, *According to city ordinance 1251.*

I. A short dash (in printing terminology, an en dash) indicates a range of time, in this case from *October* to *May.* A hyphen may be substituted. (See Chapter 8 for more information.)

J. A comma follows the introductory expression, *Should you need to check my radiators.*

K. The abbreviations for morning and afternoon may be written in capital letters (*AM* and *PM*) without periods or in lowercase (*a.m.* and *p.m.*) with periods. Whichever style you select, be consistent.

L. The closing (Sincerely) is always followed by a comma.

M. Titles following names (*Jr., Sr., Esq., Ph.D.,* and so forth) are generally separated from the name by a comma. Roman numerals, however, are not set off by commas.

LETTER TO THE EDITOR

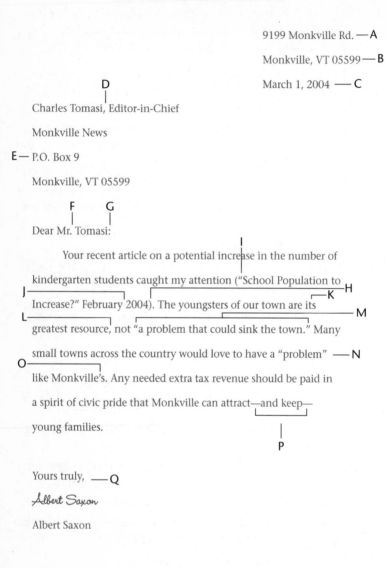

9199 Monkville Rd. —A

Monkville, VT 05599 —B

March 1, 2004 —C

D

Charles Tomasi, Editor-in-Chief

Monkville News

E— P.O. Box 9

Monkville, VT 05599

F   G

Dear Mr. Tomasi:

Your recent article on a potential increase in the number of

kindergarten students caught my attention ("School Population to

Increase?" February 2004). The youngsters of our town are its

greatest resource, not "a problem that could sink the town." Many

small towns across the country would love to have a "problem"

like Monkville's. Any needed extra tax revenue should be paid in

a spirit of civic pride that Monkville can attract—and keep—

young families.

P

Yours truly, —Q

Albert Saxon

Albert Saxon

Punctuation in a Letter to the Editor

This letter to the editor of a newspaper or magazine falls somewhere between a business and personal communication. The punctuation reflects the dual nature of this communication.

A. The abbreviation for *Road* (Rd.) is followed by a period. Abbreviations ending in lowercase letters are generally followed by a period.

B–C. See page 186 for an explanation of these points.

D. A comma separates a name (Charles Tomasi) and title (Editor-in-Chief) only when the title follows the name. Hyphens link the three parts of this title.

E. Periods follow the capital letters of the abbreviation for *Post Office.*

F. See page 186 for an explanation of this point.

G. Because this letter is somewhat formal, a colon follows the salutation (Dear Mr. Tomasi).

H. The information in the parentheses cites the article and date. The citation is part of the sentence and thus precedes the period.

I. The title of an article is placed in quotation marks.

J. See page 186 for an explanation of this point.

K. The possessive pronoun *its* has no apostrophe.

L. A comma precedes *not* because *not* begins a contrasting expression.

M. Quotation marks surround a phrase lifted from the original article. Because the quotation is tucked into the sentence, it is not preceded by a comma.

N. *Problem* is enclosed in quotation marks to show that the writer does not agree with that judgment.

O. *Monkville's* is a singular possessive form.

P. The em dashes set off and emphasize the expression *and keep* (See Chapter 8 for more information on dashes).

Q. The closing, *Yours truly,* is followed by a comma.

LETTER TO AN ELECTED OFFICIAL

1839 Southern Pkwy. —**A**

Ellison, SD 76987 — **B**   ⎤—**D**

June 14, 2005 — **C**

D— Mayor Daniel Movich

Town Hall

1 Penn Plaza

Ellison, SD 76987 **B**

E

Dear Mayor Movich: **F**

On June 1, 2005, the Town Council received a petition
containing more than 500 names. The petition asks that the Town
of Ellison increase the frequency of trash collection from
municipal litter baskets.

G—— Granted, the costs of trash collection will increase;
H————
nevertheless, the benefits to Ellison's business district are   **I**

substantial. All too often the trash baskets downtown are
J————
overflowing with litter, and every gust of wind dirties the streets.
————————————**K**
As a small business owner (I run the Cookie Cafe on Main and
L————
Penn Streets), I know that an inviting shopping area must be

clean.

Please use your political influence to persuade the council to
————**M**
pass this measure. When the bill comes to your desk, sign it

into law.   **N**

Thank you.

Sincerely,   **O**

Ralph David Morris

Ralph David Morris

Punctuation in a Letter to an Elected Official

Although this letter is personal in that it expresses the views of a private citizen, it is written to someone working in his official capacity. Thus the letter has some characteristics of both personal and business communication, and the punctuation reflects that fact.

A.   The abbreviation for *Parkway* (Pkwy.) is followed by a period. Abbreviations ending in lowercase letters are generally followed by a period.

B–E.   See page 186 for an explanation of these points.

F.   Traditionally, the year is surrounded by commas when a month-day-year date is inserted into a sentence.

G.   The introductory word, *Granted,* is separated from the rest of the sentence by a comma because it is a comment on the sentence and not part of the main idea.

H.   *Nevertheless* is not a joining word. A semicolon links two complete sentences. Words such as *nevertheless, consequently, however,* and *therefore* are normally followed by a comma when they come after a semicolon.

I.   The apostrophe and letter *s* added to *Ellison* make that name into a singular possessive form.

J.   When two complete sentences are joined by *and,* a comma precedes *and.*

K.   The statement in parentheses adds information to the sentence. Because the parentheses are part of a larger sentence, no period appears inside.

L.   A comma follows the parentheses because all the words preceding the comma, in parentheses or not, are part of an introductory statement.

M.   Introductory expressions of time, unless they are quite short, are generally set off by a comma.

N.   *Thank you* is not technically a sentence, as there is no subject/verb pair. Nevertheless, it is completed with a period.

O.   The closing (Sincerely) is followed by a comma.

LETTER OF SYMPATHY

Margaret Collis
412 Beech Street
Harbourton, New York 10110   ⎤ — A

April 15, 2006 ⌐ — B

Dear Louise, / C

I have just heard the│news about the death of your oldest E

D⎯⎯⎤ brother, Pierre. Louise│ I am extremely sorry that such a fine

young man is gone. You have often told me of his work with the

F⎯⎯⎯⎯⎯⎯⎯⎯⎯⎯⎤ poor and the homeless; he did his best throughout his life to make

the world a better place. To honor his memory, ⌐ I have made a G

donation to the Children's Home. ⌐⎯⎯ H

I know that you and he were very close, ⌐ and I am sure that it I

was a great comfort to him to have your care and support

throughout his illness.

You are in my thoughts. If you need me to do anything—mind J

the children, run errands, make phone calls, or help in any way— J

please do let me know.

Yours truly, / K

Edith J. Sinclair
Edith J. Sinclair ⌐⎯⎯⎯ L

Punctuation in a Letter of Sympathy

A–C. See page 186 for a full explanation of these points. This address is centered, as an imprinted address would be.

D. A comma separates *your oldest brother* and *Pierre.* The name is extra information, not an identifier. Identifiers are not set off by commas, but extra information is.

E. A comma follows *Louise* because the writer is directly addressing *Louise.* Words in direct address are set off by commas.

F. The semicolon links two complete sentences. If there is no joining word (*and, but, nor,* etc.), a semicolon is needed between two complete sentences.

G. The introductory expression, *To honor his memory,* is set off by a comma.

H. *Children* is an irregular plural because it does not end with the letter *s.* To make the word possessive, add an apostrophe and the letter *s.*

I. When two complete sentences are joined by *and,* a comma precedes the *and.*

J. The em dashes set off the examples from the rest of the sentence and create a dramatic effect. The examples form a series and are separated by commas. The comma preceding the joining word *or* is optional. (See Chapter 8 for more information on dashes.)

K. The closing (Yours truly) is followed by a comma.

L. A letter used as an abbreviation for a name is always followed by a period.

14

Business Letters

Business communication has come a long way since the days of "acknowledging yours of the 14th, attached hereto are the contracts" and similar expressions. Punctuation too has become simpler and somewhat more flexible than it was a few decades ago.

This chapter includes sample business letters covering basic tasks, including cover letters for job applications; information about products, programs, and the like; performance reviews; letters of recommendation; and ordering and returns.

The content and format of each letter represents only one of many options for each type of communication. If you are writing on letterhead, the company name and address has already been printed, so you need add only the date and the address of the recipient. General guidelines for addresses are described in the introduction to Chapter 13.

The company name should be separated from the abbreviations *Inc.* or *Ltd.* by a comma, unless the firm has already established a different tradition.

Also be aware of these conventions:

- The titles *Ms.*, *Mr.*, and *Mrs.* are generally, but not always, followed by a period. If you know the preference of the person to whom you are writing, follow it. If not, inserting a period is best.

- The salutation (*Dear Ms. Smith*) is followed by a colon in a business letter.

- A comma follows the closing (*Sincerely, Yours truly,* and so forth).

COVER LETTER FOR A JOB APPLICATION

Whether you are seeking a first job or the next step on the career ladder, you will have to send a resume accompanied by a cover letter similar to the one below. (For help in punctuating a resume, see Chapter 17.)

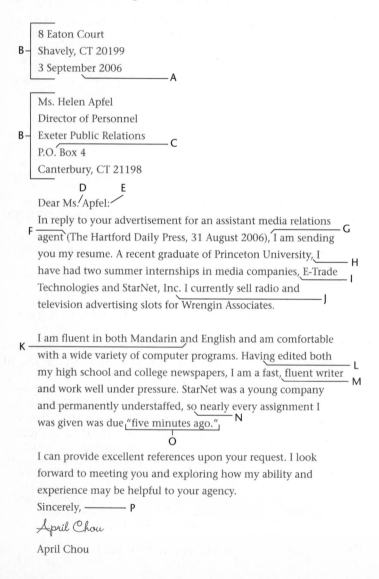

B ⎡ 8 Eaton Court
   Shavely, CT 20199
   3 September 2006 ——— A

B ⎡ Ms. Helen Apfel
   Director of Personnel
   Exeter Public Relations ——— C
   P.O. Box 4
   Canterbury, CT 21198

              D   E
Dear Ms. Apfel:

In reply to your advertisement for an assistant media relations
F agent (The Hartford Daily Press, 31 August 2006), I am sending ——— G
you my resume. A recent graduate of Princeton University, I ——— H
have had two summer internships in media companies, E-Trade ——— I
Technologies and StarNet, Inc. I currently sell radio and
television advertising slots for Wrengin Associates. ——— J

K I am fluent in both Mandarin and English and am comfortable
with a wide variety of computer programs. Having edited both
my high school and college newspapers, I am a fast, fluent writer ——— L, M
and work well under pressure. StarNet was a young company
and permanently understaffed, so nearly every assignment I ——— N
was given was due "five minutes ago."
              O

I can provide excellent references upon your request. I look
forward to meeting you and exploring how my ability and
experience may be helpful to your agency.
Sincerely, ——— P

April Chou

April Chou

Punctuation for a Job Application Cover Letter

A. When a date is written in day-month-year order, no commas are needed.

B. The introduction to Chapter 13 explains how to punctuate addresses in a business letter.

C. The abbreviation for *Post Office* (P.O.) takes periods.

D–E. See page 203 for an explanation of these points.

F. Parentheses enclose the extra details (publication and date of advertisement). A comma separates the publication and date inside the parentheses.

G. No comma precedes the parenthesis, but a comma is required after the parenthesis because the parenthesis ends an introductory statement (In reply . . .).

H. A comma sets off the introductory statement (A recent graduate of Princeton University).

I. A comma separates the general term *companies* from the names of those companies.

J. See page 203 for an explanation of this point.

K. When *and* links anything other than two complete sentences, no comma precedes *and*.

L. A comma sets off the introductory expression, *Having edited both my high school and college newspapers,* from the rest of the sentence. Introductory expressions containing verb forms are usually separated from the rest of the sentence by a comma.

M. *Fast* and *fluent* are equal (coordinate) descriptions of *writer.* Two or more of the same type of descriptions are separated by commas when the descriptions are equal in importance and precede the word being described.

N. A comma precedes the joining word *so* when *so* links two complete sentences.

O. Quotation marks surround the quoted words. The period is placed inside the closing quotation mark.

P. See page 203 for an explanation of this point.

INFORMATION LETTER

Riverside Nursery Gardens
18 Riverside Avenue
Hundred Oaks, CA 45600

A ⌐

B

January 14, 2005

Ms. Olivia Dembosk
4 Allerton Avenue
Zerega, CA 45600

C ⸻   D

E

Dear Ms. Dembosk:

F

Though the sky is gray and the air is chilly, spring is closer
than you think. It's time to plan your garden. We at Riverside
Nursery Gardens have been busy amassing a terrific array of

G ⸺ seeds, bulbs, plants, and equipment to ensure your best
growing season yet.

H

F

Now at preseason prices, we offer you the chance to stock up.

F

What's more, we'll store the items you order and deliver them

F

when you're ready. All you have to do is let us know which date
is convenient, and we will deliver within a week of the time
you select.

I

J

K

Riverside has been in business for more than fifty years; our
customers' satisfaction is our best reward. Take a look at the
enclosed catalogue or visit our website, www.rng.ca.com. ⸻ M

N

Hurry! Preseason prices are valid until March 1, 2005.

L   A

O

Sincerely,

Peter Z. Engili
Peter Z. Engili
President/Founder

P

Q ⸺ Enc. Catalogue

Punctuation for an Information Letter

A. A comma separates the day from the year in a date written in month-day-year order.

B–D. See page 203 for explanations of these points.

E. Introductory expressions beginning with *although* and *though* are followed by commas.

F. In contractions *s* an apostrophe replaces the missing letter(s).

G. Each item of a series is separated from the next by a comma. The comma preceding *and* is optional.

H. *Now at preseason prices* is an introductory expression, set off from the main idea of the sentence by a comma.

I. When two complete sentences are joined by *and,* a comma precedes the *and.*

J. A semicolon takes the place of *and* or a similar word and links two complete sentences.

K. The possessive *customers'* is plural, so the apostrophe follows the letter *s.*

L. The term *our website* is followed by the specific location of the website. When two equivalent terms are placed together, they are often separated by a comma.

M. Parts of a Web address are generally separated by periods (dots).

N. The exclamation point adds a sense of urgency.

O. The closing (Sincerely) is followed by a comma.

P. The slash indicates that Engili has two titles, *President* and *Founder.*

Q. The abbreviation *Enc.* (Enclosure) is followed by a period. Abbreviations ending in a lowercase letter generally require periods.

PERFORMANCE REVIEW

Agnes Murrey Academy
919 Wolbeck Street
Davenport, IA 63546

March 12, 2003 —— A

B ⎡ Mr. Brad Williamson
⎢ 333 Main Street
⎣ Davenport, IA 63544

C ⎡ Dear Brad:

It was my pleasure to observe your literature class on March
11, 2003. Although I arrived a few minutes late, I could see —— D
A —— that the class was already hard at work. Seated around an oval —— E
table, the 15 ninth graders were completing a grammar
exercise. Your review of their answers touched upon several
important issues, including misuse of commas and quotation
marks.   F   E G   H   I

After the grammar exercise, you quickly moved the class
into a discussion of Shakespeare's play *Hamlet.* The students
were engaged immediately by your question about Gertrude's
motivation. I do have one suggestion: The students who were —— J
unduly aggressive would benefit from a conversation with you
outside of class about the need to share the limelight.
                               K

You have done a fine job this year at AMA, and I look
forward to working with you for many years to come.

Very truly yours, —— L

Dillon Jones
Dillon Jones III —— M
Dept. Chair
            N

Punctuation for a Performance Review

A. A comma separates the day from the year in a date written in month-day-year order.

B. See page 186 for an explanation of this point.

C. Although this letter is friendly in tone, it is destined for the personnel file of the recipient and thus merits a colon, a more formal punctuation mark than a comma, after the salutation (Dear Brad).

D. Introductory expressions beginning with *although* and *though* are followed by commas.

E. Introductory expressions of place or time are frequently set off from the main body of the sentence, especially when they contain a verb form (seated).

F. The comma separates the general term (issues) from the specifics that define it (misuse . . . marks).

G. The apostrophe and letter *s* added to the name to create a singular possessive form.

H. No comma separates the general term (play) from the specific (*Hamlet*). When two equivalent terms are placed next to each other and the general term comes first, usually no comma is needed.

I. The title of a play is not placed inside quotation marks. Titles of full-length works are italicized or underlined.

J. A colon may join two complete sentences when the second sentence explains or elaborates upon the first.

K. No periods are needed for acronyms (the first letter of each word, in this case *Agnes Murrey Academy,* or *AMA*).

L. A comma follows the closing (Very truly yours).

M. Roman numerals, unlike the abbreviations *Jr.* and *Sr.,* are not separated by commas from the names they follow.

N. A period follows an abbreviation (*Dept.,* or *Department*) ending with a lowercase letter.

LETTER OF RECOMMENDATION

MODEL-TALENT, INC.
A ——— 5555 S. 5th Street
Dayton, OH 40490

30 October 2004 —— B

To Whom It May Concern: —— C

I write to recommend Clayton Harris for a position at your
firm. Clayton worked as a summer intern in my department at
Model-Talent, Inc. 2003–2004. I worked closely with him every
D ———————————————————————————————————— E
day and have frequently discussed his work and progress with
other colleagues.

Clayton prepared publicity releases and biographies for our
clients. He is a very strong writer. In fact, even before I met him I
                                                                    F
heard rumors about a freshman who wrote better essays than the
average senior. Throughout the past two years, variations of this
                                                                    G
compliment from a senior staff member have frequently reached
my desk: Clayton's work needed no editing at all.
H ———————   └—— I

His office demeanor is serious and involved, and he works   J
independently with a minimum of direction. Personally, Clayton
                                                                    K
is mature and considerate. He will excel in whatever tasks you
give him.

Sincerely,——— L

Oscar Hislop
Oscar Hislop, Jr.—— N
Talent Agent └—— M

Punctuation for a Letter of Recommendation

A. Abbreviations for compass points (north, south, east, west) are followed by periods.

B. No commas are needed for a date written in day-month-year order.

C. A colon generally follows the salutation (To Whom It May Concern) of a business letter.

D. *Model-Talent* inserts a hyphen between the two parts of its name. The abbreviation *Inc.* (Incorporated) is generally separated from the name of the company by a comma. An abbreviation ending in lowercase letters should be followed by a period.

E. A short dash (what printers call an *en dash*) is used to show a range of time.

F. The introductory expression *in fact* is set off from the main part of the sentence by a comma.

G. A long introductory expression of time (in this sentence, *Throughout the past two years*) is separated from the main part of the sentence by a comma.

H. The colon introduces the compliment referred to in the previous portion of the sentence.

I. An apostrophe and the letter *s*, added to the name *Clayton,* create a singular possessive form.

J. When two complete sentences are joined by *and*, a comma precedes the *and.*

K. A comma separates the introductory word, *Personally,* from the main part of the sentence.

L. A comma follows the closing (Sincerely).

M. A comma separates the title *Jr.* from the name.

N. Abbreviations ending in lowercase letters (*Jr.* for *Junior*) are followed by a period.

LETTER ORDERING SUPPLIES

AMERICAN FLORAL DISPLAYS
3255 W. MERCER STREET —— A
DYERS, OH 43490 —— B

C
|
5 December 2004

Mr. Arthur Lenn —— D
Sales Dept. —— E
Artistic Vase Co. —— E
10 Conduit Street
Birmingham, AL 78782 —— F

Dear Mr. Lenn: —— G

    This letter confirms our phone order of the following

H ——— merchandise, which should be sent to the above address:—— I

J ———— 15 PQ vases, catalogue #121H-5 ($5 each) $75 ——— K

            10 frames, catalogue #454B ($15 each) $150

    I understand that shipping and handling charges come to $5.95.

Enclosed is a check for the total, $230.95.

                         | | L

Sincerely, —— O   M   N

Frank Civitan

Frank Civitan

Punctuation for a Letter Ordering Supplies

A. Abbreviations for compass points (north, south, east, west) are followed by periods.

B. See page 186 for an explanation of this point.

C. No commas are needed for a date written in day-month-year order.

D. See page 203 for an explanation of this point.

E. A period follows the abbreviations *Dept.* and *Co.* (*Department* and *Company*). Abbreviations ending with a lowercase letter take periods.

F–G. See page 186 for an explanation of these points.

H. The expression *which should be sent to the above address* is separated by a comma from the word it is describing (merchandise). Descriptions beginning with *which* are usually set off by commas. Descriptions beginning with *that* generally are not separated by commas from the word being described.

I. A colon introduces a list of products.

J. The name of the item is separated from the catalogue number by a comma.

K. The price per unit is enclosed in parentheses to set it off from the total.

L. A period separates the numerals representing the dollar and cents amount.

M. Two equivalent terms, *the total* and *$230.95,* are separated by a comma.

N. A period separates the numerals representing the dollar and cents amount.

O. A comma follows the closing (Sincerely).

LETTER RETURNING MERCHANDISE

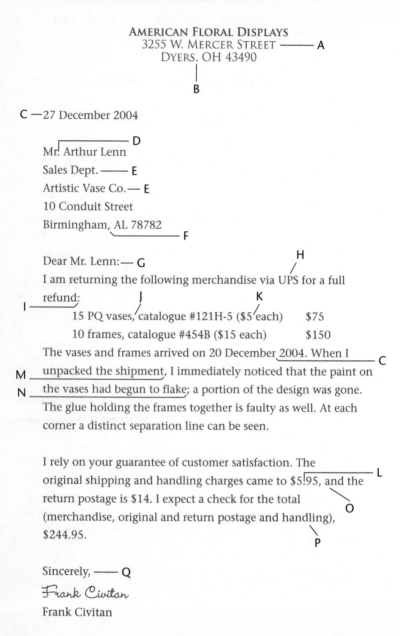

AMERICAN FLORAL DISPLAYS
3255 W. MERCER STREET ——— A
DYERS, OH 43490

B

C —27 December 2004

Mr. Arthur Lenn ——— D
Sales Dept. ——— E
Artistic Vase Co.— E
10 Conduit Street
Birmingham, AL 78782
——— F

Dear Mr. Lenn:— G

H

I am returning the following merchandise via UPS for a full
refund:

I

    15 PQ vases, catalogue #121H-5 ($5 each) $75
    10 frames, catalogue #454B ($15 each) $150

J   K

The vases and frames arrived on 20 December 2004. When I
C
M   unpacked the shipment, I immediately noticed that the paint on
N   the vases had begun to flake; a portion of the design was gone.
The glue holding the frames together is faulty as well. At each
corner a distinct separation line can be seen.

I rely on your guarantee of customer satisfaction. The
original shipping and handling charges came to $5.95, and the   L
return postage is $14. I expect a check for the total
(merchandise, original and return postage and handling),   O
$244.95.

P

Sincerely, ——— Q

Frank Civitan

Frank Civitan

Punctuation for a Letter Returning Merchandise

A. Abbreviations for compass points (north, south, east, west) are followed by periods.

B. See page 186 for an explanation of this point.

C. No commas are needed for a date written in day-month-year order.

D. See page 203 for an explanation of this point.

E. A period follows the abbreviations *Dept.* and *Co.* (*Department* and *Company*). Abbreviations ending with a lowercase letter take periods.

F–G. See page 186 for an explanation of this point.

H. Acronyms (*UPS* is an acronym for *United Parcel Service*) do not include periods.

I. A colon introduces a list of products.

J. The name of the item is separated from the catalogue number by a comma.

K. The price per unit is enclosed in parentheses to set it off from the total.

L. A period separates the numerals representing the dollar and cents amount.

M. Introductory expressions of time are generally set off by a comma.

N. A semicolon joins two complete sentences without the need for a joining word such as *and*.

O. When two complete sentences are joined by the word *and*, a comma precedes the *and*.

P. Parentheses separate added detail from the rest of the sentence. No punctuation precedes the parentheses. A comma follows the parentheses because *total* and *$244.95* are equivalent. When equivalent terms follow each other, they are often separated by commas.

Q. The closing (Sincerely) is followed by a comma.

15

Memos

Memos are such an important part of internal business correspondence that the major word-processing programs include several memo templates among the options for a new document. These templates include proper punctuation of the memo heading; all the writer has to do is to insert information into the required fields. Though they are handy, memo templates are not really necessary.

To set up your own memo, keep these guidelines in mind:

- Each heading label ends with a colon. The first two lines indicate the primary recipient of the memo (the *To* line) and who is to receive copies (the *CC* line). If more than one recipient is listed, the names may be separated by commas or listed on separate lines. The third line tells who sent the memo (the *From* line). The date and subject lines follow. The subject line may be labeled *Re* (about or "Regarding").

- A comma separates the name and title; and a colon separates the subject from a subtitle.

- The specific information in each line is not followed by punctuation, unless a line ends with an abbreviation containing a period.

- Dates written in day-month-year order take no commas. In month-day-year dates, a comma separates the day from the year. Slashes may also separate the numerals of a date.

This chapter contains sample memos addressed to a superior, an employee, and a group of employees. Subjects range from the agenda for a meeting to a retirement announcement. Some are more formal than others in order to show the range of proper, acceptable English.

TO A SUPERVISOR, REPORTING
ON A BUSINESS TRIP

Memorandum —— A

B —— **To:**   Joseph Adelson

C —— **CC:**   Ileanna Engelmeyer

D —— **From:**   Susan Garcia

E —— **Date:**   4/11/2006

F —— **Re:**   Stadium proposal

G —— Pam Carpenter and I met with Addison Industries representative Michael Khalid on 2/15/06 in his Dayton office. We discussed our proposal for a new multipurpose stadium on the site of the vacant wallpaper factory (land parcel 52-77). Preliminary work was divided between Addison and our employees. —— H

I —— **POINTS AGREED ON**

J ——
- The bid should be prepared jointly by an employee of Addison and Martin Kelso of our planning department. Work is to begin immediately and to be finished by 1/1/07. L

- Work should begin immediately on an environmental impact survey (our company), to be completed by 9/1/06. L

- Caitlin Kreegar (Addison) will prepare a report on the political issues involved in gaining approval for the stadium, to be L—M completed by 7/1/06. L

- Our engineering staff will evaluate the site and submit a report by 4/15/06. L

I —— **TO BE DECIDED**

K ——
- Role of public funding

- Estimates of necessary site and transportation improvements

- Likely supporters and opponents of the stadium

- Probable competing bids   / L

Our next scheduled meeting is 4/15/06, again in Dayton. Michael Khalid will distribute an agenda by 4/5/06.   N

CONFIDENTIAL — O

Punctuation for a Memo to a Supervisor, Reporting on a Business Trip

A. The title of the memo should not be punctuated unless it contains an abbreviation requiring a period. If there is a subtitle, divide it from the title with a colon placed flush with the last word of the title.

B–F. See page 217 for an explanation of these points.

G. The date in the body text is written in the same style as the date in the heading, with slashes separating the month, day, and year.

H. Extra information is inserted into the sentence with parentheses. No punctuation precedes parentheses.

I. Subheads are not followed by periods.

J. Bullet points that take the form of complete sentences are punctuated according to normal rules.

K. Bullet points that are not complete sentences are not punctuated with endmarks.

L. The date style should be consistent throughout the memo.

M. The phrase *to be completed by* . . . is tacked on to the end of the sentence and is separated from the main idea of the sentence by a comma.

N. The phrase *again in Dayton* is an interrupter and adds extra information to the sentence. It is set off by commas.

O. The footer, a shaded box with the word *confidential,* is not punctuated.

AN AGENDA FOR A MEETING

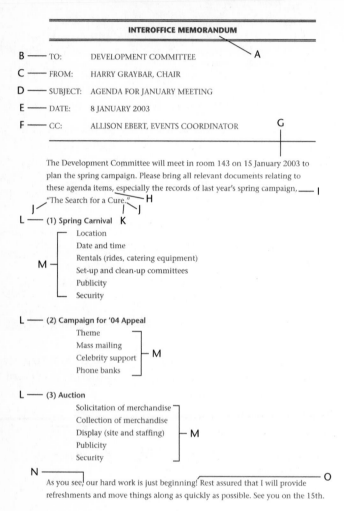

INTEROFFICE MEMORANDUM

B —— TO: DEVELOPMENT COMMITTEE   A

C —— FROM: HARRY GRAYBAR, CHAIR

D —— SUBJECT: AGENDA FOR JANUARY MEETING

E —— DATE: 8 JANUARY 2003

F —— CC: ALLISON EBERT, EVENTS COORDINATOR   G

The Development Committee will meet in room 143 on 15 January 2003 to plan the spring campaign. Please bring all relevant documents relating to these agenda items, especially the records of last year's spring campaign, —— I "The Search for a Cure." —— H

J

L —— (1) Spring Carnival   K

M
- Location
- Date and time
- Rentals (rides, catering equipment)
- Set-up and clean-up committees
- Publicity
- Security

L —— (2) Campaign for '04 Appeal

M
- Theme
- Mass mailing
- Celebrity support
- Phone banks

L —— (3) Auction

M
- Solicitation of merchandise
- Collection of merchandise
- Display (site and staffing)
- Publicity
- Security

N ————

As you see, our hard work is just beginning! Rest assured that I will provide   O refreshments and move things along as quickly as possible. See you on the 15th.

Punctuation for a Memo with a Meeting Agenda

A–G. See page 217 for explanations of these points.

H. Two equivalent terms (*all relevant documents* and *especially the records of last year's spring campaign*) appear in this sentence. The second term is essentially a definition added to the sentence. Because it is extra information, it is set off by a comma.

I. Two equivalent terms (*last year's spring campaign* and *"The Search for a Cure"*) are placed next to each other and separated by a comma. The second term is not an identifier, because the sentence already pinpoints what is being discussed—last year's campaign. Thus the name of the campaign is extra and set off by a comma.

J. The name of the campaign is placed in quotation marks.

K. The period is placed inside the closing quotation mark (American style).

L. The numbers of agenda items are placed in parentheses, and the numerals are not followed by periods. If the parentheses are removed, a period should follow each numeral.

M. The subtopics of each agenda item are not followed by periods because the subtopics are not written in the form of complete sentences.

N. Introductory expressions containing a verb form are generally set off by commas.

O. The exclamation point emphasizes the idea in this sentence.

STATUS REPORT

A ──────────────

Kelfax Storage, Inc.

Memo

B

C — **To:**   Accounting Staff

D — **From:**   Jose Perilos

E — **CC:**   Belinda Stamos, Storage Facility Director

F — **Date:**   May 19, 2005

G — **Re:**   Status Report: Unpaid storage fees

┌─ H

Our drive to collect unpaid storage rental fees stands as follows:

I ──────────────

- As of April 30, 2005, 59 customers were at least two months behind in rent for storage units.

- All customers owing rent were contacted by mail and given notice that their belongings would be sold if the outstanding fees were not paid by May 31, 2005.
                                                                    I

- More than half of customers with rental fees in arrears at the end of April (47/59) are now paid in full.
                                                              J

K ──────────────

- Follow-up phone calls to the remaining debtors

I ──────── (12 customers) were completed by May 5, 2005.

                                                              ┌──── I
- A final notice of seizure will be mailed on May 20, ──── L
  2005, to all who owe more than three months' rent.

                                                              ┌──── I
- Beginning on June 1, 2005, the storage facility staff will open the storage units of those who have not paid. The contents will be inventoried by two staff members.

- The belongings will be placed at auction beginning on

I ──────── June 10, 2005.

We appreciate your cooperation in dealing with any customer dissatisfaction. Please refer to my office any client who is particularly upset.

M

Punctuation for a Status Report Memo

A. The company name is separated from the abbreviation *Inc.* (Incorporated) by a comma. *Inc.* and *Ltd.* (Limited) are generally set off by commas.

B. Abbreviations ending in a lowercase letter are generally followed by periods.

C–G. See page 217 for general explanations of these points.

H. The introduction to the bulleted list, which is a complete sentence, ends with a colon.

I. A date inserted in a sentence is written in the same style as the date in the heading. Commas separate the day from the year and the year from the rest of the sentence (if the sentence continues on) when a date is written in month-day-year order.

J. Parentheses set off extra information inserted into a sentence.

K. Two words combined to create one description (follow-up) are generally hyphenated when the description is placed in front of the word being described.

L. An apostrophe is used to express the value of time or money. The words *of* or *for* may be substituted for the apostrophe. In other words, *three months' rent* is *rent for three months.* The apostrophe follows the *s* in *months* because *months* is plural.

M. No comma separates *client* and *who* because *who* begins an identifying statement. The writer is not asking for any and all *clients* to be referred, only those who are *particularly upset.*

ANNOUNCING A PROMOTION

MANDALAY INDUSTRIES: INTEROFFICE MEMO

A

B — **TO:**   ALL EMPLOYEES

C — **FROM:**   ART D. MANDALAY, PRESIDENT/CEO

D — **SUBJECT:** NEW VP OF MARKETING

E — **CC:**   EDITH DOMICH

F — **DATE:**   5 NOVEMBER 2003   G

H   I am pleased to announce that Edith G. Domich has been promoted to Vice-President of Marketing. Ms. Domich joined the firm in 1995 after a successful career in journalism. Ms. Domich headed the team I developing the AG-9 model, which, as you know, is one of our best- J selling product lines. Two years ago she became the Regional Director K of Sales for the Mid-Atlantic region. In her new position, Ms. Domich will oversee a staff of 289 employees; she will report directly to me and attend all executive planning-meetings. L

M

N   Ms. Domich, who was twice named "Employee of the Year," brings a wealth of expertise to our marketing department. She is expert at dealing with all media outlets, including both new and traditional L media; she is legendary for her attention to detail and her grasp of Q the overall strategy of the company.

O   P

Punctuation for a Memo Announcing a Promotion

A. The title of this memo is combined with the name of the company (Mandalay Industries). A colon divides one from the other.

B–F. See page 217 for explanations of these points.

G. Abbreviated names are followed by periods.

H. The title *Vice-President* is generally hyphenated.

I. The *AG-9 model* is named specifically, so the information beginning with *which* is extra and thus set off by commas.

J. Within the *which statement* (see letter I above), an interrupter (*as you know*) is set off by commas.

K. Two-part descriptions (*Mid-Atlantic*) are frequently hyphenated when they precede the word described.

L. A semicolon joins two complete sentences without the help of a joining word such as *and.*

M. The hyphen in this phrase helps the reader understand that the meetings are devoted to planning and that they are attended by executives, not meetings to plan executive positions.

N. The descriptive expression beginning with *who* is extra, not identifying, because the sentence has already named the person being discussed. Hence commas surround the *who* expression.

O. The title *Employee of the Year* is placed in quotation marks.

P. The comma goes inside the closing quotation mark (American style).

Q. The descriptive expression *including both new and traditional media* is extra, so it is set off by a comma.

WARNING TO IMPROVE JOB PERFORMANCE

Carver Books

A

Memo

B — **To:**   Helen Chapel

C — **From:**   Ellen Weaver

D — **CC:**   Elisabeth Searles

E — **Date:**   6 December 2004

F — **Re:**   Lateness

G — In the last two months you have arrived more than 20 minutes past

H — the beginning of your shift. True, the weather has been especially

I — bad this winter; nevertheless, punctuality is extremely important.

Every time that you were late, a worker from the previous shift had

to stay in order to take care of customers. It is not reasonable to

J — continue to ask others to cover for you, and employee morale

is suffering.

K

L — I have asked your supervisor, Ms. Searles, to monitor your arrivals

and to report to me on a weekly basis. If the situation does not

improve, I will be forced to terminate your employment.

M

Punctuation for a Memo About Job Performance

A. The company name is not punctuated.

B–F. See page 217 for explanations of these points.

G. The introductory statement, *True,* is a comment on the rest of the sentence, not a part of the main idea. It is set off by a comma.

H. A semicolon joins two complete sentences in the absence of joining words such as *and, but, nor, or,* and the like.

I. *Nevertheless* may not join two complete sentences. When it falls between two complete sentences, *nevertheless* is generally preceded by a semicolon and followed by a comma.

J. Two complete sentences are joined by *and.* A comma precedes the joining word.

K. The name is set off by commas because the person has already been identified by the phrase *your supervisor.* Identifying information is not set off by commas, but extra information is.

L. The title *Ms.* is often, but not always, followed by a period, as are the titles *Mr.* and *Mrs.* Whatever style you choose should be consistent throughout the memo.

M. When an expression beginning with *if* begins a sentence, it is separated from the main idea of the sentence by a comma.

POLICY MEMO

Memorandum

A —— **To:**   All Faculty

B —— **cc:**   Henry Guiso, Principal, 7–12

Mary Herb, Principal, K–6

Agnes Wethim, Principal, Nursery Years

C —— **From:**   Eileen August, Head of School

D —— **Date:**   3 September 2006

E —— **Re:**   Attendance Policy

F   Effective immediately, all faculty will return the attendance sheets within fifteen minutes of
G   the first period of the school day. The sheets should be sent to the office with an aide. The
H   absentee list will be compiled and e-mailed to you before the start of second period. Parents will
be called to verify absence; if there is any problem, you will receive a notice of "unexcused   J
absence" at the start of the next school day.   I

K   I remind you that accurate records are essential to our students' safety and well-being. For   L
those of you who are not familiar with school policy, absence is excused only for these reasons:
M   N

O
- Illness
- Family emergency
- Pre-arranged college visits
- Scheduled field trips

P   Q   P
No other reasons for absence—doctors' appointments, family vacations, etc.—are allowed.
R   R

Punctuation for a Policy Memo

A. See page 217 for an explanation of this point.

B. See page 217 for additional explanation of this point. The name of the person is separated from his or her title by a comma. The range of grades (7 to 12, for example) is indicated by a short dash, also known as an *en dash.*

C–E. See page 217 for explanations of these points.

F. The introductory phrase, *effective immediately,* is separated from the main part of the sentence by a comma.

G. The word *e-mail* is generally, but not always, hyphenated.

H. A semicolon joins two complete sentences in the absence of a word such as *and, but, nor,* etc.

I. Expressions beginning with *if* are frequently set off by a comma.

J. The expression *unexcused absence* is in quotation marks because it is the name of the notice that will be sent.

K. The word *students* is made possessive by the addition of an apostrophe placed after the *s.*

L. The expression *well-being* is created from two separate words joined by a hyphen.

M. The introductory statement, which is not part of the main idea of the sentence, is set off by a comma.

N. The list is introduced by a colon.

O. *Pre-arranged* takes a hyphen to help the reader see that the two vowels (*e* and *a*) should not be read together.

P. The dashes set off the unacceptable reasons in an emphatic, dramatic fashion.

Q. The make a plural possessive, an apostrophe is added after the *s.*

R. Commas separate the items in the series contained by the em dashes.

16

E-mails and Faxes

Perhaps because e-mail and faxes are nearly instantaneous, they seem less substantial than a letter mailed the old-fashioned way. Yet the same judgment attached to a paper communication may be made on a screen message or fax. Good writing signals that care and attention have been accorded the recipient by an educated person. Don't hit "send" before proofreading your work.

The computer program that transmits e-mail and faxes does quite a bit of the work for you. The heading of an e-mail is predetermined by the form the computer creates: sender, recipient, subject, copies, and so forth. All you have to do is fill in the blanks. A fax cover sheet may be created with the same subject lines used for e-mail, plus a slot for the telephone number of the receiving fax machine and, if desired, of the sender. Most word-processing programs include templates for "friendly" and "professional" fax cover sheets. The message should always follow standard punctuation rules.

A few general principles apply:

- The heading for each line (*Sender, CC, Subject,* etc.) is followed by specific information (the recipient's e-mail address, for example). Headings are usually separated from the specifics by colons, but the specific information is not followed by an endmark unless it is a complete sentence or unless an abbreviation calls for a period.

- The abbreviations *Mr., Mrs.,* and *Ms.* are usually followed by periods; some writers omit the periods. Whichever you choose, be consistent.

- Several date styles are acceptable: month, day, and year numerals separated by slashes; day-month-year order without punctuation; and month-day-year order with a comma between the day and year. Again, consistency is key. E-mails and faxes often include the time, hours, minutes, and seconds are separated by colons.

- Communication requires both the sender and the receiver to agree on meaning. Nonstandard abbreviations, such as *LOL* for "laughing out loud" or *G2G* for "got to go," are risky. What will you do if the receiver does not understand what you are trying to say?

AN INFORMAL E-MAIL TO A FRIEND

A — Tuesday, April 05, 2005 6:57:39 AM

B — From: Gillian_Stin@whs.edu

C — Subject: Trade Association Dinner

D — To: Katrina_Whatti@shw.org

E — Attachments: Dinner Agenda

G   H

F _____

I   Hi, Gillian. I hope you enjoyed a well-deserved vacation! Now
   that you're back, I think we should make plans to attend the
   Emerging Markets Trade Association Dinner together. They've
J   got a great list of speakers, and we can catch up on all the
   office gossip during the intermission. Are you free? I've   I
   attached a copy of the agenda.

   Best, —— K

   Katrina

Punctuation in an Informal E-mail to a Friend

A. See page 232 for an explanation of this point.

B. The *From* line contains the e-mail address of the sender. Many computer programs automatically underline the entire address and create a link. This address contains an underscore between the first and last names of the sender.

C. See page 231 for an explanation of this point.

D. The *To* line contains the e-mail address of the recipient.

E. The *Attachment* line usually indicates the name of the attached file and, at times, the size of the file.

F. *Gillian* is being addressed, so her name is separated by a comma from the comment *Hi.*

G. Two words combined as one description (well-deserved) are often hyphenated.

H. The exclamation point adds emotion to the sentence.

I. In a contraction an apostrophe replaces the missing letter(s).

J. A comma precedes *and* when *and* connects two complete sentences.

K. A closing is not necessary in an e-mail, but many people include one anyway. The closing should be followed by a comma.

E-MAILS TO EMPLOYEES

A — Monday, 5 November 2005 2:43:01 PM

B — From: bossman@kkg.com

C — Subject: 3rd Quarter Projections

D — To: welton@kkg.com, oliver@kkg.com, gaspar@kkg.com

E — Attachments:

Please send your 3rd quarter projections by Wednesday

F — (7 November). Once I have looked over the data, I will circulate   G
the combined projections. Be sure to include the UN contract in
your calculations.   H

Monday, 7 November 2005 5:14:41 PM

From: bossman@kkg.com

Subject: Re: Re: 3rd Quarter Projections   I

To: welton@kkg.com, oliver@kkg.com, gaspar@kkg.com

Attachments: QuarterReport.doc — J

K   I have now received all your data. We will meet on Friday (9
November) at 10 AM in the conference room to edit the final
report. If you have discovered any errors, let me know ASAP.
                                              L   H

Punctuation in E-mails to Employees

A. See page 232 for an explanation of this point.

B. The *From* line contains the e-mail address of the sender.

C. See page 231 for an explanation of this point.

D. The *To* line contains the e-mail address of the recipients. The addresses are separated by commas.

E. The *Attachment* line usually indicates the name of the attached file and, at times, the size of the file. This line is blank because no file is attached.

F. See page 232 for an explanation of this point.

G. Introductory expressions of time, particularly those containing a verb, are followed by commas.

H. Acronyms (the first letter of each word written in uppercase) do not take periods.

I. The abbreviation *Re* means "Regarding" and is followed by a colon. In the second e-mail on the facing page, the boss has presumably received e-mails from the three recipients and is now replying to them. Thus the e-mail is label as a *reply* to a *reply* (*Re: Re:*).

J. The attachment here is a file named *QuarterReport.doc*. The period separates the name of the file from the suffix, which indicates the type of file.

K. The abbreviation for "before noon" may be written as capital letters without periods (*AM*) or in lowercase with periods (*a.m.*). Whichever you choose, be consistent.

L. An introductory statement beginning with *if, though,* or *although* is separated from the main part of the sentence with a comma.

E-MAIL NOTICE OF TRAVEL PLANS

A — From: SusanMarie@csmalumni.org

B — Sent: Monday, June 11, 2004 11:33 PM

C — To: Woods

D — CC:

E — Subject: Travel Plans

                                    F   G   H   I

I am on ComAir flight #333, arriving in Nashville, TN, at 9:12 AM. I expect to be in the office no later than 11 AM. If the flight is delayed, I will call.

                 J

Punctuation in an E-mail Travel Notice

A. The *From* line contains the e-mail address of the sender. As in many e-mail addresses, a period (dot) separates parts of the address.

B. See page 232 for additional explanation of this point. The abbreviation for "afternoon" (PM) may be written in uppercase without periods or in lowercase with periods (p.m.). Whichever you choose, be consistent.

C. The *To* line contains the name of the recipient. If the recipient is in the address book of the sender, the name alone may appear. If the message is going to a stranger, the e-mail address is normally spelled out.

D. The *CC* line indicates who will receive a copy of the message. This particular message is going only to one, primary recipient, so this line is left blank.

E. See page 231 for an explanation of this point.

F. The number symbol (#) is acceptable in an informal e-mail, but in a formal communication, you should omit it and use the word *number,* or you may reword entirely.

G. The information at the end of the sentence (arriving in Nashville at 9:12 AM) is extra because the flight has already been identified by number. Extra information in a sentence is set off by commas.

H. The state abbreviation (TN for Tennessee) is set off by commas from the city and from the rest of the sentence.

I. The hour and minutes are separated by a colon. The abbreviation for "before noon" (AM) may be written in uppercase without periods or in lowercase with periods (a.m.).

J. A comma separates an introductory statement beginning with *if* from the rest of the sentence.

E-MAIL ANNOUNCEMENT

A — Wednesday, 15 October 2006 11:04:41 AM

B — From: bossman@kkg.com

C — Subject: Contest

D — To: Employees of KKG Industries

E — Attachments: Contestentry.doc

Paulson Awards for Customer Service

✦ $1000 AWARDS ✦

F

All employees are invited to nominate colleagues who have excelled in the area of customer service. These awards, named for the late Andrew Paulson, are given once a year to an exemplary member of our community. Nominees should —— H

G

- **have at least five years experience with KKG Industries.**

- **possess an excellent service record.**

- **not be the subject of any disciplinary inquiries.**

- **work in any area of customer service.**

I

You may nominate up to three people with the attached entry blank. A separate form must be downloaded and filled in for each nominee.

Winners will be honored at a gala in December 2006.

J

Punctuation in an E-mail Announcement

A. See page 232 for an explanation of this point. The abbreviation for "before noon" (AM) may be written in uppercase without periods or in lowercase with periods (a.m.).

B. The *From* line contains the e-mail address of the sender.

C. See page 231 for an explanation of this point.

D. The *To* line usually contains the e-mail address of the recipients. In this e-mail a group name is given, indicating that the program has stored a list of names in a personal mailing list.

E. The *Attachment* line usually indicates the name of the attached file and, at times, the size of the file.

F. No comma separates the word described (colleagues) from the description (who have excelled in the area of customer service). The description identifies which colleagues may be nominated and thus needs no commas. Extra information is set off by commas, but not identifying information.

G. Commas surround the extra information (named for the late Andrew Paulson). Extra information is set off by commas, but not identifying information.

H. The introduction to this list is not a complete sentence and thus is not followed by a colon.

I. Each bullet point completes the sentence started by the introductory expression (*Nominees should*), so the bullet points require endmarks. In essence, the introductory expression plus each bullet point equals one complete sentence.

J. No comma separates the month from the year when no day is given.

FAX COVER SHEET 1

A   B   C
1585 Broadway, NY, NY 10022

KKG Industries

Fax

To:	Samantha Tertelle	**From:**	Bert Lawson
Fax:	912-555-6665	**Pages:**	3
Phone: 912-555-4321		**Date:**	7/26/05 — E
Re:	Dinner Speakers	**CC:**	Alfred Mueller, — G Public Relations

D
D
F

x **Urgent**   ☐ **For Review**   ☐ **Please Comment**

☐ **Please Reply**   ☐ **Please Recycle**

Attached are the resumes of three possible speakers for the annual dinner.

Punctuation in a Fax Cover Sheet 1

A. The street (*Broadway*) is separated from the city abbreviation (*NY*) by a comma.

B. The city and state abbreviations are separated by commas. The city abbreviation, all capitals, is acceptable without periods. (An abbreviation ending with a lowercase letter needs a period.)

C. The state and zip code are not separated by a comma.

D. Hyphens separate the area code, exchange (the first three digits), and number (the last four digits).

E. Slashes separate the month, day, and year in this date.

F. The *Re* (in reference to) heading, like all the headings, takes a colon. The subject needs no punctuation unless it is a question or contains an abbreviation.

G. A comma separates the name from the title.

Figures and Illustrations

If the material you are faxing includes several drawings or other nontext visuals, you should number each illustration (photo, drawing, etc.) consecutively. Charts and graphs may be numbered separately but are often included in the figure list. Tables are frequently kept separate from other illustrations and numbered consecutively. On the label for a figure, the abbreviation *Fig.* may be used. Do not place a period after the number or after the title of the figure, as in this example:

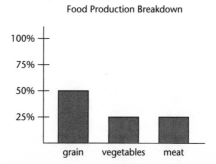

Fig. 2

FAX COVER SHEET 2

MORGAN COMMUNICATIONS, LTD.
                                         | |
                                         A   **B**

FACSIMILE TRANSMITTAL SHEET

TO:
Gail Eglanovich

FROM:
Horace Arthur

COMPANY:
Alexander Graphics, Inc.
A ⌐   ⌐ **C**

DATE:
4/11/05 — **D**

FAX NUMBER:
212-555-6766 — **E**

TOTAL NO. OF PAGES INCLUDING COVER:
16

PHONE NUMBER:
212-555-6888

SENDER'S REFERENCE NUMBER:
F ——— P.O. 50909

RE:
Advertising Flyers — **G**

YOUR REFERENCE NUMBER:
Job #30909

☐ URGENT   X FOR REVIEW   X PLEASE COMMENT   X PLEASE REPLY   ☐ PLEASE RECYCLE

NOTES/COMMENTS:

Please go over this proof copy carefully. We need your approval before going forward with the printing. Because the deadline is very tight (4/15/05), we must have your response by tomorrow (4/12/05) or delivery will be delayed.
                    |
                    H

Punctuation for Fax Cover Sheet 2

A. The name of the company (Morgan Communications) is separated from the abbreviation (Ltd.) by a comma.

B. The abbreviation *Ltd.* (Limited) ends with a period, as do all abbreviations ending with a lowercase letter.

C. The abbreviation *Inc.* (Incorporated) ends with a period, as do all abbreviations ending with a lowercase letter.

D. Slashes separate the month, day, and year in this date.

E. Hyphens separate the area code from the exchange (first three digits) and the number (last four digits) of telephone numbers.

F. The capital letters of the abbreviation for *Purchase Order* (P.O.) are followed by periods.

G. The *Re* (in reference to) heading, like all the headings, takes a colon. The subject needs no punctuation unless it is a question or contains an abbreviation.

H. Information may be inserted into a sentence with parentheses.

I. Commas or other punctuation marks do not precede parentheses. In this sentence, a comma follows the parentheses because the sentence begins with an introductory statement containing a verb (Because the deadline is very tight [4/15/05]).

Useful Abbreviations

The electronic communication world specializes in speed and thus is rife with abbreviations. Particularly useful abbreviations include *mgr.* (manager), *dept.* (department), *mfg.* (manufacturing), *mdse.* (merchandise), *qtr.* (quarter), *i.e.* (that is), *e.g.* (for example), and *enc.* (enclosure). Abbreviations ending in lowercase letters, as well as abbreviations derived from Latin, end with periods.

17

Presentations and Resumes

In the "good old days" when a business executive or a professor wanted to present information, a chalkboard or a sheet of paper was the only option. Because of advances in computer technology, little effort is now required to display all sorts of charts, graphs, illustrations, and text. As visual literacy has increased, however, so has time pressure. Readers or audiences want information quickly and coherently. Thus it is not surprising that the standard paragraph form, still a workhorse for report writers, is frequently accompanied by bulleted lists. Bulleted lists are also key in resume writing.

PowerPoint, Word, and similar programs make the writer's task easy by supplying templates for titles, introductory phrases, and bullet points. Unfortunately, computer programs don't insert proper punctuation automatically. Fortunately, today's writers have a great deal of leeway in punctuating bulleted lists. Some of the stricter rules—that all but the last bullet point in certain types of lists must end with a semicolon, for example—may seem stodgy and outdated to some readers, though such punctuation is correct.

This chapter contains several examples of presentation slides and resumes. The first two "slides" are punctuated in the traditional way. The next shows acceptable variations. Keep these general points in mind when creating presentations or writing a resume:

- Centered titles are not placed in quotation marks and do not contain periods, except as needed for abbreviations. If the title is an exclamation or a question, the title may end with an exclamation point or a question mark. If the title is followed by a subtitle, a colon separates the two.

- Bullet points that are complete sentences generally begin with a capital letter and end with a period or other end-mark.

- Bullet points that are *not* complete sentences normally begin with a lowercase letter and don't take endmarks. This sort of bullet point may end with a semicolon. As mentioned earlier, the semicolon is often omitted these days.

- If the introduction to a bulleted list is a complete sentence, it is usually followed by a colon. Many contemporary writers place a colon after an introduction that is not a complete sentence, though this practice is technically incorrect.

- An introduction that is not a complete sentence may be followed by a dash, a comma, or by no punctuation at all.

- A colon should not follow an introduction that ends with a form of the verb *to be* (*is, are, was, will be, have been,* etc.). Normally, no punctuation follows introductions ending with a form of the verb *to be.*

- A colon should not follow an introduction that ends with a preposition (*of, for, by, in, after, from,* and so forth). Again, no punctuation is placed after an introduction ending with a preposition.

Be Consistent

Bullet points should resemble each other. If the first bullet point is a complete sentence, all the bullet points should be complete sentences. If the first is a command, the rest of the bullets should also follow that pattern.

Wrong:

+ sell raffle tickets
+ silent auction

Right:

+ raffle
+ silent auction

Also Right:

+ sell raffle tickets
+ conduct silent auction

TRADITIONAL BULLETED LIST:
COMPLETE SENTENCES

Changes to Health Coverage: — A
PYB Industries Expanded
Employee Benefit Plan (EEBP) — B

C —

— D

Beginning in 2006, the EEBP for PYB
Industries will include these features: — E

- The co-pay for office visits (currently $20) will decrease to $15.
  — G

- Precertification for mental health benefits is no longer required.

- The list of participating pharmacies will be expanded.

- Primary care physician visits (in-network only) will not be
  subject to a deductible. — H

- Fertility treatment will be covered only when provided by an
  in-network facility.

- Updates to coverage will be sent via e-mail to all members. — I

- Membership in health clubs will be reimbursed (50%) for the
  employee only; spouses and dependent fees are not covered.

— F

J —

Punctuation in a Traditional Bulleted List

A traditional bulleted list may be introduced, as the example illustrates, by a complete sentence. The bullet points are all complete sentences.

A. A colon separates a title (Changes to Health Care Coverage) from a subtitle (PYB Industries Expanded . . . Plan).

B. An acronym—an abbreviation formed from the first letter of each of several words—does not include periods.

C. The left-aligned title is not placed in quotation marks.

D. Introductory expressions of time, especially when they contain a verb form (Beginning), are set off from the main part of the sentence by a comma.

E. A complete-sentence introduction to a bulleted list is usually followed by a colon, though a period is also acceptable.

F. As these bullet points are all complete sentences, each should be followed by a period.

G. Extra information is inserted into a sentence with parentheses.

H. A hyphen makes the meaning of in-network easier to grasp. Without a hyphen, the reader may perceive *inn* as the first syllable, as that combination of letters is popular in English words.

I. A hyphen is generally inserted in *e-mail,* though the word is sometimes written without one.

J. A semicolon links two complete sentences without a joining word such as *and, but, nor,* or *yet.*

TRADITIONAL BULLETED LIST:
INCOMPLETE SENTENCES

Experiment: Stage One

When you are preparing for the experiment,

- sterilize two test tubes;
- assemble the reagents;
- preheat the incubation chamber;
- gather specimens from at least three classmates.

Punctuation in a Traditional Bulleted List: Incomplete Sentences

In this presentation slide, neither the introductory expression nor the bullet points constitute a complete sentence. However, a complete sentence results when each of the bullet points is attached to the introductory expression:

> *When you are preparing for the experiment, sterilize two test tubes.* (complete sentence)
>
> *When you are preparing for the experiment, assemble the reagents.* (complete sentence)
>
> *When you are preparing for the experiment, preheat the incubation chamber.* (complete sentence)
>
> *When you are preparing for the experiment, gather specimens from at least three classmates.* (complete sentence)

The punctuation reflects the fact that the entire bulleted list is a series of complete sentences created by attaching the bullet point to the introduction. In proper English usage, the introductory expression is followed by a comma, as it would be as part of the sentence completed by the bullet point. Each bullet point, excluding the last, ends with a semicolon because the entire list is linked. A semicolon links complete sentences. The last bullet point ends with a period.

This bulleted list follows the traditional rules very strictly. If you use this sort of punctuation, be aware that some readers may find the semicolons fussy and overly precise. Modern usage gives you a few additional options. You may place no punctuation at the end of the introductory expression or at the end of the bullet points. You may insert a colon at the end of the introductory expression, and you may insert a period at the end of the last bullet point but no punctuation after the other bullet points.

Keep in mind that altering the traditional punctuation leaves you open to criticism from those who value correct usage above all else.

NONTRADITIONAL BULLETED LIST

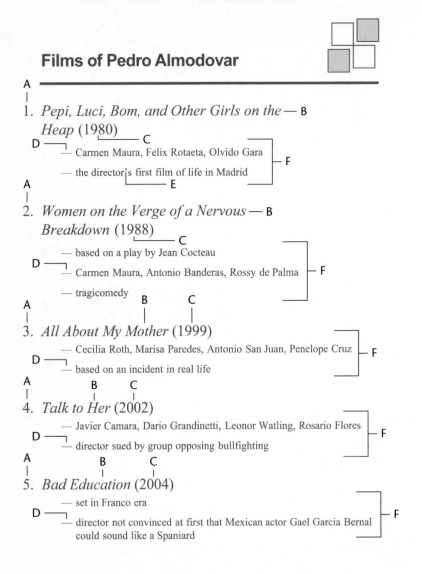

Films of Pedro Almodovar

A

1. *Pepi, Luci, Bom, and Other Girls on the* — B
   Heap (1980)   C
   D —┐
         — Carmen Maura, Felix Rotaeta, Olvido Gara
                                                    ┤ F
         — the director's first film of life in Madrid
                            E

A

2. *Women on the Verge of a Nervous* — B
   Breakdown (1988)   C
         — based on a play by Jean Cocteau
   D —┐
         — Carmen Maura, Antonio Banderas, Rossy de Palma ┤ F
         — tragicomedy

A   B   C

3. *All About My Mother* (1999)
         — Cecilia Roth, Marisa Paredes, Antonio San Juan, Penelope Cruz ┤ F
   D —┐
         — based on an incident in real life

A   B   C

4. *Talk to Her* (2002)
         — Javier Camara, Dario Grandinetti, Leonor Watling, Rosario Flores ┤ F
   D —┐
         — director sued by group opposing bullfighting

A   B   C

5. *Bad Education* (2004)
         — set in Franco era
   D —┐
         — director not convinced at first that Mexican actor Gael Garcia Bernal ┤ F
           could sound like a Spaniard

Punctuation in a Nontraditional Bulleted List

The presentation slide on the facing page varies from traditional punctuation rules but is still acceptable in formal English. The slide has a title (Films of Pedro Almodovar) with no separate introductory phrase or sentence. The bullet points are numbered, and the subtopic bullet points are preceded by dashes. A few details:

A. The numbers in a free-standing list are followed by periods. If the numbers were placed in parentheses, no periods would be inserted.

B. Titles of full-length works are not placed in quotation marks. Use italics, bold type, or underlining instead.

C. Extra information is inserted in parentheses.

D. Em (full-size) dashes set off each subtopic. No space separates the end of the em dash from the first word in the subtopic.

E. Within the bullet points, normal punctuation rules apply. *Director's* is possessive, as the apostrophe indicates.

F. The bullet points are not followed by endmarks (period, question mark, exclamation point).

RESUME 1

Albert Weiss
1544 Mosolu Parkway
Riverhead, MT 56950 —— A
—— B
C —— weiss@hmail.com
(334) 555-1212 —— D

Employment Objective

Full time position as technology director. —— E

Education

F —
M.S.   Colgen University, Richmond, New York, 1998. —— E
Major: Computer Science
—— G
B.S.   University of Wisconsin at Madison, Madison,
Wisconsin, 1996. Major: History Minor: Education
—— G

Work Experience

—— H
Computer Technician   Ran help desk for Xander H.S. (1700
2004–present   J —— students); trained faculty in word —— I
—— K
processing, spreadsheet, and e-mail
L   J —— programs; repaired computers;
supervised computer lab.

Programmer   Wrote C+++ code for Readers' —— M
2000–2004   Subscription Service (automatic
N — mailing list updates, overdue bill
L   management programs, employee
attendance records).

Sales Associate   Sold computer peripherals for RQ
1998–2000   Electronics; trained new employees;
supervised summer intern staff. —— E
L

Other Qualifications

Working knowledge of Mac and PC hardware and software;
expert programmer (C+++, UNIX); fluent in Spanish and
Mandarin. —— E

References

Available upon request.

Punctuation in a Resume

A. A comma separates the city from the state abbreviations. Two-letter state abbreviations are capitalized and written without periods.

B. No comma separates the state from the zip code.

C. An e-mail address may be underlined if it is an active link that the reader may click on. If you are submitting a resume on paper, not via e-mail, omit the underlining.

D. The area code is often placed in parentheses. Hyphens separate parts of the phone number.

E. The period here is optional, as this is not a complete sentence.

F. Traditionally, the abbreviations for university degrees (*M.S.* and *B.S.*) are capitalized and include periods. The more modern style omits periods.

G. The colon separates the general term (*major, minor*) from the specific (*computer science,* for example).

H. The abbreviation for *high school* (H.S.) includes periods.

I. Parentheses insert extra information into a sentence.

J. Semicolons separate items in a series when at least one item contains a comma.

K. Commas separate parts of one item in a series.

L. An *en dash* (longer than a hyphen but shorter than most dashes) shows a date range. A hyphen may be substituted if you wish.

M. An apostrophe indicates a plural possessive.

N. No item in this series contains commas, so the items may be separated from each other by commas.

RESUME 2

Helen Troy
A 48 Ithaca Road B
Cornella, IA 30393
htroy@marslink.net — C
(917) 555-0098 — D

Customer Service Manager, Retail, Midwestern States. — E

PROFESSIONAL EXPERIENCE
F

2001–present   Unit Supervisor, Hatch & Crombie.
Responsible for staff of 13 responding to
consumer complaints. Designed Procedures
Manual for sales clerks. Monitored consumer — E
satisfaction via written surveys and follow-up
telephone inquiries. Reported directly to
F   Regional Vice-President for Marketing. G
└─ H

1995–2001   Technical writer, Elworth Pharmaceuticals.
Researched and wrote consumer information
packets (over-the-counter medications). Edited
FDA compliance reports.
J ────   I

PROFESSIONAL AFFILIATIONS

President, Midwest Retail Customer Service Society since
2005; member since 2000. — E
K ───

EDUCATION

B.A. in English, Carmel College, 1995. — E

OTHER SKILLS

Fluent in French and Japanese, reading knowledge of Tagalog
(Philippines). Working knowledge of Word, Excel, and Lotus. — E
Expert researcher (electronic and printed sources).

PERSONAL   I

Will relocate to any city in the Midwest. Salary negotiable. — E
References available upon request.

Punctuation in a Resume

The punctuation and style of this resume differs from those used in the previous resume (see page 254). In a resume, several styles of punctuation are considered proper, so long as you are consistent throughout. The rationale for the punctuation in this resume is as follows:

A. A comma separates the city from the state abbreviations. Two-letter state abbreviations are capitalized and written without periods.

B. No comma separates the state from the zip code.

C. An e-mail address may be underlined if it is an active link that the reader may click on. If you are submitting a resume on paper, not via e-mail, omit the underlining.

D. The area code is often placed in parentheses. Hyphens separate parts of the phone number.

E. In this resume, each statement—of employment goal, professional experience, education, and so on—is followed by a period. The style is consistent in every part of the resume.

F. The job title is separated from the name of the company by a comma.

G. Two words joined together to make one description (follow-up) are generally linked with a hyphen if the description precedes the word being described.

H. A hyphen separates two parts of a compound word (Vice-President).

I. Extra information is inserted into a statement with parentheses.

J. Acronyms (expressions created with the first letter of each of several words, in this case, *FDA* for *Food and Drug Administration*) do not take periods.

K. This statement contains two elements (*President, Midwest Retail Customer Service Society since 2005* and *member since 2000*). Because one of those elements contains a comma, a semicolon is needed to differentiate one element from the other.

18

School Assignments

Regardless of the academic discipline, no one is more ruthless than a teacher with a red pen intent on ticking off every misplaced quotation mark and errant semicolon. A laboratory report or a history term paper with poor mechanics—the academics' term for grammar, spelling, and punctuation—is likely to receive a lower grade than one that follows the rules.

This chapter contains samples of the most common types of academic writing (book report, research paper, essay, and lab report), written in the most frequently assigned format. A particular teacher or school may prefer a different placement or arrangement of a heading or another element.

In general, text in the body of the assignment (the paragraphs) should conform to the rules of standard English usage set out in Part I of this book. At times manuals for specific academic fields prescribe a different approach. These variations are noted in Part I and also in this chapter.

Students at all grade levels and in every field of study should take note of these general principles:

- Centered titles should not be placed in quotation marks or underlined unless the title of the paper refers to the title of another work.

- Lines of a heading are not followed by periods.

- A colon often divides a general term from a specific (for example, *Course: The Literature of World War I*).

Note: Citations, the identification of source material, are subject to strict punctuation rules. For a detailed explanation of how to cite sources and compile a source list (bibliography), see Part III.

BOOK REPORT

Book reports are a standard assignment from elementary through graduate level. Some teachers distribute a questionnaire with blanks for the title, author, plot summary, and other information. Others expect an essay or composition format. The book report excerpted here includes a standard class heading, a title, and body paragraphs. The ellipses (three spaced dots) would not appear in an actual book report unless they were needed to show gaps in quoted material. Here they replace parts of the book report, omitted for reasons of space.

A <
Name: Stephanie Felix   Class: English 11 —— A
Teacher: Ms. Hermia   D   E   12 May 2005 —— B

F   Jane Austen's *Pride and Prejudice* —— C

In her novel *Pride and Prejudice,* Jane Austen presents a
domestic comedy that makes serious points about the roles of   G
men and women and the power of first impressions (Austen's
original title for this book). Written at a time in history when
love began to supersede financial and family considerations as   H
a motive for marriage, *Pride and Prejudice* centers on the
romance between Elizabeth Bennet, a gentlewoman of slender
means, and Fitzwilliam Darcy, a wealthy landowner.   I
I

Elizabeth and Darcy do not like each other when they first
meet at a country ball. The two are thrown together frequently
by the budding romance between Elizabeth's sister Jane and
Darcy's friend Mr. Bingley. Later in the story, Elizabeth's
younger sister Lydia makes an imprudent match. . . .

Elizabeth, one of five daughters of marriageable age, is one
of literature's most delightful heroines. She is intelligent but
opinionated and headstrong, declaring that "Mr. Darcy is all —— J
politeness" as she refuses to dance with him. The implication,
that she is not interested in mere politeness, is forceful. . . .

. . . the major theme of false expectations and unreasonable   L
prejudice is set forth in the very first sentence of the book: "It is
a truth universally acknowledged, that a single man in
possession of a good fortune, must be in want of a wife."   K
L
M

Punctuation in a Book Report

A. See the chapter introduction for an explanation.

B. When the day precedes the month and year, no comma is inserted in a date.

C. See the chapter introduction for an explanation.

D. The apostrophe indicates possession or a relationship that may be expressed with the word *by*.

E. The title of a full-length work should be placed in italics or underlined. *Pride and Prejudice* is the title of a novel.

F. A comma sets off an introductory expression. No comma divides *novel* from the title because the term *novel* is general and the title is essential, not extra information.

G. Extra information is inserted into a sentence with parentheses.

H. An introductory expression is set off by a comma.

I. If the name is given, the extra description is set off by commas.

J. The direct quotation from the text is placed inside quotation marks. No comma precedes the quotation because there is no speaker tag such as *he said* or *Austen writes*.

K. A colon introduces a long quotation.

L. The directly quoted words are placed inside quotation marks.

M. Following American usage, the period is placed inside the closing quotation mark.

ESSAYS

An essay is the mature form of what many elementary school teachers call a "composition." An essay is a written discussion of ideas or facts. This essay excerpt considers the role of the Nile River in shaping ancient Egyptian society.

Note: The ellipses in this essay mark places where words or paragraphs have been omitted here for reasons of space.

A —— The Nile in Egyptian History

┌———— B
By Bart Sovich '07

C ──── The Nile River is one of the world's most impressive bodies of ──── D
water. It winds through 6,400 km of Africa before emptying
into the Mediterranean Sea. Along its banks human beings
E ──── created settlements over 10,000 years ago. A Greek historian
F ──── once called Egypt "the gift of the Nile" because without the
river, the ancient Egyptian civilization would not have existed
in the same form.

Key to the importance of the Nile is the fact that each year
the river rises as it is fed by spring rains in the interior of
G ──── Africa. In ancient times the river was allowed to overflow its
H ──── banks, though now the flood is largely controlled by dams.
Ancient farmers quickly learned that the receding Nile left
fertile soil. . . .

. . . other achievements of the ancient Egyptians. Irrigation
techniques and the necessary technology were invented to take
advantage of the yearly flood. Mathematics and astronomy
were developed to calculate the rise of the water and the
expected volume. As historian J. Adams-Phelps writes: —— K
         I ⌐⌐   ⌐⌐ J

L —— Much of the achievements of the ancients may be traced
directly to their need to grow and harvest food and distribute it
in a fair manner. What would we have of river craft in this period
were it not for the Egyptians? . . . What would we know of
science? (44)   └— M
                    N ⌐
The Nile also facilitated trade, and in the desert areas the
river became the easiest route. . . .

Punctuation in an Essay

A. A centered title not enclosed in quotation marks.

B. Omitted numbers, in this case *20,* are replaced by an apostrophe.

C. Counting from the right, large numbers are divided by commas after every three digits.

D. Metric abbreviations do not include periods.

E. A quotation that is tucked into a sentence without a speaker tag is not set off by commas.

F. When a statement containing *because* introduces another thought, the *because* statement is usually set off by a comma from the idea that it introduces.

G. A short introductory expression of time needs no punctuation.

H. Commas set off expressions beginning with *though* and *although.*

I. To abbreviate a name, place a period after the first letter.

J. A hyphen separates two parts of a last name. The use of the hyphen in this manner is an option, and many people choose to omit the punctuation mark entirely.

K. A colon introduces a lengthy, blocked quotation. Do not use a colon after a form of the verb *to be* or after a preposition (*by, for, from,* and so forth).

L. Blocked quotations are not enclosed in quotation marks.

M. Within this quotation, words are omitted. The ellipsis (three spaced dots) signals the omission. If the last portion of the sentence is omitted, the question mark is moved up so that the reader understands the tone of the original.

N. A comma precedes *and* when the word joins two complete sentences.

LABORATORY REPORT

A lab report, written after completing an experiment, includes a statement of the problem, the purpose of the experiment, a hypothesis, procedure followed, data analysis, a conclusion, and a list of sources. Most lab reports contain visual presentations of data in the form of charts, graphs, and illustrations. Depending upon the format requested by the teacher, a lab report may also have a separate title page, a table of contents, and a list of figures and tables. The text follows the standard punctuation rules, with some special variations suited to the scientific nature

THE EFFECT OF MUSIC GENRES ON GROWTH IN
SAINTANNIA PAULENSIS —— A

Helen Chavez
Biology 201
Huntington High School   B
C —— 12 April 2003

TABLE OF CONTENTS

LIST OF TABLES AND FIGURES   E

Table 1 Height of Plants Exposed to Music; 8 June 2003–13 August 2003   D   F

Table 2 Number of Flowers

of the content. These pages show parts of a lab report. Some sections have been omitted for reasons of space but follow the same general guidelines as the material illustrated here.

Punctuation in a Laboratory Report

This laboratory report has a title page, a table of contents, and a list of tables and figures. Simpler lab reports need only a heading (title of experiment, name of student, course, date) and subheads for each section of the report.

Title Page

A. Titles that are not inserted into a sentence do not need quotation marks, italics, or underlining unless the title refers to another work. This title is set in capital letters, but initial capitals are also acceptable.

B. The centered information (name of student, course, and so on) is not followed by periods.

C. A date written in day-month-year order takes no commas.

Table of Contents

This table of contents uses dots (periods) to connect the name of the section with the page number. The dots are optional. Headings are written in capital letters, and subheads use initial capitals only. The subheads are indented. Neither headings nor subheads are followed by punctuation, with the exception of the *Appendix* heading, which is separated from its subhead by a colon.

List of Tables and Figures

If the report has many illustrations, you may list the tables and figures (charts, graphs, drawings, photos) separately. Number them consecutively, with separate numbering for the tables and figures. In the report itself, you may abbreviate *figure* (fig.) or write out the whole word.

D. A colon separates the title from the subtitle.

E. Dates written in day-month-year order do not need commas.

F. An en dash (a little longer than a hyphen but shorter than an em dash) shows a date range.

LABORATORY REPORT, CONTINUED

INTRODUCTION —— A

B —— Statement of Problem   E

Claims have been made for years about the power of music to
influence the growth rate and flowering ability of plants (e.g.—— D
C —— Miller, 1989; Shotfield & Dabnis, 1995; Colowith, 2004). All
previous studies have compared plants exposed to music with
plants grown in silence. No studies have addressed the effect of
different genres on plants.

Purpose

The purpose of this experiment is to determine whether the
genre of music played in the vicinity of growing Miniature
F —— Argentinian Violets (*Saintannia paulensis*) has an effect on the
growth rate and number of flowers produced over the course of
three months.

Hypothesis

Plants will be affected differently by rock, classical, country, —— G
and New Age music played in their vicinity.

DATA ANALYSIS

F —— The following tables indicate the growth patterns of ten
Miniature Argentinian Violet (*Saintannia paulensis*) plants.
Table 1 shows the height of the largest stem of the plant,
measuring from the soil surface, at weekly intervals over the
course of approximately three months. Table 2 indicates the
number of flowers, counted at monthly intervals over the —— H
course of three months.

The data show that the plants exposed to rock music were
on average 2 cm taller than those exposed to country music.
I —— The plants exposed to New Age and classical music were on
average 9 cm taller than those exposed to rock music. The —— J
number of flowers roughly corresponds to the height: New Age
and classical music produced the best results, with rock and —— K
country having less effect. All plants exposed to music did
better than those raised in silence.

TABLE 1 Height in Centimeters of Plants Exposed to Rock
Music

	8 June	15 June	22 June	29 June	6 July	13 July	20 July	27 July	3 August	10 August
Rock	6.3	6.6	7.1	7.4	7.6	8.1	8.8	10.0	11.5	11.7
Classical	7.1	7.3	7.6	7.9	8.1	8.2	9.6	10.7	11.8	12.1
New Age	7.1	7.4	7.7	7.7	8.2	8.3	9.5	10.8	11.7	12.0
Country	6.2	6.3	6.7	6.8	7.0	7.1	7.3	7.5	7.9	8.0
No music	5.1	5.4	5.4	5.5	6.1	6.6	6.7	6.8	6.9	7.1

Punctuation in a Laboratory Report

A. Centered titles are not followed by periods or enclosed in quotation marks.

B. This subtitle is underlined but is not followed by a period.

C. Citations are normally inserted into the text with parentheses in scientific papers. See Part III for more information on citation styles.

D. Latin abbreviations are generally followed by periods. In this sentence, *e.g.* is the abbreviation for *for example*.

E. In a series, items must be separated by semicolons if one or more item contains a comma.

F. Extra information, in this case the botanical name of the plant, is inserted into a sentence with parentheses.

G. In a series, the last item preceding the word *and* may be followed by a comma, or the comma may be omitted. Most of the major style guides call for this comma.

H. A comma separates the extra information (when the flowers were counted) from the rest of the sentence.

I. Metric abbreviations do not include periods. In this sentence *cm* is the abbreviation for *centimeter*.

J. A colon may join two complete sentences when the second sentence explains or expands the meaning of the first.

K. The comma separates extra information (the performance of rock and country music plants) from the main idea of the sentence.

RESEARCH PAPER

A —Images of Knighthood in Bernard Malamud's *The Natural*

Augusta Philbert   C

B

Hartley Moseman School
English 12
May 2005 — D

Page 5

E

Wonderboy, Roy's bat, assumes almost magical qualities and
illustrates that a knight must respect his weapons and his own
honor. In the crucial game that forms the climax of the novel,   F
G —"the ball shot past Wonderboy—which almost broke his wrists   H
H to get at it—and plunked in the pocket's of the catcher's glove"— G
   (200). The bat wants Roy to perform well, but Roy has agreed
I to throw the game in return for a bribe. Later in the game, Roy
   leaves the dugout and "to his dismay he found Wonderboy   J
   lying near the water fountain, in the mud" (204). Newly
L committed to playing well, "Roy tenderly wiped it dry" (206).
   However, his change of heart comes too late. As critic Johanna K
   Sinclair comments,—M

N —
Wonderboy splits in half during the most important moment in
Roy's career. With one section pointing towards first [base] and   O
one towards third [base], the bat magically indicates the forked
path that Roy has faced throughout the novel: Iris or Memo?
Honest or dishonest? Success or failure? (12) P

J In the movie version of this novel, the magic bat is replaced by
   one hewn by the innocent acolyte, the bat boy who has
J benefited from the hero's attention. With his substitute magical
   object, Roy conquers the ball, wins the game, and redeems his   Q
   team. In the novel no such redemption is possible. Roy strikes
   out.

Punctuation in a Research Paper

The standard academic research paper is a multi-page exploration of a particular topic reporting, as the name implies, on research into others' ideas and data. Citation of sources is crucial; the style varies according to the academic discipline. In this excerpt from a research or term paper, citations are inserted into the text with parentheses. Part III explains the three major style systems and illustrates how to cite material in the body of the paper and how to compile a source list. **Note:** Because of space limitations, only part of this paper is presented here.

A. See page 259 for an explanation of this point.

B. The apostrophe indicates possession or a relationship that may be expressed with the word *by*.

C. The title of a full length work, inserted into text, is italicized or underlined. In this case *The Natural* is inserted into the title of the research paper.

D. In a month-year date format, no comma is necessary.

E. This sentence contains two equivalent terms: *Wonderboy* and *Roy's bat.* The second term is extra and therefore set off by commas.

F. A comma follows the long introductory statement.

G. The quotation marks enclose a direct quotation.

H. Malamud uses em dashes to set off a comment on the action described in the rest of the sentence.

I. The parenthetical citation follows the closing quotation mark but precedes the period.

J. A comma sets off this introductory expression of time.

K. An introductory expression containing verb forms is generally set off by a comma.

L. An introductory *However* is set off by a comma.

M. The block quotation is introduced by a partial sentence ending with a comma. A colon would also be acceptable.

N. Blocked quotations take no quotation marks, unless the original contains quotations or dialogue.

O. Information is inserted into a quotation with brackets.

P. A colon sets up the list in this sentence.

Q. Items in series are separated by commas.

19

Desktop Publishing

Countless thousands of computer owners have taken their writing directly to the public via desktop publishing programs. Whether on paper or in a website, the advantages of this publishing explosion are obvious. No one can refuse an offer to self-publish, and the number of original voices now in print has increased readers' options.

However, self-published authors cannot rely on sharp-eyed copy editors to catch stray punctuation marks or to impose consistency and order on writing. Instead, many authors must edit their own creations. This is all the more reason to understand proper punctuation.

Newsletters, Web postings, advertisements, and pamphlets are the most common products of desktop publishing. This chapter contains samples of each form, complete with explanations of the punctuation. Some general principles apply to all these types of writing:

- Headlines and title are not punctuated with quotation marks or underlining, unless the headline refers to another work (a movie or book title, for example).

- Consistency is key. If "afternoon" is abbreviated as *p.m.* in one spot, it should be *p.m.* throughout the article, even though *PM* is also a correct abbreviation.

- Clarity is essential. If a comma or hyphen will make the reader's life easier, one should be inserted.

NEWSLETTER ARTICLE

A ⌐ **Cunningham School Parents' Association News** ⌐ B

Published jointly by the Cunningham School and the Parents' Association, March 2006

C ⌐

Robert McMillan Takes Helm of Upper Division— E   D

Intensity, breadth of vision, sense of humor, compassion, and leadership ability. These are the qualities listed in the school's advertisement for a new head of the upper division, and these are the qualities the Board of Trustees believes it has found in Dr. Robert McMillan, a graduate of Cunningham from the class of 1977. After leaving Cunningham, Dr. McMillan went on to Columbia University, where he majored in history and political philosophy. He attended Harvard University for a combined Masters/PhD program in Educational Administration. Dr. McMillan is married and the father of two sons—Eli, 8, and Mack, 12—who will attend Cunningham next fall. The Parents' Association recently interviewed Dr. McMillan about his plans for CHS.

What would you like to accomplish in your first year at CHS?
First let me say that I am thrilled to join Cunningham. I'm looking forward to working with a talented and dedicated faculty, a supportive staff, and an involved parent body. Of course, I'm most excited about the chance to be part of the lives of the intelligent, creative students of Cunningham's Upper Division.

> I'm looking forward to working with a talented and dedicated faculty, a supportive staff, and an involved parent body.

It would be presumptuous of me to make plans before I learn more about the school, something I cannot do until I am actually in the job. So I intend to devote my first year to listening—to the faculty, the parents, the administration, and the students. The Board has already been helpful, and I expect they will continue to advise me as I take over the position.

What attracted you to Cunningham?
As you may know, I attended Cunningham. After I graduated in 1977, I stayed in close touch with the school. The relationships I formed with teachers there and with my classmates—with whom I remain close friends—were extremely valuable.
(continued on page 17)

Punctuation in a Newsletter Article

A. See page 271 for an explanation of this point.

B. This organization chooses to make *Parents'* possessive. The word *parents* may also be used simply as a description, in which case the apostrophe is omitted. Follow the wishes of the organization you are describing.

C. The statement about the publication is separated from the date by a comma. The date may be set off in other ways, such as extra spaces or a separate line.

D. No comma separates the month from the year.

E. See page 271 for an explanation of this point.

F. Items in a series are separated by commas.

G. The apostrophe precedes the letter *s* in a singular possessive word.

H. When two complete sentences are joined by *and,* a comma precedes the *and*.

I. Abbreviations ending in lowercase letters are generally followed by periods.

J. Two equivalent terms—*Dr. Robert McMillan* and *a graduate of Cunningham*—are separated by a comma if the second term is extra, not identifying, information.

K. Introductory expressions containing verbs forms (leaving) are followed by commas.

L. The information following the comma (where he majored in history and political philosophy) is extra and therefore is set off by a comma.

M. The slash indicates that one program confers both degrees.

N. The abbreviation for *Doctor of Philosophy* (PhD) is generally written without a period.

O. The em dashes separate the name/age statements from the rest of the sentence.

WEB POSTING

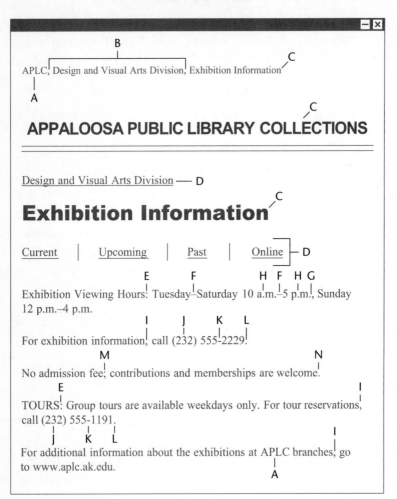

B

APLC, Design and Visual Arts Division, Exhibition Information C

A

C

APPALOOSA PUBLIC LIBRARY COLLECTIONS

Design and Visual Arts Division — D

C

Exhibition Information

Current | Upcoming | Past | Online — D

E   F   H F   H G

Exhibition Viewing Hours: Tuesday–Saturday 10 a.m.–5 p.m., Sunday 12 p.m.–4 p.m.

I   J   K   L

For exhibition information, call (232) 555-2229.

M   N

No admission fee; contributions and memberships are welcome.

E

TOURS: Group tours are available weekdays only. For tour reservations, call (232) 555-1191.

J   K   L   I

For additional information about the exhibitions at APLC branches, go to www.aplc.ak.edu.

A

Punctuation in a Web Posting

A. Acronyms—abbreviations formed from the first letter of each of several words—do not take periods.

B. In this heading the description (Design and Visual Arts Division) is set off by commas.

C. See page 271 for an explanation of this point.

D. The underlining indicates a link that may be opened with a double click.

E. A colon separates an introductory expression (Exhibition Viewing Hours, for example) from the details.

F. An en dash traditionally shows a range. A hyphen or the word *to* may be substituted.

G. A comma separates the two items in this series because they are not joined by *and*.

H. The abbreviations for morning and afternoon may be written in lowercase with periods or in uppercase without periods.

I. Introductory expressions beginning with *for* are often followed by commas when they precede a command.

J. The area code in a telephone number is generally enclosed by parentheses.

K. A hyphen separates two parts of a telephone number.

L. A period ends a sentence that gives a command.

M. Although the first part of this expression (No admission fee) is not a complete sentence, a complete sentence is implied (No admission fee is charged). Thus a semicolon links the two sentences.

N. A period completes this sentence.

Punctuation: Simplified and Applied

ADVERTISEMENT

YARD SALE— A

to benefit
The Joey Fund

15 March 2006— B

NEW AND USED ITEMS FOR SALE— A

C ⌐

- FURNITURE: DINING ROOM SET, DESK, SOFA BED
- COMPUTER EQUIPMENT: PRINTER, PRINTER STAND
- KITCHEN EQUIPMENT: MIXER, BLENDER, CAKE DECORATING SET, PRESSURE COOKER
- CLOTHING

D

Cash only! All sales final! Delivery available within town only; delivery charge, $10.

E   E   F

F   E

Joey Abbonizzi was born with a defective heart valve. He needs constant medical care. Please help us to help the Abbonizzi family. Donations for the yard sale may be dropped off at the Doubletown Fire House, 56— G Main St. (Information: [221] 555-4090)

H I   C   J   K   I

Punctuation for an Advertisement

A. Centered titles should not be placed inside quotation marks.

B. When a date is written in day-month-year order, no commas are inserted.

C. A colon separates the name of the series from the items in the series.

D. Items in a series are separated by commas. This series does not include the word *and.* If *and* appears between the last two items, a comma may or may not precede it.

E. Although many "sentences" in an advertisement are actually not complete in a grammatical sense, most writers punctuate these incomplete expressions with a period anyway if the tone is that of a statement or command.

F. This statement contains two parts (*Delivery available within town only* and *delivery charge, $10*). The second part of the statement has an interior comma, so the statements are separated by a semicolon. The semicolon allows the reader to differentiate between statement one and statement two. In this situation, a comma after *only* would confuse the reader because the list would then appear to have three items (*Delivery available within town only, delivery charge,* and *$10*).

G. When an address is inserted into a sentence, commas take the place of line breaks.

H. The period after the abbreviation for *street* also functions as the endmark of the sentence. Never end a sentence with two periods.

I. Extra information is inserted in parentheses.

J. The area code is usually placed in parentheses. However, in this case the "sentence" is enclosed in parentheses, so the area code is placed in brackets. Another solution is to place a hyphen between the area code and the phone number and omit the parenthesis around the area code.

K. A hyphen separates parts of a telephone number.

PAMPHLET COVER AND INTERIOR

Do You Know How to Care for Your New Parakeet?— B

—A

A Guide for Human Companions⌐ C Feeding, Shelter, and Training of Pet Birds

by
Sally Seton, DVM — E
|
D

F

Your pet bird drinks very little, but the water must be clean. Even if the water container is full, wash it and refill it daily.

G

May I give my parakeet table scraps?— H

The most important food for your parakeet is seed. Pet stores and supermarkets sell several different brands of seed mix that will give your bird every essential nutrient. However, you may also give your parakeet special treats. seed sticks (also sold in pet-food departments) and treat mixes are fine. Your parakeet may also like to nibble on raw leafy green vegetables, a bit of peanut butter, or a piece of carrot.

I

J

K

L

N

M

Parakeets "eat like a bird," but that doesn't mean they are light eaters. They consume large amounts of food each day and should always have seed available.

Punctuation for a Pamphlet Cover and Interior

A. A centered title should not be enclosed in quotation marks. No period is placed at the end of a title unless one is needed for an abbreviation.

B. Part of this title is a question, so a question mark is appropriate.

C. A colon separates the title from the subtitle.

D. A comma separates a name from the degree; in this case *DVM* is the abbreviation for "Doctor of Veterinary Medicine."

E. Abbreviations for college or university degrees are increasingly written without periods.

F. When two complete sentences are linked, a comma precedes the linking word (*but* in this case).

G. The introductory statement (Even if the water container is full) is separated from the main statement of the sentence by a comma.

H. Questions are followed by question marks.

I. The introductory word *however* is followed by a comma.

J. A colon may join two complete sentences when the second explains or expands the meaning of the first.

K. Extra information is inserted into the sentence with parentheses.

L. Items in a series are separated by commas. The last comma before the joining word (in this case, *or*) is optional.

M. The old saying (eat like a bird) is placed in quotation marks to show that the writer knows it is not an original phrase.

N. The comma is placed inside the closing quotation mark, in American English.

Part III

CITATIONS

20

Modern Language Association Citation

The principle behind citation is simple: Writers must credit the sources they have referenced in a particular piece of writing and must clarify which ideas and words are the writers' own and which have been drawn from the someone else's work.

Writers in the humanities—literature, history, philosophy, and so forth—are often asked to follow the guidelines of the Modern Language Association (MLA) for citation format. The MLA favors parenthetical notes inserted into the text directly following the material being cited. The writer creates a "List of Works Cited" containing complete information on each source and appends the list to the end of the paper or article. While the textual citation normally gives only the author and page, the List of Works Cited supplies the title, publisher or periodical name, the date and place of publication, and other information. If the writer has consulted an electronic database or a website, the List of Works Cited includes the *URL* (*Uniform Resource Locator* or Web address).

This chapter provides sample MLA style parenthetical citations and entries for a List of Works Cited. The works referenced are not actual publications but are set up to show you how to punctuate citations for the materials you may use in a typical research project. It should be noted that some publications alter some aspects of MLA style. If you are writing for a specific journal or publisher, ask for guidelines.

CITATIONS IN THE TEXT

Parenthetical citations make the readers' task easier; instead of switching between the text and a footnote or an endnote, the reader can read seamlessly, pausing only when curiosity requires the additional publication information from the List of Works Cited.

The placement and content of the parentheses vary, but several general principles apply:

- The parenthesis contains the author's last name unless the name appears in the text.

- If an entire work must be cited, the author's name or the title of the work should appear in the text. If only a portion of a work is referenced, the parenthesis includes the page(s) where the material cited may by found in the original source.

- If the source material occupies more than one page, the page range is given. If two separate pages or page ranges are cited, a comma separates the numbers.

- The citation is part of the sentence in which the cited material appears. If the cited material is a quotation, the citation precedes the endmark of the sentence but follows the closing quotation mark.

Examples of several different citations and explanations of the punctuation are in the sections below.

Citing an Idea

To credit material that is not directly quoted, place the parenthetical citation immediately following the idea being cited. Do not place any punctuation before the parenthesis.

Citation Software

Computer programs that format citations automatically are now available. After choosing the style, the writer simply enters information about each source into a grid and the computer takes care of the rest. One such program, StyleEase, includes the MLA format.

Showing a Page Range

Page numbers in citations should be separated by an *en dash,* which is slightly longer than a hyphen but shorter than a full-size, or em dash. The "Insert" pull-down menu on many word processing programs includes a selection of symbols, one of which is the en dash. If no en dash is available in, for example, a work produced on a typewriter, a hyphen is an acceptable substitute.

Author's Name in Text

Margot Helber's theory of armed response deals primarily with self defense (14).

In the preceding example, the *theory of armed response* argued by Margot Helber can by found on page 14 of her book or article. The List of Works Cited contains the publication information for Helber's work.

If the entire work is cited, no page number appears, and both the author and title are mentioned in the text:

Posnic's *Towards an Understanding of the Constitution* proposes a different theory of inalienable rights.

Author's Name Not in Text

If the author is not mentioned in the text, the parenthetical citation provides the name and page number(s). No punctuation separates the author from the page(s):

One theory is that armed responses are seldom counted accurately (Helber 14).

The List of Works Cited contains an entry giving information about a source written by Helber. The *14* indicates that the material about armed responses is located on page 14.

Two or Three Authors

If two or three authors must be credited, commas separate their names:

> Looting was widespread during the blackout of 1977 (Alexander, Comberson, and Zelig 188–192).

More than Three Authors

If a work has more than three authors, it is customary to cite the name of just one author and include the abbreviation *et al.*, from the Latin "and others." Place a period after the abbreviation but no punctuation before it:

> Crowd control had become a science by the time Schumacher was named Chief of Police (Gabel et al. 76).

More than One Author with the Same Last Name

If the List of Works Cited includes more than one author with the same last name, include the initial letter of the author's first name, followed by a period:

> The imposition of additional taxes resulted in a landslide for the opposition party (D. Smith 98–104).

More than One Book by the Same Author or by an Unnamed Author

If the List of Works Cited has more than one book or article written by the same author, the parenthetical information must show which work is referenced. A shortened form of the title—usually just one word is sufficient—accompanies the author's name. Similarly, if the author is anonymous or unknown, a shortened form of the title identifies the work:

> Cotton production more than doubled with the introduction of pest-resistant plants (Jones, "Egypt" 484).

> Wheat harvests, on the other hand, were not immediately affected by the climate change (*Warming* 409).

In the first example above, the author's name is separated from the title by a comma. In the second, only the title appears, indicating that no author's name is available. A book title may be italicized or underlined; an article title should be enclosed in quotation marks. No comma separates the title from the page number(s).

Nonprint Sources

Material acquired from an electronic database, a website, or a sound or video recording is cited in the text in the same way as print sources. If the author is known, the name should be given in the text or parentheses. If the author's name is unknown, a shortened version of the title is sufficient. Normally, no page number is available for nonprint sources. The exception is an electronic reproduction of a printed source. In that case, the page number that appears on the screen should be cited. Detailed information appears in the List of Works Cited, as it does for print material. Some electronic sources give chapter or paragraph numbers. If that information is available, it should appear in the parentheses, preceded by the abbreviation *chap.* (chapter), *par.* or *pars.* (paragraph or paragraphs).

Citing a Quotation

The underlying principle of citation for quoted material is that a parenthetical citation is part of the sentence in which the quotation appears but not part of the quotation itself.

Quotation at the End of a Sentence

If the quotation appears at the end of the sentence, the parenthesis precedes the endmark and follows the closing quotation mark, as in this example:

> Nestor first noted that "the means of production were entirely controlled by the workers only in the South and only for a limited period of time" (47–52).

Quotation in the Beginning or Middle of a Sentence

If the sentence continues on after the quotation, insert the parenthetical citation as close as possible to the quoted material. Punctuation needed in the sentence (a comma before a conjunction or after an introductory expression, for example) may follow but not precede the parentheses:

> Flower believed that "the economy could not be stabilized" (42), and chaos was inevitable.

In the preceding example two complete sentences (*Flower believed that "the economy could not be stabilized"* and *chaos was inevitable*) are joined by *and.* When two complete sentences are connected by *and,* a comma precedes the *and.* The parenthetical citation refers to the quotation and thus follows the closing quotation mark without any intervening punctuation. The comma preceding *and* comes after the parenthesis.

Quotation Ending in an Ellipsis

An ellipsis—three spaced dots—indicates that words have been deleted from a quotation. If the ellipsis falls at the end of a quotation that is cited parenthetically, the parenthesis appears at the normal spot immediately following the quotation. The endmark of the sentence follows the parenthesis:

> The rebels said that they were "protesting every breach of civil rights . . ." (Mascom 11).

Quotations from Shakespearean Plays

Shakespeare is in a class by himself. The title of the play may be included in the text, in which case the parenthesis includes the act, scene, and line(s) numbers, separated by periods. If the title of the work is not mentioned in the text, a shortened title should appear in the parenthesis.

> In *Macbeth* the witches may be responsible for the "dagger which I see before me" (2.1.44).

> The witches may be responsible for the "dagger which I see before me" (*Macbeth* 2.1.44).

Both of these examples quote Act II, scene 1, line 44. In the first sentence above, the text mentions the title of the play, so the parenthesis does not. In the second, the title is inserted in the parenthesis because it does not appear in the text.

If more than one line of the play is quoted, a slash indicates the line breaks. A hyphen or an en dash (slightly longer than a hyphen) shows the line range.

Quotations from the Bible

In quoting the Bible, the title of the book may be abbreviated (*Rev.* for *Revelations,* for example). The chapter and verse are separated by periods. Citations of more than one verse show the range with a hyphen. Some examples:

Luke 2.3–4 (second chapter of the book of Luke, verses 3 and 4)

Num. 4.5 (fourth chapter of the book of Numbers, verse 5)

Blocked Quotation

A blocked quotation is indented 7–10 spaces from the left margin. The indentation takes the place of quotation marks. The parenthetical citation follows the endmark of the quotation.

Billings argues that deregulation of the airline industry has not brought the promised benefits to the consumer:

The constant congressional intervention has led to a real price increase, once the cost of taxation is factored into the equation. Furthermore, the industry has little incentive for competition, despite deregulation, given the tendency for lawmakers to play such an active role. (56–58)

Notice that the citation is not part of the last sentence in a blocked quotation.

Quotation from a Secondary Source

Researchers often find a quotation reprinted in a secondary source. In such cases the citation should reflect this fact:

> Mary Oliviere notes, "The average fundraising activity earns about 50% of its potential" (qtd. in Weston 55).

In the preceding example, the quotation from Oliviere was encountered in a work by Weston, which is described more fully in the List of Works Cited. The author of the quoted material is best mentioned in the text, as in this example, with the source in parenthesis. The abbreviated *qtd.* ("quoted") is followed by a period, as are most abbreviations that end in a lowercase letter.

Some Special Cases

The preceding material in this chapter covers most citations, but a few special cases call for additional guidelines.

Citing Unpaged Material

Material retrieved from an electronic databases or other non-print sources may not have page numbers. In some cases, paragraphs may be numbered. If so, indicate the paragraph number in parenthesis along with the abbreviation *par.* (paragraph) or *pars.* (paragraphs). If the author's name is not in the text, separate the name from the paragraph abbreviation with a comma:

> Alberton's theory about the mass extinction has not yet been contested (pars. 12–13).

> Albertson writes, "My theory of mass extinction has not been effectively challenged" (pars. 12–13).

> The newest theory of mass extinction has not yet been contested (Alberton, pars. 12–13).

Multivolume Works

If the cited information comes from a multivolume work, the volume number should be included in the parenthesis, preceding the page number(s). The volume and page numbers are separated by a colon and a space:

> The earliest known legend of White Deer Woman was noted by McLean (8: 45).

In the preceding example, the White Deer Woman legend appears on page 45 of volume 8 of a work by McLean. If the author's name does not appear in the text, it should be inserted in the parenthesis:

> The earliest known legend of White Deer Woman was noted nearly 50 years ago (McLean 8: 45).

Multiple References in One Citation

Writers may need to cite more than one reference for the same bit of information. The references should be separated by a semicolon:

> Healing ceremonies are always conducted in Alegan culture before the full moon rises (Greville 98; Ashur 202).

CITATIONS IN THE LIST OF WORKS CITED

The brief references in the text and parenthetical citations direct the reader to expanded references at the end of the book, paper, or article. Because today's writers have such a wealth of resources available, many variations are possible. In this section the most common references are illustrated. Some general guidelines apply:

- Works are alphabetized by the last name of the principal author. In a work with multiple authors, the principal is the first named on the title page or in the byline. The author's last name is flush with the left margin and additional lines of an entry are indented five spaces. This arrangement highlights the author's name so that an inquisitive reader may turn from the text to a reference quickly and easily.

- Titles of full-length works are italicized or underlined. Titles of parts of a longer publication (an article, poem, song, television episode, etc.) are enclosed by quotation marks.

- Pamphlets and government publications are treated the same as full-length books.

- Most entries place the author first, then the title; and then the publication company, date, and place. Each of these three elements is followed by a period. If only part of a book (perhaps an encyclopedia entry) had been used, the page numbers are placed last and followed by a period.

- Article listings include page numbers, which are separated by a colon from the date information.

Examples of various types of entries for a List of Works Cited follow.

Hanging Indentation

MLA style calls for a "hanging indentation" in the List of Works Cited. That is, the first line of each entry begins flush with the left margin, but each subsequent line is indented five spaces. (The tab key is not a reliable way to create these spaces; instead, touch the space bar five times.) The hanging indentation places emphasis on the author, isolating the name at the left margin. Because the textual citations also rely on the author's name, the hanging indentation helps the reader to locate a reference more quickly. Here's an example:

Foster, Alan. <u>Security in the Age of Electronic Surveillance:</u>
    <u>An Assessment.</u> New York: General Press, 2006.

Books

Although the Internet has changed research considerably, most Lists of Works Cited include at least a few books.

Single Author

To list a book, include the author, title (underlined), place of publication, publishing company, and date. The "author" may sometimes be a company or an agency identified on the title page of the work:

> Smith, Robert. <u>Dog Training: A Practical Guide</u>. New York: Fenster, 2004.
>
> Thompson, J.P. <u>Woman's Best Friend</u>. Chicago: Peplum Press, 2005.
>
> United Pet Owners. <u>Puppies' Health</u>. New York: Fenster, 2003.

In the first example above, the book has a subtitle, which is separated from the title by a colon placed directly after the title. If the title ends with a question mark or an exclamation point, the colon is omitted. A colon also divides the place of publication from the name of the publishing company. A comma divides the company name from the date. The second example above follows the same pattern, though there is no subtitle.

The author's name should appear exactly as it does in the book. In the second example above, the author chose to use only initials, so the entry reflects that choice. If the full name appears in the book, the full name should be printed in the List of Works Cited as well. The initials are followed by periods, as abbreviated names normally are.

If the List of Works Cited contains more than one work by the same author, the author's name is given in the first entry. Thereafter, three hyphens, followed by a period, take the place of the name. An example:

> Cita, Agnes. <u>Teaching Reading</u>. New York: Preston, 1999.
>
> - - -. <u>Writing and Phonics</u>. New York: Preston, 2001.

Multiple Authors

Books with more than one author follow the same basic pattern as single-author works. The first author's name is given with the last name first, followed by a comma and the first name. The second and subsequent authors' names are written in first-last order and set off from each other by commas, with the entire sequence ending in a period. In the case of four or more authors, one name is followed by a comma and *et al.* (and others).

> Reese, Patrick, and Mary Vartan. <u>Constantinople: A History</u>. London: Olden, Inc., 1990.
>
> Silvers, Tabby, Martin Sirni, and Justin Armstrong. <u>The Bosporus: Its Role in Warfare</u>. New York: Peters, 2000.
>
> Werner, Robert, et al. <u>The Crusades</u>. Philadelphia: Excel Press, 2004.

Anthologies and Reference Works

If one person acts as an editor, collecting articles or shorter works from a variety of writers, he or she is identified with the abbreviation *ed.* (editor).

> Caldwell, Dennis, ed. <u>Dance Technique</u>. New York: Preston, 1990.

If only one work from an anthology has been referenced, the entry in the List of Works Cited provides information on the author and title of the work as well as information on the entire collection:

> Kolinski, Elwood. "Hip Hop." <u>Dance Technique</u>. Ed. Dennis Caldwell. New York: Preston, 1990. 80–93.

Notice that in the preceding example the article or chapter is placed in quotation marks, with the period inside. The title of the book is underlined. The abbreviation for "editor" is capitalized because it begins a new segment of the entry. The page number(s) form a separate segment and are followed by a period.

In citing an article from an encyclopedia or dictionary, the author of the article is included, if the author's name is specified. The editor of the reference work is not included in the citation. If the reference work is widely known, publication information is not necessary. If the entries in the reference work are alphabetized, no page numbers are needed in the citation. For example:

> Delafield, Herbert. "Dickens' Imagination." <u>Companion to British Literature</u>. 2nd ed. 2000.

> "Barnard's Inn." <u>British Literary Guide</u>. London: Inglewood, 1999. 23–24.

Anonymous Author

If no author is specified, the book is listed by title alone, following the standard pattern of title (followed by a period) and place, company, and date of publication:

> <u>Pet Owner's Handbook</u>. New York: Humane Society, 2002.

Volume Numbers, Translations, and Editions

If the book is a translation, the original author comes first, followed by the title. Next is the abbreviation *Trans.* (translated by) and the name of the translator:

> Cervantes, Miguel de. <u>Don Quixote</u>. Trans. Edward T. Evans. New York: Universe, 2004.

A multivolume work or a work that has more than one edition must indicate this information in the citation, even if the author referenced only one volume. The abbreviations for *volume* (vol.) and *edition* (ed.) are followed by periods:

> Cather, Willa. <u>Collected Works</u>. 3 vols. Stamford: Twain, 1989.

> Dobsir, Jessica. <u>Short Fiction</u>. 3rd ed. Halifax: Nova Press, 2003.

Articles

Citation of printed articles follow much the same format as books. The author and title of the article are identified, as are the name of the magazine or journal, the date, and the page number. (Electronically accessed material is cited differently: See the next section.)

Journals and Magazines

Citations of articles from scholarly journals generally identify the volume and issue number. The volume number precedes the issue number, separated by a period. The year of publication is placed in parenthesis, followed by a colon and the page number(s) of the source. For example:

> Stanford, Alex. "Art and Diversity." <u>Midtown Art Journal</u> 4.3 (2003) : 102–103.

In the preceding citation, an author named Alex Stanford wrote an article entitled "Art and Diversity," which was published in volume 4, issue 3 of the <u>Midtown Art Journal</u>, which came out in 2003. The article appeared on pages 102 and 103.

Some journals do not number volumes, only issues. In such cases, the issue number stands alone:

> Stanford, Alex. "Art and Diversity." <u>Midtown Art Journal</u> 3 (2003) : 102–103.

Citations of popular magazines do not require volume or issue numbers. Two examples:

> George, Rebecca. "The Harlem Renaissance." <u>Newsweek</u> 3 Mar. 2003: 45–46.

> Lopes, Felix. "The Poetry of Georgia Douglas Johnson." <u>Smithsonian</u> Dec. 2002: 55+.

In the first example above, the article appeared on pages 45 and 46. In the second example, the article begins on page 55 and does not continue on the next consecutive page but rather elsewhere in the magazine.

Newspapers

Newspaper articles are frequently accessed through the Internet or an electronic database; citation for electronic sources is explained later in this chapter. The information here applies to citations of print media.

Newspaper citations resemble magazine or journal citations (see above section) in that they include the author, title of the article, and name of the publication. The name of the city in which the newspaper is published should appear in brackets after the name of the paper, except in the case of national publications such as *USA Today* or unless the city name is part of the paper's name (*New York Daily News*, for example). The bracketed material is not underlined. The date is written in day-month-year format. The edition (*morning, late editions*, etc.) is included, but not the volume or issue number. A comma separates the date and the edition, and the edition name is followed by a colon and the page number(s). Some examples follow:

> Arthur, Manuel. "Arms System Is Flawed." <u>Morning Herald</u> [Albany] 4 Nov. 2003, late ed.: B2.

> Browning, Daniella. "Weapons Test Report Issued." <u>San Francisco Gazette</u> 12 Dec. 2003, natl. ed.: A1+.

In the first example above, the late edition of the *Morning Herald,* which is published in Albany, carried this story on page B2. In the second example above, the national edition is referenced. The plus sign after *A1* indicates that the article continues beyond the first page. (Because newspaper articles are frequently printed on nonconsecutive pages, only the first page number is specified, followed by a plus sign.) In both examples the month is abbreviated, as the MLA requires for all months except May, June, and July.

Nonprint Sources

The Internet and the World Wide Web have expanded the research opportunities for writers, but the expansion has opened the door to legitimate, factual sources as well as to what may best be called mistaken or doubtful. Furthermore, not every website supplies the author's name or other basic facts. Hence the basic principles of citation of electronic sources:

- The source must be clearly identified, to the extent possible, so that the reader may locate the original material and judge its validity. In the case of Web or Internet sites, the URL (Uniform Resource Locator or Web address) should be given. The URL should be divided, if necessary, after a slash, never anywhere else.

- The medium should be specified (website, CD ROM, etc.).

- The date that the material was retrieved should be supplied because electronic sources may change daily or even hourly.

- If the electronic material was taken from a printed source, source information on the original should also be supplied.

Internet and Websites

The basic information (author and title) is followed by information about the print version, if applicable and available; and then the name of the site; the date of electronic publication; the name of the group or person sponsoring the site; the date of access; and the URL (Uniform Resource Locator, or Web address). If the URL for a specific article is extremely long, the main page of the site should be identified, so that the reader may enter the search terms and be sent to the article by the search engine of the site. Some examples:

> Bahr, Sharon. "Nature Writing." <u>English Quarterly</u> 5.2 (2005): 34–35. <u>English Online</u>. 15 June 2005. English Teachers of America. 20 May 2005 http://www.englishteachersofamerica.edu/articles/.

> Kassel, Robin. "Birds of a Feather." <u>Natural History of the United Kingdom and the Americas</u>. Summer 2005. Audubon Affiliates. 12 Sept. 2005 http://www.aafil.com/birds.html.

In the preceding examples, both entries begin with the author's name and then the title of the article. In the first example, the article was originally published in a print medium, on pages 34 and 35 of volume 5 issue 2 of the journal *English Quarterly*. The article was posted on a website called *English Online* on June 15, 2005. The site is sponsored by the English Teachers of America and was accessed on May 20, 2005. The second entry is for an article that did not appear in print. The website, *Natural History of the United Kingdom and the Americas*, is sponsored by Audubon Affiliates (not a real group) and was accessed on September 12, 2005.

If the author of an article is not identified, the entry begins with the title:

> "Birds of a Feather." <u>Natural History of the United Kingdom and the Americas</u>. Summer 2005. Audubon Affiliates. 12 Sept. 2005 <http://www.aafil.com/birds.html>.

If an entire website, not a specific article, is referenced, the entry begins with the name of the site:

> <u>Natural History of the United Kingdom and the Americas</u>. Summer 2005. Audubon Affiliates. 12 Sept. 2005 <http://www.aafil.com/birds.html>.

If the entry is a personal home page, begin with the name of the person posting the page followed by the words "home page" and then the date of posting, access, and URL:

> Gelworth, Gloria. Home page. 30 June 2005. 1 July 2005 <http://www.gelworth.optiontoweb.com>.

Paragraph and Page Numbers

Online material is often posted without page numbers. Scholarly journals sometimes number paragraphs, for ease of citation. If the material cited has numbered paragraphs instead of page numbers, the paragraph numbers appear in the citation followed by the abbreviation *par.* (one paragraph) or *pars.* (more than one paragraph).

CD-ROM, DVD, and Tape

Material accessed from a CD-ROM, DVD, or tape should include the author and title, if available, each followed by a period. If there is an editor, compiler, or translator, that fact should be indicated with the appropriate abbreviation (*ed., comp., trans.*) The entry also includes the date and publisher of the original (if previously published in print), the publication medium the writer consulted (CD-ROM, for example), and the publication date of the electronic version. The punctuation closely follows the format for print media (explained in the previous section). Some examples:

<u>Birds of the Americas</u>. Ed. Harvey Melstein. CD-ROM. Albany: Cleson UP, 2004.

<u>Warblers: A Database</u>. Magnetic tape. Philadelphia: Natural Press, 1990.

<u>Wrens of the World</u>. DVD. New York: New Media, 2005.

Zymen, Virgil. "A Bird and Its Nest." <u>Ornithology</u>. 6.1 (2003): 102–103. <u>Natural History Database</u>. CD-ROM. New York: Prescott, 1992.

In the preceding examples, only the last indicates a previous printed version. The other entries show sources that appeared only electronically.

21

American Psychological Association Citation

Writers in the physical and social sciences generally follow the guidelines of the American Psychological Association (APA) for parenthetical citations in the text and in the reference list, where the sources consulted or quoted are described in detail. When the citations are done properly, the reader can distinguish between the writer's ideas and those of others. Furthermore, the reader can turn to the original source to evaluate its accuracy and fairness and to find more information. Because science is time sensitive, APA format gives a prominent position to the date in both the parentheses and the reference list.

One researcher surveyed 52 science journals and found 33 different styles of reference citation. Before embarking on a project, a science writer is wise to check the preference of the intended publisher, in the case of journal articles, or the teacher, in the case of school assignments. The citation format described in this chapter is the most frequently used general-science style. To help the harried researcher, some computer programs (StyleEase, for example) allow the writer to enter data in response to a series of prompts, whereupon the program automatically formats the references in APA style.

CITATIONS IN THE TEXT

Science and social science writing typically contains so many references to other works that an article with citations in the form of footnotes or endnotes would be nearly impossible to read. Parenthetical citations, on the other hand, interrupt the reader for only a moment and provide two useful bits of data:

when the study was done and who conducted it. In reference to a theory, the parenthetical citation tells the reader when the theory was put before the public in published form and who created the theory. Several general principles govern APA citation style:

- The parenthesis contains the author's last name unless it appears in the text.

- The parenthesis also includes the date of publication.

- If only part of the source is referenced, the parenthesis gives the page number(s) where the material cited may be found in the original source.

- In the case of electronic sources without page numbers, the paragraph numbers should be supplied if the original source provides such information.

- The citation is part of the sentence in which the cited material appears. If the cited material is a quotation, the citation precedes the endmark of the sentence but follows the closing quotation mark.

Examples of several different citations and explanations of the punctuation follow. All the references are to fictitious sources and serve only to illustrate the punctuation of APA citations.

Citing Previous Studies

Science writers must often refer to previous experiments or studies on the same topic. Hence the writer must give the names of one or more authors and dates. If the name is in the text, only the date appears in parenthesis. Absent a textual reference, the parenthetical citations give the author(s) and date(s).

Author's Name in Text

Bruce showed the relationship between birth order and self esteem (2005).

In the preceding example, the parenthetical citation tells the reader that study of birth order and self-esteem was published by a scientist named Bruce in 2005. The reader is free to consult the reference list at the end of the paper for complete information on Bruce's study: the full name of the author, the title of the article or book, where it was published, and so forth.

If both the author and the date appear in the text, no parenthetical citation is needed, though the reference list should include the publication information.

> Posnic's study in 2001, *Towards an understanding of childhood,* proposed a different theory of birth order.

Author's Name Not in Text

If the author is not mentioned in the text, the parenthetical citation provides the name and date. A comma separates the author from the date:

> One theory is that first-born children receive more attention and thus expect more of themselves (Gregory, 2000).

The reference list contains an entry giving information about a source written by *Gregory.* The *2000* is the publication date.

Multiple Authors

Scientific studies are frequently the product of many authors. For studies with up to five authors, the APA calls for their names to be listed in the parenthetical citation. Beyond five, the abbreviation *et al.* (and others) follows the first author's name. The reference list includes up to six authors' names and then relies on *et al.* to cover any remaining writers. Regardless of the number of authors, in parenthetical citations only the last names are used. As always in APA style, a comma separates the date from the name. Below are some examples of multiple-author citations:

Two Authors   If a study is attributed to two authors, APA style dictates that both authors' last names be included in the text or parenthetical citation every time the study is referenced. Both authors' full names must be provided in the reference list. In the first example below, the text does not mention the names, so *Zarcon* and *Zelig* are cited in the parenthesis, joined by an ampersand (&). In the second example, the authors' names appear in the text, so only the date is given in the parenthesis. Two authors' names are joined by *and* when the names appear in the text.

> The rate of decay was measured under controlled conditions (Zarcon & Zelig, 2002).

> Zarcon and Zelig (2002) measured the rate of decay under controlled conditions.

Three, Four, or Five Authors   For a study done by three, four, or five authors, the last names of the entire group appear in the first reference, either in the text or in the parenthetical citation. Thereafter, only the first author is mentioned along with the abbreviation *et al.* (and others). The year is included only in the first citation of each paragraph. In the text, the word *and* joins the last two names. In parenthetical citations, an ampersand (&) replaces the *and:*

> **First citation, names not in text:** The rate of growth was measured in full sunlight (Behr, Catalupo, & Henry, 1999).

> **Citation in same paragraph:** Eight hours of full sunlight produced the fastest growth rate (Behr et al).

> **Citations in subsequent paragraphs, names not in text:** Three hours of sunlight produced the slowest growth (Behr et al., 1999).

> **First citation, names in text:** Behr, Catalupo, and Henry measured the rate of growth in full sunlight (1999).

> **Citation in same paragraph, names in text:** Behr et al. showed that eight hours of full sunlight produced the fastest growth rate.

> **Citations in subsequent paragraphs, names in text:** Behr et al. (1999) found that three hours of sunlight produced the slowest growth.

Six or More Authors For a study with six or more authors, only the first author is cited by name, followed by *et al.* ("and others") in parenthetical citations:

> **Names not in text:** An acidic growth medium retarded the production of seeds (Ciccone et al., 2004).

> **Names in text:** Ciccone et al. (2004) found that an acidic growth medium retarded the production of seeds.

More than One Author with the Same Last Name If a paper refers to works by two or more authors with the same surnames, the initial of each author's first name is included in the citations. The initial is followed by a period:

> W. Chandler (1999) and E. Chandler (2006) found that mosquitos breed more readily in damp conditions.

Anonymous Works

Citations of works with no specified author give the name of the group responsible for the study—usually a government agency or other organization. Citations of studies with no identifiable author or sponsoring group (usually studies referred to in the popular press) may be cited with a few words from the title, which is placed in quotation marks (articles, chapters, and components of other works) or in italics (books and full-length works).

> Drug addiction in these circumstances may be traced to childhood trauma (National Institute of Mental Health, 2004).

> Obesity may be a treatable but not curable disease ("Helping Dieters," 2005).

Notice that the comma in the second example above is placed inside the closing quotation mark, as is customary in American usage.

The names of organizations may be shortened if the organizations are well known and if the names are so long as to burden the reader. In such cases, the shortened form, usually an acronym, is placed next to the full name the first time the name appears. Thereafter, the acronym appears alone. If the first use of the acronym is in the text, the acronym appears in parenthesis. If the first use is in a parenthetical citation, the acronym is placed in brackets. Examples:

> **In text:** A study completed by the National Institute of Mental Health (NIMH) in 2006 found a 36% increase in post-traumatic stress syndrome.

> **In citation:** The study found a 36% increase in post-traumatic stress syndrome (National Institute of Mental Health [NIMH], 2006).

More than One Study Cited in the Same Parenthesis

In a survey of previous research, writers must often list several works in one citation. Commas separate the name and years. Semicolons separate each citation.

> Several studies addressed the resistance to pests of genetically engineered plants (Jones, 1984; Watson & Peters, 2000).

> Rust-resistant wheat fared best in controlled studies (Warer, 1999, 2003).

In the first example above the two authors' name are separated by an ampersand (&). In the text the ampersand would be replaced by *and*. The second example indicates two studies by the same researcher. Commas separate the name and years.

Citing Part of a Source

Most APA citations refer to the entire book or article. Occasionally a writer must refer only to a section of a longer work. In such cases the page number(s), chapter number(s), or paragraph number(s) should be supplied. Page numbers are preceded by *p.* or *pp.* and paragraph numbers are identified with the ¶ symbol or with the abbreviation *para.*

> Children between the ages of 4 and 7 are most likely to identify with a television superhero (Brand, 2001, p. 3).

Children between the ages of 4 and 7 are most likely to identify with a television superhero (Brand, 2001, chap. 9).

Children between the ages of 4 and 7 are most likely to identify with a television superhero (Brand, 2001, para. 8).

Nonprint Sources

Material acquired from an electronic database, a website, or a sound or video recording is cited in the text in the same way as print sources. If the author is known, the name should be given in the text or parenthesis. If the author's name is unknown, a shortened version of the title is sufficient. The date is included in the same way as print sources. The entry in the reference list includes the URL (Uniform Resource Locator or Web address) or the name of the database. For more information, see "Citations in the Reference List" later in this chapter.

Citing a Quotation

Science writers seldom quote as frequently as writers in other fields. Nevertheless, quotations are sometimes necessary. The underlying principle of citation for quoted material is that a parenthetical citation is part of the sentence in which the quotation appears but *not* part of the quotation itself. Hence the citation is placed *after* the closing quotation mark but *before* the endmark or subsequent words of the sentence. Ellipses (three spaced dots) show where words have been omitted from a quotation. Citations for blocked quotations are placed immediately following the final word of the blocked quotation, which is not enclosed by quotation marks. Examples of quotation citations are included in Chapter 20, which explains MLA style. The placement of citations is the same for APA style, though the contents of the parentheses differ, as described previously in this chapter. Some examples:

Although Chapman reported that "post-traumatic stress is unusual" (2000, p. 450), Olivier (2003) disagreed.

The previous conclusion that "post-traumatic stress is unusual" (Chapman, 2000, p. 450) is now in dispute.

CITATIONS IN THE REFERENCE LIST

APA style parenthetical citations direct the reader to an expanded "Reference List" at the end of the book, paper, or article. A reference list must include every source cited by the author, but not works read as general background. The general guidelines of an APA reference list are as follows:

- The reference list must include all the information the reader needs to locate the original source, including author(s), title, medium of publication, publisher, and place of publication. The date is given a prominent position because scientific studies are time-sensitive.

- Personal communications are not included in the reference list because they are not generally accessible to the reader. Information gained from a private letter or interview should be identified as such in the text, not in a formal citation.

- Some parts of a reference-list entry may be abbreviated. The APA uses the two-letter postal abbreviations for states.

- Most entries place the author(s) first, then the date in parenthesis, followed by a period. Next is the title of the book or article: APA style, in contrast to most humanities writing, calls for capital letters only for the first word and for any proper names in the title. The publication venue (company or journal or magazine) and related information follows. All the words in the name of a journal or magazine are capitalized, with the exception of articles and prepositions, unless the article or preposition is the first word of the name. Each of these three elements is followed by a period. If only part of a book (perhaps an encyclopedia entry) has been used, the page numbers are placed last and followed by a period.

- Citations of electronic sources include the URL (Uniform Resource Locator, or Web address) or other information to help the reader access the original.

- The Reference List employs a "hanging indent"—a first line flush with the left margin with subsequent lines indented five spaces. This format allows the reader to locate the last name of the author quickly, a useful quality given that the parenthetical citations or textual references refer to the author(s). This example illustrates the hanging indent:

  Thomas, K., & Adams, L. 2003. *The effect of sunlight on the growth rate of deciduous trees.* NY: Fenster.

More detail on APA Reference List format follows.

Listing Authors in APA References

Because scientific papers often have multiple authors, the format for citing their names is somewhat complicated.

One author: Author's last name followed by a comma and the initial of the author's first name followed by a period. Example: Adams, J.

Two authors: Author One's last name followed by a comma and the initial of his or her first name, followed by a period. Next is an ampersand (&) and Author Two's last name, which is separated by a comma from the initial letter of his or her first name, followed by a period. Example: Adams, J. & Catapano, R.

Three, four, five, or six authors: The authors' names are listed in last name-first initial format, with commas between these two components. Commas also separate one author from another. The last two are joined by an ampersand (&), which is preceded by a comma.

More than six authors: The names of the first six authors are listed in last name-first initial format, with commas between the name and initial. After the sixth name the abbreviation *et al.* (and others) appears.

If the author is an organization or a department of the government, the entire name should be written out in the Reference List: *National Institutes of Health, Drug Enforcement Agency,* etc. If the author has chosen to withhold his or her

name, the reference-list entry should include the word
Anonymous in place of the author's name. If no author is identified and the word *anonymous* does not appear on the original source, the reference-list entry begins with the title.

Journals and Other Periodicals

Citations of articles from scientific journals usually make up the
bulk of references in an APA style paper. Depending upon the
topic and the purpose of the paper, writers may also refer to
popular magazines or newspapers. The general format is simple:

- **Author(s):** See the preceding section of this chapter for
  details on how to cite one or more authors.

- **Date:** The year is placed in parenthesis; the closing parenthesis is followed by a period. If the article comes from a
  popular magazine with a month or a month-day designation, that information is included in the parenthesis, following a comma. For example: *Newsweek* (2003, May 13).

- **Title of the article:** The title is followed by a period.
  Only the first word of the title and subtitle (if present)
  and any proper names are capitalized. A subtitle is separated from the title by a colon. Neither quotation marks
  nor underlining appears.

- **Title of the journal or magazine:** The title of the journal is italicized and followed by a comma.

- **Volume number:** The italicized volume number is followed by a comma and is not labeled *vol.* or *volume.* If
  the publication does not use volume numbers, the
  month or other time designation used by the periodical
  (*Summer*, for example) is included. The issue number
  appears in parenthesis after the volume number only if
  each issue of the periodical starts on page 1. (Many journals number pages consecutively, with one issue ending
  at, for example, page 121 and the next issue beginning
  with page 122. With this sort of numbering, the issue
  number is unnecessary.)

- **Page number(s):** An en dash (slightly longer than a
  hyphen) shows the page range. Most word processing

programs include the en dash on a pull-down, insert/symbol menu. A hyphen may be substituted for the en dash. The last number is followed by a period. If the periodical is a newspaper, the page numbers are preceded by the abbreviation *pp.* (pages).

Following are some examples of reference-list entries for print sources, written in APA style. Journal, magazine, and newspaper articles are frequently accessed through the Internet or an electronic database; citation for electronic sources is explained later in this chapter. The examples below are citations of print media.

Journal

> Patterson, H. (2004). Fluidity of selected gasses at high-temperature. *Materials Science, 23,* 304–308.

> Schiller, N., & Benno, F. (2005). Cognitive dissonance in survivors of childhood trauma. *Journal of Psychoanalytic Treatment, 45*(2), 45–59.

> Walton, I., Gringich, H., Mulhanpt, C. & Williams, E. (2006). Food-gathering strategy: Evolutionary perspectives. *Anthropological Theory, 12,* 14–18.

In the three preceding examples, all have volume numbers, but only the second example includes an issue number (2). The journal titles are italicized, as are the volume numbers. The dates are placed in parenthesis and followed by periods.

Magazine

> Haxley, Q. (2005, June) Why our kids can't read. *Popular Psychology, 4,* 50–56.

> Arthur, C., Bennard, S., & Compeyson, R. (2005, January 3). Houses of glass. *Mechanics Weekly, 67,* 2–9.

In these examples the parenthetical dates include the month (example one) and the month-day (example two). The co-authors of entry two are separated by commas, with an ampersand (&) connecting the last two.

Newspaper

> Erdich, L. (2004, May 11). Stain resistant glass on the horizon? *Mercury Times, 66,* pp. A20–A30.

> Holofield, G. & Brantly, W. (2006, July 15). Ozone pollution rises. *Houston Daily Mirror, 49,* pp. B12, B14.

In the above examples, *pp.* (pages) precedes the page number. The second example gives two page numbers separated by a comma, indicating that the article begins on B12 and continues on B14. The title of the newspaper is followed by a comma and the volume number. The year, month, and day are included in the date parenthesis.

Books

In APA style, entries for books or for portions of books resemble entries for periodicals, with a few differences.

- The authors are listed in the same way (see preceding section for detail), in last name-comma-first initial-period order. In multiauthor works, the names are separated by commas, and the last two authors are joined by an ampersand (&). Works with more than six authors cite the first six and then add the abbreviation *et al.* (and others).

- Anonymous authors are alphabetized under the word *Anonymous,* which appears in place of the name.

- Editors are identified with the abbreviation *Ed.* in parenthesis after the last name.

- The year of publication is placed in parenthesis following the author(s).

- The place of publication precedes the name of the publishing company and is followed by a colon (for example, *New York: Dutton*). If the name of the publishing company includes its location, no further place designation is necessary (for example, *New York University Press* needs no added place name). Two-letter state abbreviations are acceptable.

- Book titles are italicized. Chapter titles (in references to part of a book) are neither italicized nor placed in quotation marks.

Some examples of citations of books or parts of books in APA style:

> Smith, R. (2004). *Conditioned responses in canines.* NY: Fenster.

> Thompson, J.P., & Wilson, B. (2001) *The predatory instinct* (3rd ed.). Chicago: Peplum Press.

> Uniarians, L. (2003). Hunting from scarcity. In G. Seweall (Ed.), *Evolution of Behavior* (pp. 134–156). New York: Fenster.

In the first example above, the book has only one author, in contrast to the second, which has two authors, whose names are joined by an ampersand (&). The second example includes the edition number (3rd ed.) in parenthesis after the title. The last example is a reference to a portion of a longer work. The author of the article (Uniarians, L.) precedes the title of the portion cited. The editor (G. Seweall) is identified by the abbreviation *Ed.,* which appears in parenthesis following the name. The page numbers follow the book title and are placed in parenthesis followed by a period.

Nonprint Sources

The APA calls for electronic sources to be cited in much the same way as print sources, with the addition of information that enables the reader to locate the original source:

- In the case of Web or Internet sites, the URL (Uniform Resource Locator or Web address) should be given. The URL may be divided, if necessary, after a slash, but nowhere else. If the material has been retrieved through a search engine from a database, the database should be cited.

- The URL follows the phrase "Retrieved" or "Available." *Retrieved* indicates that the URL takes the reader directly to the source. *Available* takes the reader to a page with a search command that may be used to arrive at the source.

- No punctuation follows the end of a URL, even if the URL is at the end of an entry.

- Since most material may be retrieved from a number of different media (website, CD-ROM, etc.), APA citation does not call for the medium to be specified, so long as adequate information about the source—enough so that another researcher can locate the material—is provided.

- The date that the material was retrieved should be supplied because electronic sources may change daily or even hourly.

- If the electronic material was taken from a printed source, source information for the original should also be supplied.

Sample citations of electronic sources follow.

Journal Article

Conor, E., & Danko, R. (2003, November 29). Antisocial tendencies. *Sociopathology Report, 5,* 2004–2005. Retrieved January 12, 2004, from the PsychART database.

Jester, L. (1999). Progressive decay of radioactive samples. *Physical Chemistry, 8,* 123–145. Retrieved December 18, 2003, from http://www.pchem.org/journal

In the preceding examples, both entries begin with the author's name(s) and then the title of the article, the title of the journal, the volume number, and the pages. Last is the "Retrieved" statement; the first example is an article from a database, and the second an article accessed on the Web. When the "Retrieved" statement ends with a Web address, no period follows (see example two above).

If the URL (Web address) for a particular source is very long and the home page of the site contains a search function, the URL of the home page is sufficient. In such cases "Retrieved" is changed to "Available," indicating that the reader may find the source by means of the given URL, but that the URL is not the site of the article itself.

Newspaper Article

More major and many minor newspapers maintain searchable websites. A reference-list entry for an article from such a site appears below.

> Carson, K. (2004, January 12). Why anxiety is a cultural phenomenon. *New York Times.* Retrieved February 1, 2004, from http://www.nyt.com

Note: No punctuation follows a Web address.

Online Newsletter

> Halpern, D., Pennybaker, J., & Crawford, B. (2004, April). Responding to clients' sense of abandonment. *Therapist Monthly, 4*(4). Retrieved May 2, 2004, from http://www.thermonth.net/subscribe/newsl_56.html#3

In the above example the newsletter title, which is italicized, is followed by the italicized volume number and the issue number, which is not italicized but enclosed in parenthesis. The URL is not followed by a period.

Undated Web Document on a Private Website

Many websites do not specify the date or author of the articles they display. In such cases the name of the sponsoring organization is given along with the abbreviation *n.d.* (no date). An example:

> American Council on Stress, Task Force on Workplace Stress. (n.d.) Are you working for an unreasonable boss? Retrieved September 5, 2000, from http://www.stress.org

In the example above, the title of the article ends with a question mark, so no other endmark is needed. (Normally a period follows a title in APA style.)

Section of a Document

Some Internet material is divided into sections or chapters. Or, the paragraphs may be numbered in lieu of page numbers. The section or chapter number should appear in the reference list. If the paragraphs are numbered and only a portion of the document is referenced, the paragraph numbers should be supplied. Two examples:

> Harryford, K. (2000, September 12). Income distribution and health coverage. In *American Health Care* (chap. 12). Retrieved August 22, 2001, from http://www.healthcareUSA.org/library/harryford.html

> Merry, X. (2001, December 18). Health coverage in Canada. In *International Health Care* (¶ 12). Retrieved January 2, 2002, from http://www.healthworld.com

Abbreviations for APA Reference Lists

These abbreviations may also be useful in reference lists:

ed. (edition)

Eds. (editors)

Trans. (translator or translators)

Vol. or Vols. (volume or volumes)

n.d. (no date)

No. (number)

p. or pp. (page or pages)

22

The Chicago Manual of Style Citation

The University of Chicago Press has long issued style guidelines for the works it publishes. The rules set forth in *The Chicago Manual of Style,* 15th edition *(CMS),* the collected wisdom of the university press, serve the general-interest writer in any field—science, humanities, business, and so forth. If the intended recipient of a writer's work has not specified another style manual, the CMS is a good choice. The CMS, like all style manuals, calls for writers to differentiate between their own ideas and those of others.

The Chicago Manual of Style allows more options than the Modern Language Association (see Chapter 20) or the American Psychological Association (see Chapter 21). Citations in the text may be in parentheses or in the form of footnotes or endnotes. The CMS also permits several variations in the reference list or bibliography, the portion of the work that provides complete publication information about each source. This chapter explains the choices, with emphasis on those the CMS sees as preferable.

Fortunately for the busy writer, word processing programs such as Microsoft Word automatically number foot- and endnotes, and, in the case of footnotes, format the text so that the footnotes fit on the appropriate pages. Other programs, such as StyleEase, allow the writer to enter publication information on a grid and then take care of the reference-list format.

Note: The notes and bibliographic entry examples in this chapter do not refer to real sources. They simply illustrate the correct format and punctuation.

CITATIONS IN THE TEXT

The guidelines of the Modern Language Association and the American Psychological Association call for parenthetical citations only, with information on the author and date in parentheses, tucked into the text as close as possible to the material being cited. The CMS also strongly recommends the author-date parenthetical style of citation to writers in the physical or social sciences. The CMS allows footnotes and endnotes for writers in the humanities but states that these writers too should consider adopting the author-date parenthetical system. The key, according to the CMS, is consistency. Unless very good reasons exist for mixing styles, the writer should choose one system and stick with it.

Author-Date Parenthetical Citations

Parenthetical citations alert the reader to the fact that some information in the preceding sentence or paragraph is not original. Parenthetical citations provide the bare minimum of information—just the author and date—and serve as a small identification tag that leads to an expanded entry in the reference list. A reference list is, as its name implies, a list of all the references the writer has made. It corresponds exactly with the citations; every citation appears in the reference list, and everything in the reference list is cited somewhere in the writing. (See "The Reference List or Bibliography" later in this chapter for more information on the format of reference list entries.)

The term *bibliography* is generally used for a larger list that also includes works not directly cited that served only as background information. An article written with author-date citations is usually paired with a reference list. An article or paper written with footnotes or endnotes is normally accompanied by a bibliography.

The APA format of author-date parenthetical citations is described in detail in Chapter 21. The general principles of author-date citations are the same in both APA and CMS formats. Briefly, the parentheses contain the last name of the author(s) and the date of publication. If a portion of a work is being cited, the page, chapter, or paragraph numbers may appear as well. The abbreviation *et al.* (and others) is used for works written by a large group. If the text contains the name of the author or the date, that information is omitted from the parentheses. Some examples:

> Gavin (2003) found that the bacterium was resistant to penicillin.
>
> The bacterium was resistant to penicillin (Gavin 2003).
>
> Penicillin did not affect the growth of the bacterium (Gavin 2003, 489–499).

In the first two examples above, the entire work by Gavin is cited. The third example directs the reader to a few pages of Gavin's work. The reference list contains a detailed entry on Gavin's work, whether it be a book, an article, or an electronic source. Notice that the parenthetical citation is part of the sentence and thus precedes the period. The CMS prefers a comma between the year and the page numbers. The page numbers are not preceded by the abbreviations *p.* or *pp.* (page or pages) unless there is a chance that the reader may not understand what the numbers represent.

Multiple Authors

For multiple authors, the CMS prefers that the word *and* be spelled out:

> Gavin, Hoolway, and James (2006) tested the effect of penicillin on the bacterium.
>
> The effect of penicillin on the bacterium was negligible (Gavin, Hoolway, and James 2006).

Notice that the authors' names are separated by commas and that there is a comma before the *and*. No comma sets off the date.

Multiple References in One Parenthesis

Semicolons separate two or more references in the same parentheses:

> The antibiotic effect of the compound has been demonstrated (Kingsly 1999; Albert 2005).

Nonprint Sources

Material acquired from an electronic database, a website, or a sound or video recording is cited in the text in the same way as print sources, though in most cases no page number may be appended. The exception is an electronic reproduction of a printed source. In that case, the page number that appears on the screen is included. The reference list provides the URL (Uniform Resource Locator) or other information so that the reader can find the original source.

If only part of a nonprint source is cited, the parenthetical citation includes whatever location identification is available, often the paragraph or chapter numbers. (Many nonprint sources number paragraphs since these sources do not have "pages" in the traditional sense.) The paragraph symbol (¶) of the abbreviation *chap.* (chapter) is set off by a comma from the date. An example:

> Gilooley's study of the bacterium (2005, ¶ 3) concluded that it was resistant to broad-spectrum antibiotics.

Citing a Quotation

If the quotation is at the end of the sentence, the parenthetical reference precedes the endmark but follows the closing quotation mark:

> Cullen first noted that "the growth of the bacterium was entirely controlled by penicillin" (2004, 12–34).

An en dash (longer than a hyphen but shorter than an em dash) indicates the page range. Word processing programs normally include en dashes in the insert/symbol menu; if no en dash is available, a hyphen may substitute.

If the sentence continues on after the quotation, insert the parentheses as close as possible to the quoted material. Punctuation needed in the sentence (a comma before a conjunction or after an introductory expression, for example) may follow but not precede the parentheses. An example:

> Cullen further stated that if "the prescription of antibiotics could not be stabilized" (2004, 33), resistant strains were inevitable.

Quotation Ending in a Question Mark or Exclamation Point

If a quotation ends with a question mark, the question mark is included within the closing quotation mark. Next comes the parenthetical citation, followed by a period:

> Hitchcock asked, "Can the prescription of antibiotics be controlled?" (2004, 24).

The same pattern is followed for a quotation ending in an exclamation point. The exclamation point is placed inside the quotation marks and a period follows the parenthetical citation.

Ellipses

An ellipsis—three spaced dots—indicates that words have been deleted from a quotation. If the ellipsis falls at the end of a quotation that is cited parenthetically, the parentheses appear at the normal spot immediately following the quotation. The endmark of the sentence follows the parentheses:

> The scientists said that they were "exploring all avenues of prescription control . . ." (Maslom 2005, 11).

Quotations from Literary Sources

The author of a literary essay may need to refer frequently to one work. In the case of plays or poems, an author following the CMS format may cite the act, scene, and line (for a play) or the line numbers (for a poem) in the text. The citation format for this sort of quotation is the same as the MLA format described in Chapter 20.

If more than one line of verse is quoted, a slash indicates the line breaks. A hyphen or an en dash (slightly longer than a hyphen) shows the line range.

Blocked Quotation

A blocked quotation is indented 7–10 spaces from the left margin. The indentation takes the place of quotation marks. In CMS format, the parenthetical citation follows the endmark of the quotation, if the quotation is prose:

Billings argues that deregulation of the airline industry has not brought the promised benefits to the consumer:

> The constant congressional intervention has led to a real price increase, once the cost of taxation is factored into the equation. Furthermore, the industry has little incentive for competition, despite deregulation, given the tendency for lawmakers to play such an active role. (56–58)

Notice that the citation is not part of the sentence, in contrast to the citation in unblocked quotations.

The citation for a blocked poetry quotation is placed in parentheses on the line following the last line of the quotation, flush with the right margin:

> Herbert Alexander's "Manhattan Dusk" establishes a unique setting:
>
> The harbor lights and the ferries
>
> heading to the island, the fog of pedestrians
>
> flowing through the sound of horns.
>
>   (45–47)

Footnotes and Endnotes

Though parenthetical citations are the preferred form, footnotes and endnotes are still widely used for writing in the humanities (literature, history, philosophy, and so forth). Note citations are usually paired with bibliographies. (See "The Reference List or Bibliography" later in this chapter for more information on the format of entries in a bibliography.) Notes on sources are most often indicated in the text by a small raised number following the material cited, as in this example:

> Harrison claims that the Trojan War was not a dispute over territory.[8]

The *8* in the above sentence is a "superscript," written above the line. Most word processing programs have a command for "superscript" in the font/format menu. If the material cited is blocked—indented from the left margin—a full-sized number is placed on the same level as the rest of the text. Either way, the numeral directs the reader to a note that is numbered 8. The note may be at the bottom, or *foot,* of the page on which the citation appears; or it may appear at the end of the chapter or document. Most writers and editors prefer endnotes for ease of reading and composing; allowing enough room at the bottom of a page for the footnotes is an art, even with the help of a word processing program. Regardless of placement, an entry for each source is included in the bibliography at the end of the entire work.

The format of footnote and endnote numbers is the same:

- All the notes are numbered consecutively. If the work is divided into chapters, each chapter's notes may begin with the number 1. Alternatively, the notes may be numbered consecutively for the entire work.

- The note number follows the cited material and all punctuation marks except the dash. If the cited material is at the end of a sentence, the note number follows the end-mark (period, question mark, or exclamation point) or the closing quotation mark, if that is the last punctuation in the sentence. For a blocked quotation, the number follows the last word and is not raised above the line.

- The first citation of a particular source is the most complete. Thereafter, shortened forms are permissible.

The following are some examples of the proper placement of note numbers:

Standford argues that Hamlet is not so much tortured as thoughtful.[9]

Standford argues that Hamlet is not so much tortured as thoughtful,[9] but her evidence has been refuted by Allison, among other critics.[10]

Standford argues, "Hamlet is not a tortured soul, unable to make a decision. As a prince, he is responsible for the welfare of the state and must consider his options carefully."[9]

Standford's argument is simple:

> Hamlet is not a tortured soul, unable to make a decision. As a prince, he is responsible for the welfare of the state and must consider his options carefully. Were he to rush into action, the citizens of Denmark would possibly be subject to risk. 9

Format and Contents of Notes

The CMS calls for an indentation on the first line of a note. The elements of a note (author, title, publication information) are separated by commas. The first note referring to a particular source contains everything the reader needs to know: the author(s), title, publication place, company or periodical, and date of publication. In the case of an electronic source, the URL (Uniform Resource Locator or Web address) or database should be specified. The CMS does not call for the date that an electronic source was accessed unless the material is extremely time-sensitive (medical or legal information, perhaps) and the source is subject to frequent updates.

Later references to the same work may be shortened. If a second or later note is distant from the first reference, the complete information may be repeated for the convenience of the reader. Some professors and publishers allow shortened forms even for the first note, if complete information is included in an alphabetized bibliography.

The following examples illustrate the correct note format for several types of sources.

Books   The Internet now contains many sites that reprint the full text of books, especially those no longer in print. The citation format for electronic sources is different from that of print sources. The examples and explanations in this section refer to print sources; electronic sources are explained later in this chapter.

2. Helena Greenwalk, *Nature Imagery in the Poems of W.B. Yeats* (London: Dilson Press, 2003), 77.

3. George Castille, *The Diary of George Castille*, ed. Peter Burnham, 2 vols. (New York: Crown, 1998), 1:56–60.

4. Martin Cryzich and Albert Khan, *Growing Up in East Anglia* (Toronto: Carpson, 2000), 52.

5. Richard Ames, Charlotte Donadi, and Romeo Harper, *A Study of East Anglia* (London: Dilson Press, 1999), 108.

In the above examples, the first line is indented three spaces. A period follows the note number. Next is the name of the author in first-name/last-name order. In the case of two authors, the names are joined by *and.* Three authors are separated by commas, with the last two names linked by *and.* If a work has more than three authors, one name only is listed, followed by the abbreviation *et al.* (and others).

After the author segment comes a comma and then the title, which is italicized. No period or comma follows the title, just parentheses enclosing the place of publication, the publisher, and the date. A colon separates the place from the publisher; a comma divides the date from the publisher. A comma and the page number(s) follow the parentheses.

Note number 3 earlier cites an edited work. The name of the editor (Peter Burnham) follows the title. The fact that the work has two volumes is explained after the editor's name. A colon divides the volume number (1) from the page numbers (56–60).

Articles   Many writers now consult electronic media for articles. The notes for those sources, explained later in this chapter, are slightly different. The examples below refer to print media.

Journal, One Author

19. Harvey L. Peders, "End of an Era," *History Today* 15 (May 2001): 44.

Journal, Two Authors

20. Richard Ellison and Mary Quanti, "Fashion in the Sixties," *Journal of the Recent Past* 16 (Oct. 1999): 89.

Magazine

21. Hong Li, "Band Music: The Best Hope for Ailing Arts Programs," *Newsweek*, 26 Feb. 2003, 7.

Newspaper

22. Martine Freedman, "Graduation Woes for the Class of 2006," *Chicago Sun-Times*, 14 July 2006, late edition, sec. 3, 1.

In the first example above, the author's full name (Harvey L. Peders) is followed by a comma. The title of the article ("End of an Era") is enclosed in quotation marks and followed by a comma, which is placed inside the closing quotation mark. The title of the periodical (*History Today*) is italicized and followed by the volume number. Next, in parentheses, is the month and year of the periodical (May 2001). After the closing parentheses, a colon precedes the page number (44).

The second example above is similar to the first, with the exception of the fact that two authors are named. Two authors' names are joined by *and*. Three authors' names are separated by commas and the word *and* between the last two names. An article with more than three authors cites just the first in a note, followed by the abbreviation *et al.* (and others).

The third example above cites an article from a popular magazine. No volume number is needed, just the date in day-month-year order, followed by a comma and the page number(s).

The last example above cites an article from a newspaper. The edition (late edition) is specified after the date, as is the section (sec. 3). The page number is not essential but may be helpful to the reader.

Electronic Sources   The general principle for notes on electronic sources is simple: The reader should be given everything needed to locate the original. Thus the citation should include these elements, if they are available:

- Author and title
- Print publication information, if the work appeared in print form prior to being posted on the Web or entered in a database
- Medium (website, CD-ROM, DVD, etc.)
- URL (Uniform Resource Locator) or database name
- If available, the page number(s), chapter number(s), or paragraph number(s)
- Date the material was accessed, if the source is a website that is frequently updated and if the material is time-sensitive (scientific or legal information, for example)

Some examples of notes for electronic sources:

44. Glenda Karnia, ed., *The Computerized Office* (New York: Pelli Associates, 2006), chap. 5, http://bookonline.uhalifce.edu/articles.

45. Alvie Wu and Thomas M. Spicer, *Paperless Business* (Oxford: Penning Press, 2003), Microsoft Reader e-book.

46. Kathryn Nessling, "Confirmation Rituals," *Sociology Quarterly*, 5 (May 2001): 104, http://www.socio.org/article.

47. Alex McQueen et al., "Menopause and estrogen replacement: An assessment of risks," *Journal of Gynecology* 43 (May 2006), http://jog.org/issues (accessed June 9, 2006).

If the URL does not fit on one line, the break comes after a forward slash. If the URL cannot be broken there, the CMS format allows a break *before* a period. The first example cites *chap. 5* as the location of the information in the original source. The third example above cites *104* as the page number of the original. The last example above, to a fictitious medical journal, does not cite a page or chapter number but does include the date of access, implying that the information may change over time and should be assessed accordingly.

Shortened Notes

After the first, complete note, shorter notes inform the reader of the source and page number referred to in the text. In scholarly journals, the shortened form includes only the last name of the author, a comma, and the page number. If more than one work by the same author has been cited, a shortened title should be placed between the author and the page number. Commas separate each element. Some examples of subsequent notes:

> 26. Li, 8.

> 27. Ellison and Quanti, 91.

Some publications call for a key word from the title, even in a shortened note. In that case the three elements—author, title, and page number(s) are separated by commas. The comma precedes the closing quotation mark, if there is one:

> 26. Li, "Band Music," 8.

> 27. Ellison and Quanti, "Fashion," 91.

Abbreviations in Notes

A few Latin abbreviations help space in foot- or endnotes.

Ibid.   The Latin expression *ibidem,* "in the same place," may be used when a note refers to the same source as the preceding note. *Ibid.* takes the place of the author's name and title of the work. It is followed by a comma and the page number(s). If the note refers to the same source but to a different volume, the volume number is inserted before the page number. An example of two consecutive notes:

> 11. Harvey L. Peders, "End of an Era," *History Today* 15 (May 2001): 44.

> 12. Ibid., 46.

The second note indicates that the material cited comes from page 46 of Peders' article.

Id.   Latin for "the same," sometimes abbreviated as *id. Idem* or *id.* replaces the author's name if several works by the same author are cited in the same note. The first reference states the author's name; subsequent references include *idem* or *id.* and the title:

> 9. Henry Morris, "Orthography," *English Journal* 4 (March 2001): 33–34; idem, "New Orthography," *English Journal* 5 (April 2002): 56–60.

Notice that *idem* is not followed by a period. Also, a semicolon separates the two references to Morris's work.

Extinct Latin Abbreviations

Two Latin abbreviations—*Op. cit.* and *loc. cit.*—were once popular in foot- and endnotes. *Op. cit.* (in the work cited) replaced the title of a work that was referenced earlier. *Loc. cit.* (in the place cited) fulfilled the same purpose. Neither is considered appropriate today. Instead, a shortened version of the title is inserted in a note.

THE REFERENCE LIST OR BIBLIOGRAPHY

Author-date parenthetical citations do not usually contain enough information to help the reader locate the original source. Hence a work with author-date citations in the text needs a "reference list" that expands the source information. Authors using a footnote or endnote citation system, on the other hand, may rightly claim that the first footnote or endnote for a particular source may be complete enough for the readers' needs. Nevertheless, most writers append a bibliography anyway. The bibliography includes the author, title, and publication information. All sources cited in the paper as well as those used for background reading are listed in the bibliography.

The Chicago Manual of Style allows several formats for the reference list or bibliography:

- **Author-date system:** The reference list is alphabetized "by the last name of the principal author. In a work with multiple authors, the principal is the first named on the title page or in the byline. The author's last name is flush with the left margin and additional lines of an entry are indented three spaces. This arrangement highlights the author's name so that a curious reader may quickly and easily turn from the text to a reference. Immediately following the authors' names is the date of publication. Next is the title and publication information (company or journal, place, volume number, and similar data).

- **Note citations:** If footnotes or endnotes have been used in the work, the source list is still alphabetized according to the last name of the principal author. (Works with no identified author are alphabetized by title.) The source list places the author first, then the title and then the publication company, date, and place. Each of these three elements is followed by a period. If only part of a book (perhaps an encyclopedia entry) has been used, the page numbers are placed last and followed by a period. Article listings generally include page numbers, which are separated by a colon from the date information.

- Entries for electronic sources contain the same information (if it is available) as print sources, with the addition of the format (CD-ROM, e-book, website, etc.). The CMS does not recommend including the date the material was accessed except for time-sensitive material, such as medical or legal information.

Examples of various types of entries for a source list follow, first for the author-date system and then for the notes system.

Author-Date System: The Reference List

The author-date system gives a prominent position to the date of publication and thus is considered the best arrangement for science writing, a field in which an older study may be superseded by newer scholarship. The recommended format for the

CMS author-date system is similar, but not completely identical, to that of the American Psychological Association described in Chapter 21. Also, many publishers dictate minor variations. Science writers would do well to inquire of the intended recipient which format is preferred.

Titles in a Reference List

Article titles in reference lists, which accompany citations in the author-date system favored by scientists, are capitalized differently from titles in a bibliography, which accompanies a humanities paper. Only the first word of a book or article title is capitalized. So is the first word of the subtitle, if present. All the other words, with the exception of proper nouns (names of people or places—Mary, Germany, and so forth), are written in lowercase. This practice is sometimes called "sentence style" capitalization. The titles of journals, newspapers, or magazines are capitalized in "headline style"—the first and last words of the title and subtitle, proper nouns, and what CMS calls "major" words are capitalized. Major words include nouns, pronouns, adjectives, and adverbs. Articles (a, the, an) and prepositions (*by, from, for,* and so on), unless they are emphasized, are not capitalized. Neither are conjunctions (and, or, but, for, nor).

Identifying the Author(s)

Because scientific works often have multiple authors, the format for citing their names is somewhat complicated. Reference lists frequently abbreviate the author's first name, and bibliographies (used for humanities writing) often spell out the full name. The style chosen should be followed consistently. The illustrations below use the full names.

> **One author:** Author's last name followed by a comma and the first name followed by a period. Example: Elroy, Thomas.

> **Multiple authors:** CMS style permits two options: (1) all the authors' names in last-name, first-name order or (2) last-name, first-name of author one and first-name, last-name

order for the rest. In both styles, a comma follows the name of author one and the names are linked by *and.* Example of style (1): Elroy, Thomas, and Weitz, James. Example of style (2): Elroy, Thomas, and James Weitz.

Three to ten authors: The last name of the first author is listed in last-name, first-name format, with commas between these two components. The next names are written in first-name, last-name order. Commas also separate one author from another. The last two are joined by the word *and.* Example: Elroy, Thomas, James Weitz, and Delroy Runk.

More than ten authors: The names of the first seven authors are listed in the format prescribed for 3–10 authors (see above). The last author's name is followed by the abbreviation *et al.* (and others).

If the author is an organization or a department of the government, the entire name should be written out in the Reference List: *National Institutes of Health, Drug Enforcement Agency,* etc. If the author has chosen to withhold his or her name, the reference-list entry includes the word *Anonymous* in place of the author's name.

To cite several works by the same author, give the name in the first entry. A three-em dash (three times as long as a dash) takes the place of the name in subsequent listings. The three-em dash is followed by a period, just as the name would have been:

> Smith, Janet. 2003. *Computer Problems for the Young Programmer.* Baltimore: Univ. of Monroe Press.
>
> ———. 2004. *Programming in Visual Basic.* New York: Columbia.

Books

If the author-date system has been used in the paper, the entry for a book in the reference list also gives prominence to the date:

> Singhe, Anna. 1999. *A study of peptides.* 4th ed. New York: Columbia.

The example above cites the fourth edition of a book written by *Anna Singhe* that was published in 1999 by a company named *Columbia* that is located in *New York*.

Journal Articles

The reference list entry for a printed (not electronic) journal article includes the author(s), title of article, title of periodical, volume and number and date, and page reference. The title of the article is not placed in quotation marks in the reference list. The title of the journal is italicized:

> Hines, Bradford G. 1999. The unconscious behavior of pedestrians. *Sociology Today* 67:421–451.

The example above cites an article by Bradford G. Hines that was published in 1999 in volume 67 of *Sociology Today*, a scholarly journal. The volume number is followed by a colon and the page numbers. The issue number is not given because the journal numbers its pages consecutively, not beginning with page 1 in each new issue. An en dash, which is slightly shorter than a hyphen, indicates the page range (421 to 451). A hyphen may be substituted if no en dash is available.

Magazine Articles

An article from a popular magazine, in contrast to one from a scholarly journal, is generally identified by date (month and year or month, day, and year), not by volume and issue number or by page number. The date of a magazine is not enclosed by parentheses:

> Hines, Bradford G. 1999. Preventing pedestrian accidents. *Time Today*, Oct.

In the above example, the year of publication follows the author's name. (In the magazine were published weekly, the date would appear following the month).

Newspaper Articles

Newspaper articles are cited in a reference list by date and edition, not by page number:

> Jefferson, Margaret S. 2001. A scholar studies pedestrian paths. *New York Journal*, July 5, late edition.

Each element of the entry—author, title, and publication information—is followed by a period. The title of the article is not placed in quotation marks. The title of the newspaper is italicized.

Electronic Sources

Entries for electronic sources in the reference list state all the same information as those for printed sources, if the same facts are available. The nature of the Internet or the Web, however, is that at times the author, publication date, or other important information is *not* obtainable. In such cases, as much data as possible should be supplied for the reader, with the goal of enabling the reader to locate the original source, should he or she wish to do so.

The CMS does not generally ask that the date the source was accessed be stated in the reference list. Only when information is likely to change frequently, and only when those changes may have an impact on the paper's content or conclusions, should the access date be given.

In citing electronic sources, punctuating the URL (Uniform Resource Locator or Web address) may be a problem. The ideal is to fit the entire URL on one line. If the URL must be broken, the CMS calls for a break after a slash (the preferred spot) or before a period.

Some sample reference list entries:

Books

> Kunde, Peter. ed. 2005. *The Physics of Barbershop Quartets.* New York: John Wilay. http://www.cs.wilay.edu/web-books/.

> Masters, Arthur, and Joseph Pirrip. 2006. *Understanding Music.* London: Preston Press. Microsoft Reader e-book.

Notice that the format is appended to the end of each entry. Each entry also ends with a period, even if the period follows a Web address.

Journal Articles

Kunde, Peter. 2001. Music as an antidepressant. *Journal of Depression and Treatment,* 130, no. 4 (March): 551–560, http://www.journals.unewyork.edu/JDT/issues (accessed February 1, 2002).

Rotman, Kenneth. 2003. Crime and social responsibility. *Journal of the Medical Society,* 33, no. 5 (May 9), http://jms.org/issues/220049.html.

These journal articles include the volume number directly following the title and set off by a comma. The issue number, identified by the abbreviation *no.,* precedes the date, which is enclosed in parentheses. (Entries for printed journal articles seldom include the issue number because the page number is sufficient to locate the information. In an electronic source, however, page numbers may be absent. Hence the issue number is helpful to the reader.) Both examples end with periods, though only the first includes an access date.

Magazine Articles

Magazine articles accessed online normally don't include page numbers. If page numbers are available, they may be included.

Weinstein, Ruth. 2000. Enjoying jazz. *Music Today,* June. http://www.music.com/jazz/article/.

Francis, Frederick. 2003. New German style. *Architectural Review,* October 4. http://magazineart.time.com/index.html.

Newspaper Articles

Weinstein, Ruth. 2004. What does Johnny listen to? *Chicago Herald,* March 30, 2004. http://www.chicagoherald.com/.

Francis, Frederick. 2005. German court to rule on tariffs. *New York Journal,* December 20, 2005. http://www.nyt.com/2005/articles (accessed May 16, 2005).

Notes/Bibliography System

Writers in the humanities who have used foot- or endnotes to document their sources may complement those citations with a bibliography, which is similar but not identical to the MLA style described in Chapter 20. In this system the date appears at the end of an entry, not after the author's name.

While a reference list includes only sources that have been cited in the paper, a bibliography may include some sources that served as background and were not cited. Some general principles:

- A bibliography is alphabetized according to the last name of the principal author. Up to ten authors may be listed. For a work with more than ten co-authors, the entry in the bibliography lists the first seven, followed by the abbreviation *et al.* (and others).

- If no author's name is available, the source may be alphabetized according to the first important word in the title.

- If more than one book by the same author is listed, the author's name appears with the first entry. Thereafter, the spot normally filled by the author's name is occupied by a three-em dash (three dashes in a row).

- All entries end with a period.

Following are samples of various types of sources as they would appear in a bibliography.

Books

If a book has more than one author, the first author is listed in last-name, first-name order, with a comma separating the two elements. Subsequent authors are listed in first-name, last-name order, with commas between each element and commas between the authors' names. The last two authors' names are separated by *and,* which is preceded by a comma. If the book has been edited or translated, the abbreviation *ed.* or *trans.* appears as well.

> Kogan, Deborah, and Lynn Hirsch. *Gender Roles in Greek Tragedy.* New York: Prescott, 2003.

Kussel, Nancy. *Jocasta's Dilemma.* London: Old Market
Books, 2004.

Lane, Gene, trans. *The Plays of Lope de Vega.* London:
Prescott Books, 1999.

Journal Articles

Articles published in scholarly journals generally include the
volume number and date, as well as the page numbers on
which the article appears. The principal author's name is written in reverse order, with a comma separating the author's last
name from his or her first name. Other authors' names appear
in normal first-name, last-name order. Commas separate all
the authors' names. The last two in a series of authors are
joined by *and,* which is preceded by a comma. Titles of articles are placed in quotation marks. Journal titles are italicized.
The volume number precedes the date, which is placed in
parentheses. The page number follows the closing parentheses
and a colon. The page range is indicated with an en dash,
which is slightly longer than a hyphen. (A hyphen may be
substituted if necessary.)

Kogan, Deborah, and Lynn Hirsch. "Examining Oedipus and
His Mother." *Journal of Classical Literature* 44 (March
2001): 43–51.

Willard, Scott. "The Language of Tragedy." *Classics Revisited*
51 (September 2004): 90.

Magazine Articles

Citations of popular magazines do not require volume or issue
numbers. In CMS format, the page number of a magazine article is not usually given in the bibliography, though it is cited
in the foot- or endnote. The title of the magazine article is
placed in quotation marks, and the magazine title is italicized.
Two examples follow:

Perrey, Roberta. "The New Renaissance." *Newsweek,*
March 2005.

Tans, Frank. "The Sculpture of Ellen Wiganton."
Smithsonian, December 2, 2000.

Newspapers

Newspaper articles are frequently accessed through the Internet or an electronic database; citation for electronic sources is explained later in this chapter. The information here applies to citations of print media.

Newspaper citations in CMS format are minimalist. The foot- or endnote includes the author, title of the article, and the name and date of the publication. The bibliographic entry, however, is alphabetized under the name of the publication, followed by the date and edition. Commas separate each of these elements:

> *Morning Herald*, November 4, 2003, late edition.

> *San Francisco Gazette*, December 12, 2003, national edition.

Electronic Sources

In citing a nonprint source, the medium should be specified (CD-ROM, database, etc.). A URL (Uniform Resource Locator or Web address) is sufficient to identify a Web or Internet site. The date that the material was retrieved should be supplied only for sources that are likely to change frequently. The date retrieved is placed in parentheses. If the electronic material was taken from a printed source, source information on the original should also be supplied.

Fairly often a nonprint source does not identify some basic information (author, date, or page, for example). What does not exist cannot be cited; the best path is to give as much information as possible so that the reader can turn to the original source. Examples of bibliographic entries for electronic sources follow.

Books

Bibliographic entries for books retrieved from websites should include the URL (Uniform Resource Locator or Web address):

Bahr, Sharon. *Nature Writing*. Philadelphia, PA: UPA Writers' Research Group, 2004. http://www.upawg.org/onlinebooks/.

Kassel, Robin. *Birds of a Feather*. New York: Summer Press, 2005. http://www.aafil.com/birds.html.

In the preceding examples, the entries begin with the author's name and then the title of the book.

If the author of a book is not identified, the entry begins with the title:

Birds of a Feather. New York: Summer Press, 2005. http://www.aafil.com/birds.html.

Journal Articles

Bibliographic entries for journal articles in CMS format do not require date of access unless the material is time-sensitive. Some publishers require such dates, so writers planning to publish their work should check with the intended recipient. In the second example below, the access date is included.

Slossberg, James, Gabrielle Roi, and Agnes Delany. "Investigations into the Creative Mind." *Journal of Literary Biology* 34, no. 6 (January 8, 2004), http://jolb.org/articles.

Wren, Arthur. "Creativity and Mental Strain." *Journal of Psycholinguistic Study* 9, no. 8 (February 9, 1999), http://jops.org/articles/creativity (accessed August 12, 2005).

Magazine Articles

Online magazines have proliferated in the last few years. Their bibliographic entries include the usual information (author, title, publication and date) separated by periods. Next is the URL (Uniform Resource Locator or Web address):

Castleman, Mark. "Bridges and Tunnels of America." *Lifetime,*
June 5, 2004. http://www.lifeti.com/nation/article/
778%.html.

Holloway, Stanley. "Exploring America's Backroads." *National
Report,* September 4, 2002. http://www.nr.org/article/
current/.

Newspaper Articles

The URL (Uniform Resource Locator or Web address) of a
newspaper article is unlikely to remain valid, as many newspaper sites place the day's lead story on the home page and
shift older stories to the archives or to other pages. The citation of a newspaper article obtained online, therefore, generally includes the URL of the newspaper's home page. The
reader can then search the site for the desired material. The
date accessed is given only for time-sensitive material:

Goodman, Eloise. "Bridge Repairs Completed." *Philadelphia
News,* October 4, 2004. http://www.pnews.com/ (accessed
October 4, 2004).

McArthur, Hillary. "Going to Grandma's House: Thanksgiving
Detours." *Chicago Herald,* May 15, 2000.
http://chiher.news.com/.

Index

A

abbreviations
    for APA reference lists,
        316
    e-mails and faxes, 231,
        232, 243
    in footnotes and
        endnotes, 328–329
    without periods, 12
    and slash, 164–165
American Psychological
    Association (APA). *See The*
    Publication Manual of the
    American Psychological
    Association
American system
    and abbreviations, 12
    direct quotations in
        sentences with
        speaker tag, 26, 68,
        70, 94–95, 96
    and embedded
        quotations, 9, 29, 105
    and endmark, 7, 8, 101
    and punctuation, 17,
        18, 67, 68, 101
    and single quotation
        marks, 93
apostrophe
    and American
        handbooks/manuals
        of style, 172–173
    in expressions of time
        and value, 180–181

    function and definition
        of showing
        possession, 169–170
    and multiple
        apostrophes, 182
    and possessive forms,
        170–173, 174
    and words, specific,
        170–171, 174–178,
        179–182
Apostrophe Protection
    Society, 169
asterisks, 153

B

blocked quotations,
    103–105, 153–157
brackets, 133, 142–144
British system
    and direct quotations in
        sentences with
        speaker tag, 26, 68,
        70, 94, 95–96
    and embedded
        quotations, 9, 29, 105
    and period with
        numbers, 17, 101
    and quotation marks, 8,
        67, 68, 101
    and single quotation
        marks, 26, 93
business writing, 90–92,
    234–239. *See also* letters,
    business